WE GOT THE WATER

Jill Gabrielle Klein

ISBN 978-0615806969

Author photo by Brad Cansler
Cover photo by Jill Gabrielle Klein
Layout and Design: Jon Hofferman, Carissimi Publications

To my father, Gene Gabriel Klein, my aunts,
Lilly Isaacs and Oli Klutsik, my uncle, George
Isaacs, and my grandmother, Bertha Klein.

Most of all, to my grandfather Herman Klein.
You were stolen from us, and this book is the
closest I can come to bringing you back home.

PROLOGUE

Herman carried the sapling across the yard, his boots crunching in the snow with each step. The young silver pine he held in his gloved hands was about three feet tall. Its roots were wrapped in canvas, and only a few thin branches bent away from the narrow trunk. It was not heavy.

At the back corner of the yard, he gently lay the sapling down in the snow next to the bare gooseberry and raspberry bushes, careful not to snap any of the branches. He walked past the walnut tree and the small chicken coop and pulled a shovel from inside the doorway of the shed, then returned to the small tree and began clearing the snow from the earth. Then, with great effort, he dug into the frozen ground, prying out small clumps of damp, dense soil, stopping occasionally to wipe the brown hair off his forehead. Herman was a sturdy man—not tall, but strong—and was more than up to the task.

The winter of 1928 was a strange season for planting: the sky hung grey and low, looking as if a new covering of snow would fall before the day's end. But the sapling had to be in the ground today. It commemorated the birth of a healthy son, and it would grow as the baby grew.

The baby was not Herman's first child. Bertha had given birth to Lilly eight years previously, and Oli was born two years later. The baby was also not his first son. Two years before they'd had Michael, a small baby born with a lump at the back of his neck. Michael didn't grow, and left them only a month after he arrived.

Earlier that day, just hours before he had begun to plant the tree, Herman had stood outside, waiting in the cold for news from the midwife who was inside with Bertha. Lilly and Oli waited outside too, looked after by Mariska, a young woman the Kleins had taken into their home eight years earlier. The four of them had been banished from the house when the mid-wife arrived. A steady stream of friends and relatives had come to join them, including Bertha's parents and sisters, until there was a small crowd participating in the vigil. Herman was anxious and impatient.

Everyone heard the baby's first cry. When the midwife flung open a window and announced that Herman was the father of a healthy baby boy, he ran upstairs and was handed his tiny son. He and Bertha decided to name the boy Gábor, but within his first minutes of life they were already calling him Gabi. Now, as Herman planted the tree only a few hours later, the baby rested with his mother, healthy and strong.

Herman continued digging through the hard soil, pushing further into the earth and building a pile of dirt next to the hole. He was worried about the tree. Spring was still months away, and the cold might be too much for it. He lifted the sapling pine and, as he removed the cloth from around its roots, small clods of dirt dropped into the hole. He lowered the base of the tree into the ground and gently covered the roots with cold soil. Pulling off his gloves and shaking the dirt from them, he considered the chances of his newly planted tree.

He hoped for the best.

Chapter 1
HERMAN

By February 2, 1928—the day the silver pine was planted—thirty-eight-year-old Herman Klein had already had quite an eventful life.

Berehovo, his current home and the town of his youth, was part of the Austro-Hungarian Empire. At the age of twenty-four, with World War I just beginning, Herman was drafted to fight on the side of the Germans. He joined reluctantly, having no particular penchant for fighting or allegiance to Germany, and departed for the Russian front, leaving his fiancée Bertha behind. His service on the battlefield was short-lived, however, lasting only a few weeks. Consistent with the proclivity for easy surrender that was the fashion among the men of his region, Herman was captured by the Russians and sent to Vladivostok, a town on the east coast of Russia near the border with China.

During his four years in captivity, Herman learned from his fellow prisoners of war how to play the violin and how to speak four new languages to add to his native Hungarian: English, French, Russian and German. He also became acquainted with a young local woman. The prisoners were allowed to fraternize with the residents of the town because there was nowhere for them to escape to—it was unlikely that anyone would risk a suicidal trek across Siberia, and if so, to what? If they avoided recapture in Russia, they would end up right back on the front, fighting again. No, the prisoners stayed put, and Herman's cold and dark winter days were brightened by his Siberian girlfriend.

Meanwhile, Bertha waited at home for her fiancé for four long years, not knowing if Herman was still alive. She was twenty-one years old when he left, a solidly built young woman with wavy brown hair, strong features, stark blue eyes, and an alluring smile. Most of the time, Bertha waited in expectation of Herman's return, but on more solemn, lonely days in her parents' house, she feared that she would spend the rest of her life alone, mourning him. They were second cousins, and Herman had been part of her life for as long as she could remember.

The war ended in November 1918, and Herman made the long journey back to Berehovo and Bertha. Within a few days of his return in the early spring of 1919, the families began to prepare for the wedding; Bertha had waited long enough, and she saw no reason to delay her marriage any longer.

The day before the ceremony, Bertha noticed a young woman pacing up and down the street outside Herman's house. Bertha approached the stranger and learned that she had traveled all the way from Vladivostok, a journey that took weeks by train. Slowly, Bertha came to understand that the woman had followed Herman home. Right there, in the middle of the street, Bertha explained that Herman was betrothed, that the woman's long trip from Siberia had been in vain, and that she should go home. The Siberian woman stood in the street, her hands covering her face, and cried.

Herman tried to console her. He was shocked and embarrassed by her presence, but he was also concerned for this woman who had meant so much to him during his imprisonment, and had come from so far away to find him. Still, Siberia was his past, Berehovo was his home, and Bertha was his future. Herman told the woman, somewhat more gently than Bertha had, that she had to go.

Upon learning of Herman's extracurricular wartime activities, Bertha tore off her engagement ring and refused to marry him. Eventually, however, after numerous apologies and promises from Herman, she relented and the wedding took place. Naturally, the mysterious woman from Siberia and the scandalous scene in the street was a hot topic of town gossip for years to come.

Soon after Herman and Bertha's marriage, Berehovo—which lies in the foothills of the Carpathian Mountains—became part of Czechoslovakia. This change was part of the 1918 dissolution of the Austro-Hungarian Empire in the aftermath of World War I. Within a few years, Czechoslovakia would be well on its way to becoming a prosperous industrialized nation, a democracy with a constitution based on that of the United States, and although most of the inhabitants of Berehovo were Hungarian-speaking, they enthusiastically accepted the rich cultural life of their new nation. All of the shops in town listed their wares in both Hungarian and Czech, and some of the schools taught lessons in both languages.

Herman went to work in a hardware store while Bertha looked after their first home. They rented a small carriage house located behind a large home owned by a woman who had been royalty during the empire, but who now needed the income. When Lilly was born, they brought Mariska, a thirteen-year-old orphan, into their home to help Bertha with the baby. Mariska soon came to be a loved member of the family. After Oli was born, they all moved to a three-room apartment in town. The apartment was small for five people, and Herman knew it was time to provide a larger home for himself and the women surrounding him. He was up to the challenge—he had started his own household goods store in the center of Berehovo, and his business was thriving. He proudly built his family a new home, only a five-minute walk from his shop. The family moved into their new house on the day that six-year-old Lilly started school. With all of the excitement of making friends, Lilly had forgotten about her new home by the time school was dismissed, and walked back to the empty apartment. She then ran to her new house to tell her mother all about her day.

Herman sold everything from buckets to ice skates in his store, and he prided himself on the displays he produced from his varied stock. The aisles of his shop were filled with neatly stacked goods and appliances. The year that Gabi was born, Herman entered a display contest sponsored by one of his suppliers. He arranged his pots, pans, buckets and cans into the form of a robot that stood at the front of the store. His creativity won him first prize among all the household goods shops in Czechoslovakia; he was awarded a silver cigarette case, elegantly carved and engraved with the year 1928.

Herman was a popular figure around town. Because of his linguistic skills, people would bring him letters written by relatives in languages they could not read, and he would translate for them. He was respected and well-liked. He dressed well, keeping up with the styles, and he was always clean-shaven, visiting the barber every morning for a steam-towel shave on his way to work. He had a strong and loving marriage and two beautiful daughters full of personality and laughter. And now, with the birth of this baby boy, he felt that his family was complete.

RECOLLECTION
(Written 2000)

Reconstructing an event that is as old as my father is not an easy task. I know that my grandfather Herman planted the silver pine; it was still standing when I stood in the backyard in 1989. My father's older sisters, Lilly and Oli, provide two direct, living recollections of the birthday planting, and my father grew up knowing the history of the tree. But I don't know for sure if Herman dug through a layer of snow, if the sky was threatening, or, more essentially, what he was thinking as he shoveled the earth.

I can be quite sure that Herman worried about Gabi. In addition to the family stories that attest to his concerns, there are also postcards written in his hand. One, written to Bertha when she was vacationing with the children at a spa, makes his anxiety clear: "Take care of Gabika when bathing," he writes, as if, lacking this warning, Bertha might fail to pay close attention to her four-year-old son when he was in the water. In addition, the story of the woman from Vladivostok is a family legend often told. Its recitation became more guarded, however, once I started writing this book, largely due to Lilly's fear that her father's image would somehow be tarnished by the retelling of this event.

Memory, like communication, is imperfect, and my knowledge of the past depends on both. I am more fortunate than many of the second- or third-generation Holocaust survivors who would like to document the experiences of their relatives, as I have been able to conduct extensive interviews not only with my father and his sisters, but also with Lilly's husband George. Now aged from seventy-two to eighty, they still have sharp memories, but sharp is not the same as perfect. They saw the same events from different perspectives, and they remember some occurrences very differently. Particularly in times of horror and suffering, each possessed different levels of understanding and different abilities to process what was happening.

The latest neurobiological research tells us that we form strong and lasting memories of life-threatening events. Sustained threat and prolonged emotional stress, however, can interfere with the making of memories. So what happens with the protracted emotional pain and trauma of the Holocaust? My father remembers almost nothing of the three-day ride in the cattle car, probably because he was in shock, which mercifully limited his comprehension of his surroundings. He recalls in vivid detail, however, his first hours in Auschwitz, starting from the moment the train doors were opened. Generally, my father and his sisters all seem to have a punctuated recall: through the physical and emotional pain of their everyday experiences, moments and events disrupt the deep malaise, and lasting memories are made.

For any of us, recollections of our lives lose many of the mundane details of daily experience, while specific events, either positive or negative, that depart from the mundane, are more likely to be recalled. Any single moment in our lives that brought even a fraction of the psychological and physical pain experienced in the daily life of a concentration camp prisoner would be notable and remembered for years to come. For survivors, however, many of these "normal" moments of camp experience are lost. What remains in memory are the events that generated change from the dire status quo, either negative—beatings, the death of someone close—or positive—the relief of surviving a close call, a moment when hunger was eased slightly by an extra ration of food, or a small act of human kindness. Much of the rest vanishes.

How, then, do I write a story—their story—based on these staccato memories? All biographers face this challenge, but it becomes a central concern when one writes about the Holocaust, both because of the provocations of Holocaust deniers, and because of our duty to the victims to get it right. I could bypass this dilemma by calling this book a "novel based loosely on actual events," but the actual events are too important, and I want to document the facts of my relatives' story.

I started conducting interviews with them for this book over ten years ago. My dad was in his early sixties and Lilly, George, and Oli were nearing seventy. I knew then that my time was limited, that I would not have them forever, and that the details and colors of my paragraphs would fall away with them. And now they are ten years older. I write with my stacks of transcribed interviews next to me, but I still sometimes need to ask them to fill in the missing pieces: "What were you wearing?" "How old was the soldier?" "What were you thinking when that happened?" To aid me, I have careful translations of the diaries Lilly and Oli kept while they were in the camps. I have also studied dozens of survivor memoirs, and while each individual account can suffer from the distortions of time and memory, the overall structure and norms of the camps emerge, providing a context for my father's and aunts' experiences.

Where, then, to draw the line? What are the rules that guide my writing? I know that in Herman's backyard there were gooseberry and raspberry bushes, a chicken coop, and a walnut tree—I have photos and there are clear memories of these. When I describe the planting of the silver pine, I paint the sky grey and put snow on the ground because those are the probable conditions for Czechoslovakia in February, and it is impossible to have Herman dig without describing the state of the soil. I do not rely on any guesswork, however, about how the historical events of the Holocaust played out for Herman and his family. Details of their ghetto and camp experiences come directly from their memories. When there are discrepancies in their perceptions or what they can remember, these are laid out in the text and openly wrestled with. Where I draw on other witnesses, I do so explicitly.

Many individuals played important roles in my family's

various narratives: friends from home, people they met in the camps, and so on. Sadly, the names of some of these individuals have been forgotten, but because I do not want them to be nameless, I provide them with names (and I identify which are known and which are not in the Author's Notes at the end of the book). Further, I am careful with dialogue in the narrative. Obviously, no one remembers the exact words spoken—and of course, with one or two exceptions, none of the conversations were originally in English. However, there were things said that have been reported to me consistently over the years, in similar or identical words. In such instances, I have used quoted dialogue.

I sometimes fantasize about interviewing the key missing witness, about seating Herman on the living room couch and setting up my video equipment. I would give so much for just a two-hour conversation with him. I'd spend the first hour telling him how surprisingly well things turned out for his family, far better than he must have feared when he left them. I'd tell him about his grandchildren and great-grandchildren. I'd tell him that the passion for football (soccer) that he instilled in his son lives on in me today, and in his great-granddaughter as well. I'd tell him about the day when my niece, Claire, scored her first goal, and that I think about him every time I step onto the football pitch, even as I wonder whether my aging body can make it through another match; that every time I step into position to tend goal I touch each post, picturing him sitting in the shade of a tree, watching me play. I'd tell him that I am dedicating this book to him.

Then I'd say, "I have a few questions to ask, if that's okay."

"Of course," he would reply.

"Okay, Granddad. What were you thinking about when you planted the tree the day my father was born? And also, what was the deal with that woman from Vladivostok?"

There is one part of the story that I will never know with certainty and in full detail: the final moments of Herman's life. We all know that Herman died in the gas chambers, but no one remembers this, so there is no one who can tell me about it. Gabi saw him last when they were separated upon their arrival at Auschwitz, when an SS officer sent my father and grandfather in opposite directions. We now know that one direction meant slave labor and almost certain future death, while the other direction meant immediate death, but Gabi and Herman didn't know that then. No one who went with Herman survived, so I know nothing about his walk to the gas chambers, or his experience in the changing room before the shower that would provide no opportunity for cleansing. I want so much to know this part of the story, because I ache to think of Herman's loneliness. Separated from his wife and daughters just after getting off the train, and then finally from his beloved son, he took this walk alone. I want to be able to walk with him, and to see what he sees.

Thus, throughout this book, I attempt to reconstruct his passage. I start with the very little that I knew initially, with the moment Herman and my father part. I learn more, studying maps, photos, and the testimonies of prisoners who had a clear vantage point—workers in the crematoria and political prisoners who had a broader view of the camps.[1] I do this with the goal of reconstructing Herman's last moments so that, in my imagination at least, I am able to accompany him.

---

1. Birkenau map used for "The Walk" from Martin Gilbert, *Auschwitz and the Allies* (New York: Henry Holt and Company, 1981).

THE WALK

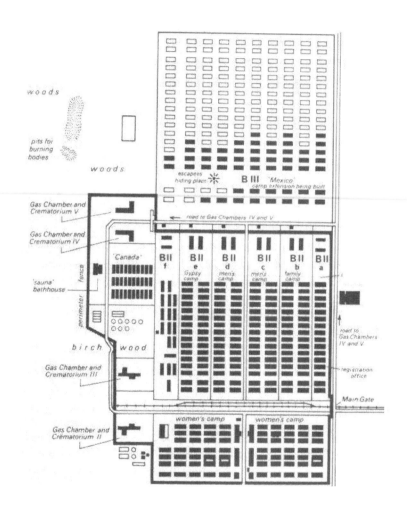

Herman turns, and over his shoulder he watches Gabi go off in the other direction. His son moves further away, and is soon lost from sight, obscured by the men who fill the growing space between them.

Chapter 2
CHILDHOOD STORIES

As a little boy, my father was a bit of a wiseass. Gabi was over-protected and indulged, the "little prince" of the family. Over the years, several stories have been told again and again, first among the family at home in Berehovo, and later to my sister, my cousins, and me—always with laughter and a sense of wonder at the audaciousness of this smiling, brown-haired mischievous boy, and the family's attempts to protect him. The story most often told is of the hole in the fence, and whenever I ask my father for details as we sit together on the blue couch in my parents' living room, he has no trouble recalling one of his earliest memories.

Herman, ever protective of Gabi, only allowed him to play in the backyard with the gate doors closed. But four-year-old Gabi complained that he couldn't see or talk to anyone on the street. Herman went to work with a saw and hammer on the tall wooden fence that ran about ten meters from the front of their house to the edge of their property. He cut a diamond-shaped hole in the wood and covered it with chicken wire. He then built a bench for Gabi so that he could sit and look out through this window onto the grey, cobblestoned street, and across it to the large green gate of his neighbor's house.

But the plan backfired—Gabi's mouth was bigger than the rest of him. Protected by the locked gate, he called the older children names, and sometimes poked at the kids passing by with a stick he pushed through the chicken wire. In the end, Herman's efforts simply led to a new set of worries.

In July of 1932, Bertha and the three children went to a vacation resort. Herman stayed in Berehovo to tend his store.

Although he enjoyed the quiet, Herman missed his family and didn't like being alone. He filled his evenings by eating out with friends and relatives. He wrote a postcard to the family:

HERMAN KLEIN

Dear Mum and Children,

I'm not sure about your address but I hope this postcard will get to you. I received your postcard and letter. I've found the stockings, so there are no more worries. I'm spending all my time with Dudi, yesterday we were in Slaia until 12:30 together with Lenke. Everybody stares at Dudi, he's so elegant. Maritz and Iren were at our table, too. I wonder how and when the parcel arrived. If you need something just write me. Take care of Gabika when bathing. We planned to go to Badalo today, but the weather is cloudy so I'd rather we didn't leave.

The business is fine. There's a great demand for big harvest vessels.

Please write.

Kisses, Herman

❖❖❖

The following winter, Bertha went to the town square to buy some sausage from the butcher. It had snowed heavily, and was still snowing, so she decided to pull little Gabi behind her on his sled. She was a strong, muscular woman, and she easily dragged him along.

Gabi heard the metal blades of the sled scratching into the ice beneath the snow, and he watched the movie theater on the corner grow bigger and bigger as they approached the end of their block. Finally they passed two more streets and arrived in the town square, stopping in front of the delicatessen located just outside the arcade.

Gabi waited outside on his sled, watching the snowflakes fall onto his coat sleeves, while his mother bought the sausage.

When she came out of the shop, she handed Gabi the meat wrapped in white paper and told him to hold on to the package and not to let go until they got home. He gripped the package tightly, determined not to let it drop.

Every dozen steps or so, Bertha asked, "Do you have the package?"

"Yes, I do," he called to his mother.

A few yards further: "Do you still have the package?"

"Yes."

And so it continued all the way home, until they were just a few feet from their front door.

"Do you have the package?"

"No," Gabi said.

Bertha stopped pulling the sled and turned toward her little boy, inspecting the round face wrapped in wool. "You don't have it? But you had it just a few seconds ago!"

To this day, my father isn't sure whether the package simply slipped out of his hand, or whether he threw it from the sled because he was fed up with Bertha's repeated questioning.

They retraced their tracks in search of the missing sausage, but the white paper package was lost in the snow.

One Sunday when Gabi was five, he rode on his father's bike to the football stadium at the edge of town. He sat in a small seat, his feet dangling over the handlebars. The bike swayed from one side to the other as Herman pedaled through the town square, and Gabi felt every bump of the cobblestones below.

The shops were closed and it seemed that the entire town was heading toward the stadium. There was a very important game that day: Berehovo was playing its biggest rival, the team from the neighboring town of Mukačevo. Gabi was impatient to get there. He wanted to see the team take the field, and to call out the names of his favorite players. By the time they arrived at the stadium, he could hardly wait to get inside. He walked through the gates with his father, and the field came into view just as the Mukačevo team entered the small arena. He could hear the fans yelling and cheering, and he hoped they wouldn't be as noisy when the game ended and Mukačevo had been defeated.

Just after taking his seat on the bench next to his father, Gabi jumped up because the home team was making their appearance. Dressed in their green-and-white-striped shirts, white shorts, green socks, and brown leather boots, the Berehovo players ran in a straight line across the field. The line dissolved as the players broke into small groups and passed the ball to one another. The fans, Gabi and Herman included, yelled loudly to their favorite players, chanting the team name and making as much noise as they possibly could in order to make it clear to the Mukačevo fans that the home team would be victorious.

The Berehovo goalkeeper approached the goal, and several other players began to take turns shooting the ball at him. This was one of Gabi's favorite moments. He hoped to be the Berehovo goalkeeper one day, and he watched carefully as the keeper kept the ball from going into the net. As the goalkeeper stretched to reach a shot heading toward the upper corner of the goal, he hung horizontally in the air for the slightest moment, and then dropped to the ground with the ball in his hands.

The players moved into their positions while the substitutes walked toward the team bench. The referee, dressed in black shirt and knickers, blew his whistle and the game began. Gabi and Herman cheered, watching intently as their team passed and shot the ball. There was pandemonium in the stands when the Berehovo team finally scored. Herman lifted Gabi high in the air in celebration, enabling Gabi to see over the heads of the people standing in front of him, down to the field where the players embraced.

When the game ended, with Berehovo victorious, Gabi and Herman walked from the stadium with their friends and neighbors, retelling the story of the goal to one another, each one of the group recalling a new detail and adding to the narrative. An hour after the game had ended, its history had been written and rewritten. Herman lifted Gabi onto the bicycle and began to pedal home, shouting the happy outcome of the game to the people they passed as they rode through the town square.

Chapter 3
GROWING UP SKINNY

Gabi started school in 1933 at the age of five. His public school was a two-story building with a pine-lined walkway that led to two sets of tall, narrow front doorways. Each door was topped with transom windows and stone archways that decorated the façade of the building. Like many of the buildings in Berehovo, its walls were painted a light pinkish brown and the roof had rust-red tiles.

By all accounts, including his own, Gabi was a happy kid. In spite of the remarks he had made through the protected window in his father's fence, he had plenty of friends by the time he started school. Berehovo was a charming town. The streets were lined with cafés, where people sat outside in the summer sunshine, and found cozy warmth inside in the winter. There was ice skating in January and swimming in July, and a big pink strawberry torte of a hotel stood on one side of the central square.

Families were large, extended, and close. Gabi had twelve aunts and uncles, most of whom lived in Berehovo or in nearby towns and villages. His days were filled with cousins and friends, football whenever possible, and piano lessons when they could not be avoided. Football was the only sport in town, and in all but the coldest of months small games were played in side yards and in the streets, the ball lost among a pack of boys. Gabi liked being the goalkeeper, a position in low demand among the other kids.

Hobbies were simple. A favorite was to collect pages from the writing tablets of the local pharmacists. Each pad had a different advertisement from the drug companies, each with a picture—perhaps of a city or someone playing a sport. The kids would finagle the pages from the pharmacists, and then trade them with each other.

There were no tensions between Christians and Jews in Berehovo in those days. The Kleins socialized often with both their Jewish and non-Jewish neighbors. When Herman built a fence at the back of the yard, he left a walkway that allowed them to easily visit Mrs. Riha, a Christian woman from Prague who lived in the house behind their own. She often invited the family to join her in the celebration of her holidays. The three Klein children marveled at her Christmas tree, decorated with real candles. Best of all were the homemade candies, wrapped in colorful paper, that were tucked into the branches. Lilly, Gabi and Oli were invited to choose some of their favorite colors and take the candies home. Herman and Bertha reciprocated the sharing of holidays with Mrs. Riha, including her in their celebrations of Jewish traditions.

On most Saturdays after temple, the extended family of grandparents, aunts, uncles and cousins would gather at the home of Bertha's parents, Záli and Toni. Bertha, Herman and the kids would join Bertha's sister Bözsi—who looked just like her—together with Bözsi's husband and their two young daughters for the walk to their parents' home. When they arrived, Toni would go down to the cellar and bring up a glass of wine for everyone, including the kids. He would then preside over the gathering from his bentwood chair, dressed in his three-piece navy-blue suit—his standard Sabbath uniform.

On some Sundays, the whole gang, including Herman's brothers and their families, would gather at the Klein home. (Herman's parents, Simon and Ida, both lived past eighty and died in the mid-1930s.) In warm weather, the summer kitchen—a small building in the backyard—was used for cooking, and food was spread on the table under the gazebo just outside the back door to the house. The guests would feast on Bertha's *challah* and chicken liver, and Herman would serve the wine, siphoned straight from the barrel in their shed. His family had a vineyard in the foothills of the mountains just outside of town, and they kept him well supplied. At the end of the meal, he would pull a watermelon up from the well where he had placed it the day before, and cut cool slices for all the guests.

The Kleins were one of the first families in town to own an electric refrigerator. Herman had bought one to sell in his store, but it was priced higher than the market could bear. It sat in the store for months without a buyer until Herman eventually decided to bring it home. The house had most of the modern amenities: Bertha still had to heat the water that was used in the kitchen, but there was an inside bathroom, and the bathtub had its own heating unit. In the kitchen pantry, Bertha stored her hand-packed jars of fruits and sauces above the small hand-lettered labels on the shelves that Herman had written to identify the contents of each jar. He had also hammered nails along the top shelf, above the bins of wheat flour and rye, where he hung bunches of grapes harvested from the trellises next to the gazebo.

The family had a vegetable garden in the yard, as well as a prolific walnut tree and several fruit trees. Fresh fruits were among Herman's favorite things to eat. Once they owned the electric refrigerator, he would pick two apricots on summer mornings and put them in to cool, enjoying them when he came home for lunch, or at the end of the day. After lunch, Herman always stretched out and took a nap, waking an hour later with the question, "Did I sleep any?"

On weekends and early evenings, Gabi would watch as Herman tended his sand garden. He used the rake like a brush, sifting through a patch of white sand that he had spread at the side of the house. Herman had read about this Japanese gardening technique, and he had taken up the hobby. The tongs of the rusty rake dragged like fingernails through the granules of sand, reminding Gabi of his mother's fingers working flour in her big mixing bowl. When the sun was low in the sky and the light just cleared the top of the fence, shadows were thrown by each small ridge of sand, creating the illusion that Herman was painting black lines on white paper. Gabi was amazed at the pictures his father could create, at the way he could move the rake so delicately. Whenever Gabi tried, he found it was so hard to keep the straight lines straight or to keep the curved ones bent smoothly. And then he would forget, and step where he had already created a design.

In the summer of 1935, the big event for the Klein family was the visit of Uncle Manny, Bertha's brother. He had emigrated to the United States before World War I, and was now running a successful department store in Scranton, Pennsylvania. Manny's family was quite affluent, particularly in the eyes of Lilly, Oli, and Gabi. The children marveled at their aunt Helen's smart American outfits, their twelve-year-old cousin Betty's skirts and matching socks (navy blue or red, while they only wore white), and fourteen-year-old Irving's white linen knickers. Lilly couldn't speak a word of English and Betty didn't know Hungarian, but by the end of their first day together they were best friends. Oli and Lilly paraded Betty down the main street of town, where they met their girlfriends and flirted with the boys.

Irving was allowed to borrow Herman's bike, and he and seven-year-old Gabi spent much of their time together riding through town. One Wednesday, Gabi and Irving rode their bikes around the marketplace. It was market day, and the vast square was crowded with horse- and mule-drawn carts filled with produce, dairy products, and meat sold by the local farmers. Irving rounded a corner in the busy market and slammed on his brakes. Gabi came to an abrupt stop behind him. Irving dismounted and knelt beside the bike, showing Gabi that the chain had fallen off. Gabi watched as Irving replaced the chain onto the sprocket, and then stood and wiped his greasy hands down the front of his white knickers. Imagining the trouble he would be in if he did such a thing, Gabi guessed that this was the sort of thing you were allowed to do if you were rich and lived in America.

The visit of Manny, Helen and their children was the highlight of 1935, and the Klein family continued to tell stories of their time together for years to come. When Herman said goodbye to his brother-in-law at the end of the six-week visit, he wished that he, too, were going to the United States. He imagined life for his family in Pennsylvania, and resolved that he would continue to work on his English, so that maybe, someday, they would join their family there.

Gabi was very skinny, which was unacceptable for the only male child of a middle-class East European family. Bertha could not get Gabi to eat much, and if she forced him to eat, he threw up. Occasionally, Gabi would eat next door at the Shimbergs' house. The Shimbergs owned a bookstore a few doors down from Herman's hardware store. Bertha was horrified when Mrs. Shimberg told her, "Your son eats fine when he eats at our house. Maybe you aren't feeding him the right things."

Bertha and Herman decided to pull the money together to send Gabi to an expensive health resort for kids in order to fatten him up. Herman spent the first few days there with him and sent home a postcard reporting that Gabi had gained some weight:

> I got your postcard and I will take your advice—will stay until Sunday. Taking the morning train and will stop at Legenje to visit with Lenke and Sanyi for a couple of hours, then I will stop at Helinec to visit Helen and Jozsi.
>
> Gabi looks good, he put on 80 dekas in 4 days, which is a good result. I am at ease to leave him there, he is in very good hands. He gets a massage at morning and at night, the doctor said it was beneficial for him. We'll have to send him a few things from home. I am looking forward to being home tomorrow. I saw a lot of beautiful things, taking walks. Maybe I'll see Poldi's children. Don't write anymore because I will be home soon.

Shortly after Herman rejoined Bertha and the girls in Bere-hovo, they received a postcard from Gabi saying, "I put on 100 dekas [about three ounces]. But I saw a squirrel and lost them." He came home the same skinny kid he had been when he left.

Lilly claims she was very pretty as a teenager and very popular with the boys. Based on the photographic evidence, I believe her. Her old album is filled with photos of her in glamorous poses, showing off her dark wavy hair, large brown eyes, pretty smile, and petite figure. There is usually a handsome, proud-looking young man standing next to her. She assures me that she did spend time doing more useful things than posing for photos. She wasn't very interested in sports, but had a particular talent for jumping great distances. This won her a broad-jump competition at school. She was an avid reader, consuming everything from Descartes to Fitzgerald, and while she played the piano with less enthusiasm than her sister Oli, she did so with much greater zeal than her younger brother. Even as a child she knew she had it good, and she was proud of her home and Herman's beautifully kept gardens, which, ever changing, were often admired by passing neighbors.

Oli was a very different sort of girl. She loved to play football with the boys, and she was a strong athlete. When she was twelve, she won first place in the large tricycle race that ran down the main street in town. In many ways—temperament, tastes and interests—Oli had more in common with Gabi than with Lilly, and she was very close to her younger brother. When Gabi was four, he and Oli became ill and convalesced together in the same bed. Oli kept him entertained by playing a game called "The Lions are Coming," which required them to hide under the covers. Both girls loved the little prince of their family, but Oli and Gabi shared a special connection.

Oli loved the piano, and played well beyond what was required for her lessons. She spent hours at the keys, impressing

The Kleins in 1935: *(from left)* Bertha, Oli, Gabi, Lilly and Herman

her parents with her talent. She imagined that she might make a career of music, and hoped to study one day at a conservatory.

The girls also helped Bertha in the kitchen, particularly at holiday time. Lilly and Oli loved Purim, the spring holiday that commemorates the saving of Jews from extermination in Persia. Baking was a huge part of the celebration, and Lilly and Oli joined Bertha in preparing the *hamentaschen, rugelach,* and various other breads and sweets. These were made in abundance—the tradition of the holiday called for the sharing of food with friends and family, and particularly with the poor. Lilly and Oli traveled the streets of Berehovo delivering cakes and sweets to relatives and to poor families in town. Some of these families were very observant, and as dictated by their beliefs, had many, many children. For these children and their parents, the generosity of their neighbors on holidays and on Friday evenings was a very welcome, often essential, gift.

Lilly frequently took trains to nearby towns and villages to visit relatives and friends. After Herman's father died, she visited her widowed grandmother Ida and brought her food from Bertha's kitchen. Ida would tell Lilly, "You are so good to do this. God will look after you and protect you always."

One day, while taking the train back home, Lilly struck up a conversation with Nina, a young woman about her age who was also traveling to Berehovo. They took a liking to each other, and when Lilly told her mother about this, Bertha suggested that she invite her for dinner. As Nina and Bertha casually conversed about their family histories, Bertha became suspicious that the daughter of the woman who had followed Herman home from Vladivostok was sitting in her living room! Bertha confirmed this through a round of questioning when her children were out of the room. After leaving Berehovo many years before, the mother had married a Slovak, settled in Czechoslovakia and had a daughter. Herman had been imprisoned with many Slovaks, which invited the question of whether Herman was the only former prisoner she found after the war. Bertha didn't ask, and the evening remained friendly.

During most summer vacations, Lilly and Oli visited Bertha's sisters, Lenke and Irene. Both aunts were married, but neither had children, so the girls were spoiled with new clothing and other treats. Oli started the summer with one aunt and Lilly with the other, then they switched halfway through their vacation. Lenke and her husband Csányi lived in Slovensko, about a two-hour train ride from Berehovo. They owned an apothecary where Lilly helped out during her visits. She enjoyed the work—packaging the medicines and talking with the customers. She liked the way everything in the store had its own place on the shelf, and especially took pleasure in the careful sequence of the colored bottles. Basic drugs were delivered to the store prepackaged, but for the others her uncle carefully mixed the ingredients, stirring precisely weighed powders with his pestle.

Herman, Bertha, and Gabi would also come to visit Lenke. Eleven-year-old Gabi made friends with Tibor, the older boy next door. Tibor had a marvelous talent for carving, and with his sharp knife made a variety of children's toys carved out of soft wood. He made ducks that could be pulled by a string and airplanes with landing wheels that rolled. Gabi's favorite by far was the plane, with its delicate double-decker wings.

His aunt and uncle received free samples of face cream with their deliveries of toothpaste and other toiletries, and Gabi asked for some of the small jars. He passed them on to Tibor, who gave them as presents to his mother. In exchange, Gabi got one of the coveted biplanes. With a flick of his finger, he could make the propeller spin.

THE WALK

I am sitting in my office at INSEAD, a business school in France where I am a faculty member. It is a Saturday afternoon and my desk is covered with maps of Auschwitz-Birkenau. No one would ever guess from looking at this mess that I'm a marketing professor.

On my computer there's a photo of the Birkenau ramp, the area where the prisoners were unloaded from the trains and selected for work or death. I'm trying to solve a mystery: which gas chamber did Herman die in? There were four in Birkenau, numbered II-V. (Crematorium I was in the original Auschwitz camp, three kilometers away.) Most Hungarian Jews were killed in Crematorium II, III and V.[1]

If Herman went to V, or IV if it was in operation on the day he arrived, he would have had a long walk to the far side of the camp, and he might have been among those who were kept in a small wooded area, waiting their turn. They sat in the grass under the trees, ignorant of what was to come. Photos discovered later show the families—old men and women, children, and some young mothers. You might think they are picnicking, until you notice there are no blankets, food, or wine. Upon closer look, you can see the stress and fatigue on their faces, the soiled clothing, and the way they are crowded together. Still, I like to think of Herman having this time in the woods after three days locked in the cattle car.

Then again, those prisoners were sitting in the woods because their number exceeded the capacities of the crematoria. On some of the days, around the time of their May arrival,

---

1. Jean-Claude Pressac and Robert-Jan van Pelt, "The Machinery of Mass Murder at Auschwitz" in *Anatomy of the Auschwitz Death Camp*, Yisrael Gutman and Michael Berebaum, eds. (Bloomington: Indiana University Press, 1994; First Paperback Edition, 1998), 238.

bodies were burned in open pits near the woods. If Herman guessed what was to come, then those hours waiting in the woods would have been agonizing. Better, perhaps, to have gone in the other direction, toward Crematorium II—a short walk and then straight inside.

Looking at the aerial photos and the maps, I realize that those going to Crematorium II or III would probably take a different route from the train tracks than those going to Crematorium IV or V. If I can determine which way Herman went when he and my father, Gabi, were separated at the selection point, then I can narrow things down.

My dad is at home in Miami, and I call him. In response to my questions, he has trouble remembering if everyone went right or left when they got off the train. He was only sixteen when all of this happened, and he is now seventy-three, twenty years older than his father was when they were separated upon arrival at Auschwitz-Birkenau. He doesn't remember which way they were facing when they reached the selections—the point where SS officers decided who would be worked to death and who would be killed immediately. I look again at the photo of the ramp on my screen. One track breaks into three just after the arch that marks the entrance to the camp. His train could have been on any of the three tracks, and the door could have been on either side of the train.

With my mom's help (she is the computer-literate member of the couple), I direct my dad to www.remember.org/camps/birkenau/bir-ramp-03.html, and now we are both looking at the same photo of the ramp.[2] I have a printout of the photo so that I can take notes.

"Dad, the entrance, the big archway that the train went through entering Birkenau, is behind where the picture was taken."

---

2. Alan Jacobs, "The End of the Line," <http://www.remember.org/camps/birkenau/bir-ramp-03.html>, originally accessed 2000, most recently accessed February 19, 2013.

Birkenau train ramp. Used with permission.

I know that by leading him to this picture and asking my questions I am evoking one of his most painful Holocaust memories. He was having an uneventful and quiet Saturday morning, and now he is looking at the Birkenau train ramp. When I was sixteen years old, he and I watched the TV movie *Kill Me If You Can*, in which Alan Alda plays Caryl Chessman, a prisoner who spent twelve years on death row before being executed. The movie depicts Chessman's death in the gas chamber in vivid detail: he struggles for air, crawls on the ground, wets himself, and eventually dies. The next day I noticed that my dad was not himself. He was quiet and withdrawn. I asked my mother what was wrong and she said, "Daddy's upset about seeing that man die in the gas chamber. It made him think about how his father suffered before he died."

Now, more than twenty-five years later, I listen carefully to the pitch in my father's voice as we each look at our respective computer screens. I am relieved that his tone is characteristically upbeat and matter-of-fact.

"Ah, okay. We got out on the right-hand side of the train, the same side we got in. I was in the second-to-last car. I remember seeing barracks." The photo is doing the trick.

"There were barracks on both sides of the train tracks. Do you remember which way you went after you got off the train?"

"We jumped down and went to our left, toward the front of the train. That's where the selections were, in the big sandy area between the middle and right track. All the men were in rows of five. There was one guy to my right, so I was in the second spot. My father was next to me on the left, and then there must have been two more guys. We approached the SS officer who was pointing a stick to one side or the other. I went right, and my father went left."

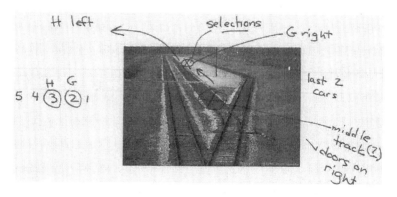

After I hang up, I look at more photos from *The Auschwitz Album*.[3] I find a picture of the selections on the ramp at the same spot my father indicated. Consistent with his recollections, women with children (who would be bound for the gas chambers) are turning left.

---

3. *The Auschwitz Album* is a series of photos taken at Birkenau in late May/early June 1944, shortly after my father's arrival at the camp. The photos were taken by an SS officer and depict the arrival of trains carrying Hungarian Jews, victims being led to the gas chambers, and other prisoners being processed into the camp. <http://www1.yadvashem.org/exhibitions/album_auschwitz/home_auschwitz_album.html>, accessed 2000, most recently accessed February 19, 2013.

The Auschwitz Album, FA 268-34.

Herman turns to the left, and over his shoulder he watches Gabi go off ~~in~~ to the ~~other direction~~ right. His son moves further away, and is soon lost from sight, obscured by the men who fill the growing space between them.

RECOLLECTION
(Written 2000)

It is the third day into the new millennium, and I gather my dad and his two sisters around Lilly's dining room table in Miami. With Oli in town and the three siblings all together, I seize the opportunity to get some things straight. I've made a list of partial stories I have heard, and different memories that need to be reconciled. Oli sits with her hands in her lap, her beautiful wavy grey hair framing her face. Her hair is still a bit out of place from the nap she has just taken, necessitated by fatigue from her recent trip over from Budapest. I'm tired too, from my flight in from Paris and the New Year's Eve celebrations by the Seine a few days before. Lilly looks eager to start, always happy for the opportunity to talk about the past. My dad, I think, is just enjoying the fact that we are all together. I turn on my video camera.

> *Jill:* One of you once told me that you were playing in the yard when you were little and he [Gabi] grabbed his chest, fell down, and said he was having a heart attack.
>
> *Oli:* Your father?
>
> *Jill:* Yes, and someone went for the doctor. Do you remember this at all?
>
> *Lilly:* No.
>
> *Oli:* I remember. He said, "My heart! My heart!"
>
> *Dad:* Oli went for this guy who was a doctor, but he was also a teacher, right?
>
> *Oli:* No, just a doctor.
>
> *Jill:* So she actually went to get a doctor?
>
> *Oli and Dad:* Yes.

33

Jill (to Oli): And did you come back with him?

Dad: He was in the coffeehouse.

Jill (to Oli): So did you go to the coffeehouse?

Oli: Yes.

Jill: And then you brought him?

Oli: He said nothing. He said, "He'll stay alive!"

Dad: It was nothing serious.

Jill: Did he get in trouble?

Oli: No.

Dad: I was only young.

Jill (to Oli): But you were scared?

Oli: Yes.

Jill: How old was he?

Lilly: Thirteen.

Oli: No, younger.

Jill: Ten?

Oli: Maybe…. Before bar mitzvah.

Lilly recounts things with absolute certainty and Oli often disagrees, at which point Lilly usually agrees that her younger sister is probably right. I don't have a sense of who actually has the best memory, because there are some things they each remember in greater detail. My father tends to be pretty sketchy on specifics, probably because he was so much younger when a lot of these incidents took place, and he's more of a general picture kind of guy, anyway.

I look for verification of every detail that they tell me, seeing if they agree with each other or not. In this manner, I hear stories I have heard before, and some that I have not. Herman, I learn, jumped out of the second floor of a building to try to avoid being drafted in World War I, though after the interview is over I remember that long ago I also heard that he jumped off a balcony when he thought Bertha wouldn't marry him because of the woman from Vladivostok. Either Herman had a daring penchant for jumping from great heights—for self-preservation, or just to make a point—or these two stories had become conflated in their minds, probably when they were children. I will have to ask them about this when we are all together again, though I know it may well be impossible for me to get this particular story sorted out.

Chapter 4
LILLY AND GEORGE

Lilly and George were third cousins who had grown up knowing each other, but George's attraction to Lilly didn't become apparent to either of them until an event that took place when they were thirteen. George had just had an operation on his toe. Neither George nor Lilly can remember what was wrong with the toe, or why it needed a surgeon's attention, but, for whatever reason, George was in a hospital bed with his toe bandaged up, and his friends came to visit. George had received a large bag of chocolates from one of his relatives, and when Lilly and some of his friends visited, he gave one piece to each. To Lilly, however, he gave the entire remainder of the bag. It was love. Within a couple of years, Lilly moved George to the top of her list of admirers, and he stayed there, most of the time.

George had been through a rough couple of years, watching his father die slowly and painfully of tuberculosis of the throat. While fighting the early stages of the disease, Moritz, who was a well-known attorney in Berehovo, defended over 100 peasants in a case against a landowner. The case added to his fame, but it was the last case he ever brought to trial. He traveled to Vienna for radiation treatment and lost his voice. He died soon after, when George was fifteen.

After Moritz's death, George's mother struggled to keep the family afloat. She had George and his younger brother Frank to care for, and she had been left with little money. Moritz had been famous for his work, but his practice was not terribly lucrative. Each year, from the spring through the fall, she worked in her parents' vineyard outside of town. Her parents also owned a hotel in town; the revenues from that helped support the family.

George gave Lilly a slim, gold engagement ring when they were fifteen. Yet, truth to tell, George's prospects of marrying her were not good. Not only was there competition—including Csányi Donat, a boy whose family owned the other hotel in Berehovo—but George's young age was a problem. Girls at that time tended to marry men who were eight or nine years older, already established, and able to support a family. Lilly was the same age as George, and so she expected that her parents were unlikely to view him as a suitable husband. Still, they were crazy about each other, and George became a frequent visitor to the Klein's house. He attended temple with Herman on the Sabbath, along with Herman's father-in-law, Toni, who had advised George that he definitely had no chance with Lilly if he didn't come along every Saturday.

By the spring of 1938, near the end of gymnasium (high school), George knew that he wanted to follow his father's example, and planned to start law school in Prague in the fall. Meanwhile, Lilly's early experiences in her aunt and uncle's pharmacy led her to decide on a career as a pharmacist. After graduation, she would leave for an internship at a pharmacy near Prague, where she could learn Czech—a requirement for attending a Prague university.

As graduation approached, Lilly prepared with anticipation for the dance that would mark the end of their gymnasium days. Her mother hired a local tailor to create a beautiful dress made of white chiffon—sleeveless, with a wide, flowing skirt. Once the dress had been tailored, it was embroidered with flowers: poppies, bachelor buttons, and daisies. Small solitary flowers at the top turned into large bouquets of flowers on the skirt. She also had a matching pocketbook of the same design. On the night of the dance, she wore her shoulder-length brown hair back from her forehead, held in place with a white hairband.

George was also well prepared for the evening. Arrangements had been made for a tailor in Prague to make his suit. It was dark grey with maroon pinstripes; he wore it with a white shirt and a matching grey and maroon tie. Lilly thought he looked very stylish and sophisticated. Their parents were able to see the results of their efforts because they, too, attended the dance. The older generation sat together at one end of the room, leaving the new graduates to socialize among themselves.

As the evening got underway, Lilly and George danced to popular tunes played by local musicians. Lilly was so proud to be with George, handsome in his new suit, with his stunning blue eyes and straight blond hair combed across his forehead. He looked much too young to be finishing gymnasium—he could pass for fourteen. She also danced with Herman, who couldn't resist the opportunity to lead his pretty daughter around the room. Lilly felt beautiful and grown-up in her lovely dress. On the dance floor, she felt that everything was in place for this to be the best night of her life.

She was wrong.

About an hour before midnight, Lilly and George were dancing together, when suddenly everything went dark. The music ended abruptly, and everyone stopped dancing, confused, their eyes adjusting to the sudden darkness. After a moment, the lights came back on, revealing a group of about ten teenage boys who had entered the room. They were dressed in a makeshift version of the Nazi Youth uniform, with high white socks pulled up to their knees. George recognized his next-door neighbor as one of the group. The boys shouted Nazi slogans and anti-Semitic insults. At first, Lilly thought that it was some kind of a joke the boys were playing. The parents, who were quicker to understand what was happening, rushed across the room, pushing the boys out the door.

When the troublemakers were gone, the dancing continued, and everyone tried to carry on as before. But the festive mood couldn't be restored, and Lilly knew that the special evening had been ruined.

At the end of summer vacation, Lilly left home to begin work in the pharmacy in Kasejovice, a small town near the Czech city of Pilsen. She had arranged her internship with an elderly Czech couple, who gave her room and board in exchange for her work in their pharmacy. She ate her meals with them, and being in a warm and affectionate home helped mitigate the homesickness she felt. For their part, the couple enjoyed having Lilly there. At meals, she took the seat of their grown son, who had recently moved out of the house.

But this arrangement did not last long. Two weeks after Lilly arrived in Kasejovice, Herman sent her an urgent telegram telling her that she must come home immediately. Czechoslovakia was falling apart or, more accurately, it was being dissolved. The German chancellor had delivered an ultimatum to the Czechoslovakian government demanding that they hand over the Sudetenland, a region that had been part of Austria prior to World War I. The deadline given for the handover was the end of September. Disappointed at having to abandon her plans, Lilly rode home on a train filled with soldiers. It seemed to take forever to get home.

Within weeks, the bulk of Czechoslovakia was under German control. As part of Hitler's dissolution of Czechoslovakia, the southern part of the country, including Berehovo, was annexed to Hungary in November of 1938. The Czechs, who had mobilized their army in the area, did not resist, and the citizens of Berehovo watched the soldiers and tanks leave town. In their wake, Hungarian troops carrying flags and guns marched into Berehovo in a grand parade. A ceremony was conducted in the market square, with the citizens of the town—now renamed Beregszász—lining the walks in front of the shops. Many cheered the "liberators"; older men wore their World War I uniforms, some of the women dressed in traditional Hungarian clothes, and flowers were thrown.

For the Jews, however, this shift in nationality was disquieting, to say the least. The Czech government had provided Jews with rights to live and work equal to those of their non-Jewish compatriots. Hungary offered no such protection, and in fact had laws on the books that actively discriminated against Jews. Six months earlier, the Hungarian government had enacted the *numerus clausus*, a law restricting the number of Jews who could hold jobs in commerce, industry, administration, and the professions to 20 per cent. This ratio would be dropped to 6 per cent in the coming months. More frightening still was the current demand from the Hungarian Nazi party, the Arrow Cross, for *numerus nullus*, a Hungary free of Jews.

These new laws were particularly hard on young people trying to prepare for their chosen careers. Lilly's plans were dashed, as were George's. Instead of going to university to train for his legal career, George stayed in Beregszász and got a job in a pharmacy, spending his days serving customers and filling aspirin capsules. At least the couple could see each other every day, but they were frustrated at the roadblocks in their path, and apprehensive about what was to come.

RECOLLECTION
(Written 2006)

Hugo Gryn, who was three years younger than my father, also grew up in Berehovo and survived Auschwitz. He eventually became a renowned rabbi in London. His daughter published his memoir, *Chasing Shadows*, after he died in 1996.[1] The book reached bookstore shelves in 2000, in the early days of my research for my own book. Much as I was curious to read his story, I purposely left the book unopened until I had written my own descriptions of Berehovo life based on the recollections of my father and aunts. My family's memories and those of Rabbi Gryn are similar in many ways. Mr. Gryn describes the town as elegant and full of energy, excitement and fun, and recounts many of the same rituals of life that my father remembers.

The greatest divergence in accounts seems to emerge from the fact that the Gryns were much more religious. Both the Kleins and the Gryns observed Sabbath and attended temple, but the Gryn children attended religious schools, whereas the Kleins did not. "Home life and religious life were inseparable," Rabbi Gryn writes in his memoir. He remembers that "meat and dairy dishes were strictly separated, and it would never have occurred to anyone that any of the biblically forbidden foods were even tempting!"[2] Bertha kept a kosher household, but her husband's behavior was not always in keeping with tradition. My dad remembers the day when Herman came home and surreptitiously motioned the kids out into the backyard, avoiding Bertha's notice. Once outside, he revealed a ham sandwich, and let each child sample the delicacy. He was clearly breaking

---

1. Hugo Gryn (with Naomi Gryn), *Chasing Shadows* (London: Penguin Books, 1996).

2. Ibid., 26.

religious (and Bertha's!) rules, but he really loved to eat ham, and he wanted to share this pleasure with his children.

Rabbi Gryn recalls the town's rapid transition from Czech to Hungarian, from Berehovo to Beregszász. He describes standing on the main square and watching with dread as the newly arrived Hungarians conducted their parade. A few weeks earlier, his uncle's farm, close to the old border with Hungary, had been attacked by pro-Nazi Hungarians. All of the cattle were gruesomely slaughtered, and his uncle was nearly killed when one of the assailants plunged an axe deep into his back. Thus, by the time the Hungarians marched into town in November 1938, his family had already experienced the consequences of hatred. The Kleins' first brushes with anti-Semitic violence were still a few weeks off.

Chapter 5
LIFE IN HUNGARY

With the dawn of 1939, the Jews of Beregszász were still anxious about the new government and the growing anti-Semitism that the Hungarians brought with them. The transition from Czechoslovakia to Hungary had little impact on Gabi's daily life, however. Herman and Bertha did their best to shield their son, who was about to turn eleven, from what was happening around him; for quite a while they were successful.

There was even some excitement for Gabi in the new regime. All of the boys in his school were given Hungarian army hats—black and blue with white stripes. They were taught to march like the Hungarian soldiers, their chests leaning forward ahead of their legs, their feet gliding close to the ground. One day his school held a ceremony, and all of the boys displayed their marching skills while Hungarian soldiers looked on. Two of the soldiers told Gabi that he was the best marcher in the crowd. His ability to mimic the Hungarian soldiers even helped him pass one of his classes. A militaristic math teacher told him that he was between a failing and a passing grade. Then he added, "I heard that you stand at attention like the soldiers very well. Show me how you do it." Gabi struck the pose, leaning his chest as far forward as possible without falling over. He held the position until the teacher said, "Okay, you passed."

While Gabi remained oblivious to the dangers of the new regime, others were confronting their changing world head on. A short while after the Hungarians took control of the town, George, who was nineteen, was walking home at around eight o'clock in the evening. He had gone to visit Lilly at the Kleins' house, and was taking a shortcut behind the synagogue. In the darkness, a small gang of young men suddenly confronted him. George recognized them as self-styled "freedom fighters," young Hungarians who took it upon themselves to police the Jews. A voice from the group yelled, "He's a Jew. Let's kill him." Though terrified, George did not panic, and as he stood facing them, an idea popped into his head. He picked out one of the men at random, looked directly into his eyes and said, "I'm not Jewish. I go to your church." Perplexed, the man looked back at George, whose blond hair and blue eyes did make the diagnosis of Jewish heritage difficult. The man hesitated a moment, looked confused, then called off his comrades.

Not everyone was as fortunate as George. Soon after this incident, the Kleins learned that the teenage brother of Bertha's sister's husband had disappeared from his small village outside of Beregszász. His parents searched for him for months. Eventually, a witness told them that a local gang of Hungarian fascists had murdered their son, and revealed where they could find his buried body.

Many Hungarian officials, civil servants, and engineers began arriving in Beregszász to work in the new administration. The Kleins had decided to rent out one of their bedrooms, the whole family now sleeping in one room. Their first boarder was a hunchbacked lawyer named Potfia. He helped Herman file papers to demonstrate that his ancestors had been in Hungary for many generations. In late December of 1939, Herman traveled to Munkács (formally Mukačevo) to collect his "Identity Papers," which allowed him to retain some rights as a Hungarian. Most importantly, these papers permitted him to keep his hardware store open for business, and to continue working. (When customers haggled with him at the store, he would joke that the *numerus clausus* said that this was the price at which he had to sell.)

By late 1939, in the wake of Germany's attack on Poland and the start of the war, other more transitory guests began to pass through Beregszász, fleeing Poland for the east. One day, Lilly was approached by her friend Miki, who lived on the corner and often walked with her to school. He told her that there were refugees arriving who needed shelter. The Kleins, habitually generous to those in need, took in a middle-aged couple who spent one night on the kitchen floor before continuing their journey. They appeared to have been very wealthy before escaping from Poland: both were impeccably dressed, and the woman wore a beautiful fur coat. They were not Jewish.

After Lilly, Oli, and Gabi had gone to bed, Herman and Bertha sat up late in the kitchen and listened to the couple describe terrible scenes from Poland. They told of large groups of civilians being gunned down by German soldiers. They told of Jews, in particular, being rounded up and shot. The conversation was hushed: Herman and Bertha were doing their best to shield their children from the effects of the war and the news of the growing anti-Semitism in the region. The kids still managed to overhear what was being said, but they told themselves that Poland was very far away, and at war, and that in war, people got killed. Here in Hungary, they were safe.

Through his parents' efforts and his own instinctive defenses against the malevolent undertones of the times, Gabi was able to maintain a remarkably normal life and routine. He continued to focus on playing football, going to school, and not playing the piano. By the spring of 1940, when he was nearly twelve, Gabi started joining the older boys of the town at the field where they played after school. He sometimes played forward, but most of the time he tended goal. There were no goalposts, so he guarded the space between two shirts placed on the ground. A shot was considered "over the bar" if the ball went higher than the goalkeeper's outstretched arms; this rule was to Gabi's benefit, since he was among the smallest of the group.

Sometimes, younger children would watch the games and retrieve the ball for the players. On most days, though, Gabi spent a lot of time running through the tall grass at the edge of the field to collect the heavy brown ball after it went out of play. As he fished it out from the undergrowth peppered with spring flowers, he would hear the jokes and laughter of his friends behind him—either taunts for the kid who had sent the ball wide of the goal, or cheers for the one who had scored. He would turn and kick the ball back toward the field, the ball would be put back into play, and they'd start all over again.

Every day after school the boys met at the field, set up their makeshift goals, and played until dinnertime. As summer turned to fall and the evenings came earlier, their games grew shorter. There were days when playing was so much fun, and everyone was joking and laughing so hard, that Gabi wished that the sun would take an hour to cast its last moments of light. They played until the first snows came.

When enough snow had fallen, the sport changed to skiing. On Sundays, Gabi and George would set off in the early morning. They walked through the farmland at the edge of Beregszász to a vineyard just outside of town. The planted hillsides were lined with narrow paths that allowed room for the horse-drawn rigs that carried away the grapes at harvest time. In the winter the vines were dormant, the horses were stabled and these paths made excellent ski trails.

The boys worked their way up the hill, using their bamboo poles to pull themselves up the incline. Each pole had a disk made of woven leather near the bottom that kept them from going too deep into the snow. The heels of the boys' boots were harnessed to the skis. After the hard work of reaching the top, they whirled their way down the slope. George, being older and heavier, usually reached the bottom first, and would turn to watch Gabi riding the last of the decline. Then they would face the hill, dig their poles into the snow ahead of them, and pull their way back up the path once again. When they got hungry, they would stop to eat a lunch of chicken liver sandwiches that Bertha had prepared and drink from her thermos of tea. They would ski all day, returning at dusk to Bertha's table and the warmth of the kitchen stove.

On school days in the winter, Gabi usually came straight home from school and ran errands for his mother. One of his favorite jobs was to take the bread dough that Bertha had mixed and kneaded during the day to the baker. Carrying the dough in a basket, Gabi walked the three blocks into the center of town, and then on to the arcade filled with stores. At one end of the arcade was the delicatessen of the lost-sausage expedition, and at the other end was Herman's store. The bakery was in the center.

The baker would take the loaf, write a number on two small bits of paper, give one to Gabi, and push the other into the top of the dough. Gabi would then go to visit his father at the shop. When he returned to the baker's an hour later, he showed the baker his number and in exchange received a warm loaf of bread to carry home. All purchases were on credit, and accounts were settled at the end of the month. Often, walking back to his house in the early evening, he could not resist the scent of the fresh bread. He'd tear off the end of the loaf and stuff the warm morsel into his mouth. "The baker ate it," he'd tell his mother. Of course, he never did this with the Friday *challah*, which was broken only by his father, and only after the prayer, said in words that Gabi recognized but did not understand.

If taking charge of the bread was one of his favorite errands, the job he hated the most was taking a chicken to the courtyard of the synagogue to be killed. Bertha would pull a noisy, flapping chicken from the small coop in the backyard, tie its feet together, and hand it to Gabi. He put the chicken under his arm and walked it into town to its death. He could feel the warmth and life of the bird tucked against his chest, and he knew he was complicit in bringing it to slaughter. He was glad the chicken didn't know what was coming.

At the small building in the garden of the synagogue, a prayer was said over the chicken. Gabi turned away when the knife was lifted, and did not turn around again until well after he heard the thud of the steel blade against the wooden chopping block. The bird was then hung upside down from a hook to drain. When the carcass was emptied of blood, it was handed to a woman for plucking. Once the chicken was bare, Gabi took it home to Bertha. She butchered the chicken into quarters, then salted it heavily and placed it in the sun to draw out any remaining blood.

It was also Gabi's job to make the weekly trek to the bakery on Friday afternoons to deposit his family's heavy pot of *cholent*—a mixture of barley and beans—that was to be eaten on the Sabbath, a day when no cooking was allowed. The ceramic pots were cooked in huge ovens, and collected again on Saturday after the morning services at the temple. In this way, the Jewish families of Beregszász had a hot meal to eat on the Sabbath. Gabi went to the courtyard outside the bakery after leaving the synagogue and looked among the many numbered pots for the one he had brought the day before. He placed the hot vessel into a mesh sack woven from yarn, wrapping the top of the sack around his wrist. This allowed him to carry the load without burning his hands.

These daily routines, these seasons of football and skiing, these years of growing and learning, were a gift from Gabi's parents. These were better times for Gabi because of the ignorance he was allowed to preserve. He knew about the war, of course, and about Hitler and his hatred for the Jews. But he was encouraged to hold to the beliefs that kept many of the Jews of Beregszász feeling secure. The war was being fought in other countries. The government was in an alliance with Germany and so would not be overrun. The Jews of Hungary, though not treated as equals, were safe from Hitler's wrath. As 1940 passed into 1941 and 1942, it would become more difficult for the Kleins and their neighbors to maintain this optimism. And as Gabi progressed into adolescence, he would become more vulnerable to the anxiety, anger, and sense of betrayal that his world forced upon him.

But as 1940 was nearing its end, Gabi was still living his life of happy ignorance, with his biggest concern being his upcoming bar mitzvah. Some months before his thirteenth birthday, he began private lessons with a tutor whose job was to teach him the songs and prayers he would need to recite at the ceremony. Though not studious by nature, Gabi was nevertheless determined to learn what was necessary to get through the ceremony and make a good impression. The tutor was a young man with long, curly sideburns that hung from beneath a black hat. He also taught Lilly and Oli to read some Hebrew, but Lilly found him very unattractive, not at all like the boys she dated. Gabi dutifully learned how to read from the Torah and sing prayers. He was able to sound out the words, but he didn't know what most of them meant.

Bertha and Oli planned the festivities. Family, friends, neighbors and customers were all invited to celebrate at the house after the ceremony. Several days ahead of the event, Bertha, her sisters, and Oli began the baking and cooking. Lilly managed to avoid helping with the preparations, instead spending her time with George, her other suitors, and her girlfriends.

When the Saturday of the event arrived, Gabi sat with his father in the synagogue, several rows from the elevated platform where the rabbi stood. Herman was called up to join the rabbi as the cantor removed the Torah from its case behind the podium. Gabi watched nervously as the velvet-covered cylinder, embroidered with Hebrew characters, was laid on the table. The rabbi held the handles at the bottom of the Torah as the cantor removed the silver ornament with its bells from the top and slid the cover off the scroll. The ringing echoed throughout the synagogue. The Torah was unrolled, and Gabi was called forward.

Standing next to his father, Gabi looked out at more than 400 people, completely unsure of whether he would make it through the ceremony. In front of him were the men, and up in the balcony, the women, including his mother and sisters. The rabbi pointed to a page of the Torah and Gabi read the prayer. He sounded out the Hebrew words. He sang the prayers with only a passing resemblance to the correct notes. Finally, he completed all of the necessary tasks. He was done. Relieved, he returned with Herman to their seats for the closing of the services.

By the time they arrived home, guests were already standing in front of the house, and before long, the living room was packed with people. To create extra space, Herman had covered the bathtub with plywood, upon which Bertha had spread a tablecloth. There, in the bathroom, the products of the women's labor were displayed: the pastries with poppy seeds and walnuts, the sweet rolls garnished with preserves from the previous summer, and the chicken liver in the shape of one of the many fancy molds from Bertha's arsenal. The bathroom was next to the living room, so Bertha, Lilly and Oli could serve the guests easily.

The rabbi arrived with other leaders of the Jewish community. He called Gabi over and spoke to him in Yiddish, but Gabi didn't understand him and tried to answer him in Hungarian. The rabbi took Gabi's right hand and formed it into a fist, then covered the curled fingers with his large hand. When he squeezed tight, Gabi's littlest finger took the force of the rabbi's grip and he yelped, pulling his hand back. Moving away, he wondered why the rabbi had done such a thing. Was it a test of his strength, of whether he had become a man? If it was a test, he clearly hadn't passed, but he was not disappointed in himself. If anything, he was annoyed at the rabbi for doing something so unexpected and strange. He had passed his test for manhood that morning in the synagogue, and finger squashing had not been part of the deal.

The celebration continued on in a manner more cordial for Gabi. A clear plum liquor was passed among the guests, and the rabbi toasted the new young man. Then Gabi was given his gifts. His Uncle Hugo presented him with a small flat package. As he opened it, he was expecting to find a pen, something nice but not very different from the gifts he had received on birthdays and holidays in the past. But when he saw inside the box, he realized that he had been given something of a completely different caliber. He marveled at the gold trim along the edges of the rectangular face, the band of black leather. This was a gift given to a man. He strapped his new watch onto his wrist.

THE WALK

Once again my office floor is covered with maps and pictures of Auschwitz, but now I'm in Singapore. I have moved from INSEAD's European campus in France to our Asian campus, but I'm still reconstructing that same 500-meter walk in Poland. Comparing aerial photos, maps, and pictures from *The Auschwitz Album*, I'm retracing Herman's steps.

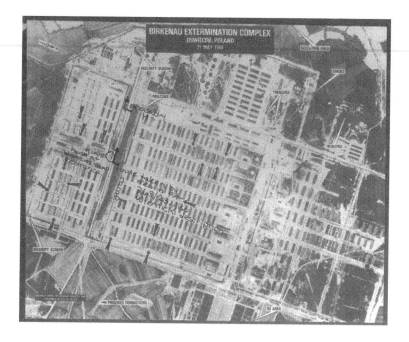

Given that he turned left at the front of the train at the end of the ramp, I can, with good probability and some thankfulness, rule out Crematoria IV and V. He must have been moving in the direction of II or III. From this conjecture, together with survivor accounts and more *Auschwitz Album* photos, I can en-vision—with high probability—what Herman saw on the first part of his journey to the gas chambers. The photograph below depicts men on their way to the crematoria, although these prisoners crossed the tracks in the middle of the ramp, not at the end as I believe Herman did.

The Auschwitz Album, FA 268-23.

Herman turns to the left, and over his shoulder he watches Gabi go off to the right. His son moves further away, and is soon lost from sight, obscured by the men who fill the growing space between them. Together with the other men, Herman rounds the front of the train, where he sees a barbed wire fence and, through the wire, long wooden buildings. He follows those in front of him as they approach the wire and then turn right.

RECOLLECTION
(Written 2007)

An impressive number of the Kleins' prewar photos and documents survive to this day. My grandfather's identity papers,
obtained in 1939 to establish the family's Hungarian heritage,
reside in the safe at my home. We still have those postcards
sent by family members when Gabi was a boy. And there is
the photo album, with a preponderance of pictures of Lilly ("I
never dated a boy who didn't own a camera," she once told me).
These precious possessions were saved during the war by Laci,
Oli's boyfriend, and by Mrs. Riha, who lived in the house behind the Kleins. The fact that we still have the identity papers
surprises me, because I thought that Herman would have taken
them with him when the family was forced to leave their home.
They were each allowed to take a small suitcase, and I would
have expected any identification documents to have gone with
them. Maybe by then Herman knew his papers would be of no

help to him, just as his service in World War I meant nothing, both trumped by the fact that he was a Jew.

The most remarkable of the surviving documents are the diaries written by Lilly and Oli in early 1945, while they were in Sömmerda, a camp in Germany. The sisters worked in a munitions factory, where Lilly surreptitiously pilfered labels used to identify bullet calibers. She sewed these labels together to make small books and—in very tiny letters—she and Oli wrote about their fears and hopes.

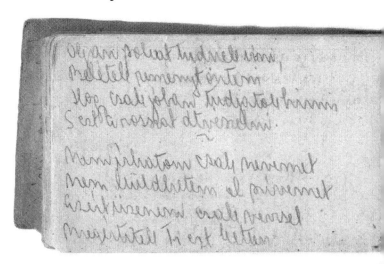

I have always known about Lilly's diaries, which are now on exhibit at the United States Holocaust Memorial Museum. But I didn't know about Oli's diary until one day in 1998, when I was visiting her in Budapest and asking my usual questions about life during the war. As she was trying to remember something, she said, "It's in the diary."

"What diary?" I asked.

"My diary from the camp."

"You kept a diary, *too*?"

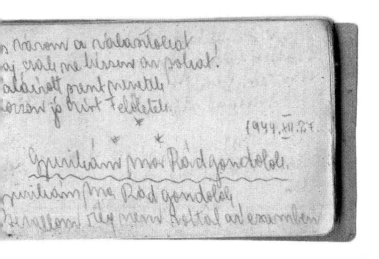

"Sure," she said, removing the top of her coffee table and revealing a cluttered compartment below. She pushed some objects around and pulled out the small, makeshift book with yellowed pages and a red cover. She opened it so that I could see the tiny, penciled writing that filled every spare space on the pages.

"Oli," I said, "is there a place to make photocopies near here?"

Within minutes we were on a bus heading to a shopping center, where I stood at a copying machine for over an hour.

Lilly and Oli's diaries are amazing historical documents that provide me with details of their daily life in the camps, and so they are a critical resource for this book. They also give me insight into their relationships. Lilly writes her diary to her father, and it is clear that she feels a strong connection to him and views him as her protector, even though he is not with her. Oli writes to her boyfriend, Laci, and from the depth of winter in a concentration camp, she recounts memories of their romance.

There is one other set of documents that survived: the "Grey Papers," a newsletter that Oli and Lilly wrote while in the camp. They "published" the "Grey Papers" by going from barracks to barracks on Sundays and reading the poetry and farcical stories from their pages. Oli accidentally left their only copy of the "Grey Papers" on a train as they made their way home after liberation. Remarkably, a man who was also returning home after the war to his town near Beregszász found the papers and returned them to Oli some months later.

Chapter 6
OLI AND LACI

On a winter's day near the end of 1940, eighteen-year-old Oli left her house with her skates hanging over her shoulder. She met up with her friend Benedek, and together they walked to the frozen river that served as the town's skating rink. Benedek was a dentist in his late twenties and a longtime companion of Oli's. But Oli had no romantic feelings for Benedek. In any case, he wasn't Jewish, which made him an inappropriate suitor as far as her parents were concerned.

Oli was going skating in syle, wearing her new dark brown skirt, the latest style that had just reached the Beregszász shops. It wasn't really a skirt, because it had an inseam that created two billowy pants legs that fell to just below her knees. It was perfect for skating. Underneath she wore thick, warm stockings, and on top she wore a heavy beige pullover.

When they arrived and began to put on their skates, Benedek saw a friend of his and called him over. Oli was instantly struck by Laci's bright white smile and wavy blond hair. The three of them talked for a few minutes and then stepped onto the ice. Many people were out on the river that day, including Herman, who loved to skate and was terrific on the ice, and Herman's friend György Orosz, a Latin and Hungarian teacher who had taught Lilly's class several years before.

After a while, Oli and Laci broke away from Benedek and skated off together. The ice on the frozen river was rough, cut by the many blades that shaved the surface. But Laci skated gracefully and competently, and Oli watched his skates gliding easily across the ice. Looking up, she took in his beige knickers, his white turtleneck sweater, his handsome face, and his beautiful hair. Oli was falling in love.

They met at the ice again a few days later and had coffee

at a café afterward. Laci was twenty-seven and worked for his father's business, constructing and selling furnaces for home heating. He spent much of his time installing furnaces in neighboring villages and towns. Even as she listened to him talk, Oli knew she had to stop seeing him before her feelings became too strong. It was unacceptable to marry someone who was not Jewish, and her parents would simply not allow her to date a Gentile. So, on their third meeting, as they again sat together in a café, Oli told Laci that she could not continue seeing him, and that it was best to end things sooner rather than later. For several months, they kept to their agreement.

In the spring of 1941, the people of Beregszász gathered in the town square for the May Day open-air music festival. Oli spotted Laci moving through the crowd, making his way to where the musicians were playing. He was accompanied by a local gypsy man with a violin. A few minutes later the violinist was given the stage and began playing. Oli saw Laci watching her from across the square.

The next morning at breakfast, Herman mentioned the gypsy's song. "The violinist seemed to be playing the music for someone in particular. Who was it for?" he asked. He looked at Lilly, the most likely culprit, but she feigned ignorance. Oli just shrugged her shoulders. But she knew that her agreement was about to be broken. She and Laci began to see one another again in secret.

From the deep and despairing winter of 1945, Oli recounts happier days spent with Laci:

Oli's Diary, January 22, 1945:

I want to tell you how much my heart is aching because I would like to be with you so much, walking along Fö street with a flushed face and talk, talk, talk. Now we are entering a nice and warm confectionery, and are sitting next to each other in the last private box. There is soft music on the radio, we are looking at each other and feel how much we love each other. Then another picture appears... We are skating, we have got used to each other on the ice and are talking about how we shall continue doing sports when we are married. We are taking photos then we are sliding home with a flushed face, our skates on our shoulder. You are taking my arm and playfully kiss me. Interesting, your kiss is warm and soft even in this cold weather. Another picture, it's a winter evening, I'm hurrying to the station to meet you. I am waiting happily excited until the snow covered train arrives. You get off, see me and come to me smiling. We spend together only a few minutes but it's enough for us because this little time is so good. I can see now how much we loved and understood each other.

Oli had hoped to be studying at a music conservatory by now, but with the dissolution of Czechoslovakia, studying in Prague was no longer an option, while restrictions on Jewish enrollment in universities made it impossible to study in Budapest. Instead, she had begun working in a laboratory making dentures. Her routine was punctuated by her discreet rendezvous with Laci. They took walks in the woods and met in places where they were unlikely to be seen by people they knew. Gabi was enlisted as a postman, carrying the lovers' messages back and forth across town. Remarkably, their clandestine meetings went undiscovered for more than a year, but in such a small town, they were sure to be found out eventually.

One Saturday, as Herman left the temple, someone slipped him an envelope. It contained an anonymous letter, demanding to know how, in these times in particular, he could allow his daughter to date a Gentile. Herman was incredulous. He had taken great pains to prevent Lilly from becoming romantically involved with Gentile boys. Every time the boy across the street tried to watch as Lilly played the piano, Herman would close the shutters. But there were so many boys courting Lilly it was hard to keep watch on everything that was going on.

When Oli came home that evening, Herman told her about the letter. He was furious: Lilly was dating a boy who wasn't Jewish. Oli nodded and vaguely agreed with Herman's concerns. But later, when he confronted Lilly and she denied the allegation, Herman realized his mistake and turned on Oli. He was livid, and in a rare outburst he yelled at her, demanding that she break off her relationship with Laci immediately. Oli arranged to meet Laci three days later, on the eve of her twentieth birthday.

Oli's Diary, April 2, 1945:

I used to have such happy birthdays, I used to get beautiful flowers, nice presents, rings, watches. Now all of them are in your wardrobe telling you about those past birthdays. Open the door of your wardrobe and the past, our past, will appear. Let the nice presents I received from you talk to you about my birthdays. The golden signet ring will talk about a sad birthday when we had to part because of bad people. It was drizzling, it was an awful 31 March. My parents urged me to promise that I would give you up, but it was terribly difficult for me. I had bought you the complete works of Ady some days before because I knew that you liked Ady's poems and I could hardly wait to make you happy. When I bought it I didn't know that I would give it to you on the horrible day when we had to part. I remember that when I told you about "my plan" I saw you crying for the first time and I was crying with you.

The following day, on 1 April, you brought me beautiful flowers and in the evening you sent me the golden ring with our names engraved in it. I was very surprised and happy. I wasn't afraid to wear it, I wasn't afraid even of Mum and Dad and I wore it until the day I gave it to you as I don't need any jewelry for my present life and anyway it would have been taken off my finger. Of course I couldn't keep my promise and I couldn't break up with you.

On Christmas Eve of 1942, Oli waited in the Inglik confectionery and café for another clandestine meeting with Laci. They purposely scheduled their meetings far apart so that they would be safer from discovery. Oli was excited to be seeing her love again. She had a small wrapped package with her for Laci: a book by Kant.

Oli's Diary, February 1, 1945:

December 24, 1942. We were the only guests of the Inglik confectionery. It was quiet, there was organ music on the radio and I was waiting for you. Every meeting was a treat for us and I was particularly excited to see you then. You soon arrived, wearing a dark blue coat and when you took your hat off, your lovely blond hair was sparkling in the light. You gave me a porcelain figurine, a little Amor holding two hearts on a golden ribbon in his hand, our two poor hearts. You brought me red carnations and I was so happy about it like about every flower I had received from you. Is there a better, more innocent present than flowers?

As Oli prepared to leave, she pocketed the figurine and gently placed the carnations under her coat. In the empty street outside the café, she wished Laci a Merry Christmas and kissed him goodbye.

Oli and Laci's affair continued to cause great tension and discord within the Klein family, for Herman and Bertha kept learning of their meetings. Lilly could not understand why Oli would hurt her parents over a boyfriend. To Lilly, the choice was clear: Oli should obey their parents' wishes. Oli, however, continued seeing Laci and Gabi remained her confidant, passing messages between the lovers. He knew his parents would be angry if he got caught, but he could see how being apart from Laci pained Oli, and he was happy to help his sister. Plus, these errands allowed him to pretend that he was a spy on a clandestine mission, navigating the streets of Beregszász to deliver his critical messages.

In the spring of 1943, on Oli's twenty-first birthday, the couple had another secret meeting.

Oli's Diary, April 2,1945 (one day after her twenty-third birthday):

Now the watch is coming out of your wardrobe and it's ticking to you about another birthday. It was raining cats and dogs when we met on the promenade and after your raincoat had gotten soaking wet we went to the office to Pista. It was so good to be sitting in the semi-dark office in the afternoon and in the evening, to frolic and to laugh at Pista fooling about. Nobody disturbed us, nobody came to the office that late. Then Pista, as if having something very urgent to do, went to the neighboring room for a few minutes. You came to me, took my hand, kissed my forehead, my eyes, my face and then my mouth, which was meant to be my birthday kiss. Of course our dear Pista came back that very moment saying, "There we are. Is that why I left you alone?"

We continued frolicking then went home. I stopped in a dark spot of the promenade to bid farewell and before we kissed goodbye you gave me a thin box. I opened it frantic with joy and saw a nice and elegant watch with a thin strap. I was so happy that I didn't know what to say. I remember that after regaining my composure I looked up at you with a radiant smile, passed my hand over your face and I wanted to say thank you for the beautiful present but I was so moved that my voice failed me so we shook hands and parted.

Herman remained angry and hurt by Oli's behavior. Decades later, Oli still vividly remembers passing her father on the street and Herman refusing to acknowledge her, looking the other way as he walked by. But it would take much more than Herman's disapproval to separate the couple.

RECOLLECTION
(Written 2007)

I am bookended by survivors. Not only is my father a survivor, but my daughter, Paris, is as well. She suffered a calamity very different from the Holocaust of World War II. As she describes it to people who ask, her arms outstretched to show the magnitude of what happened, "A big wave came and knocked down my house. It killed my first mommy."

We met her over two years ago. Three of our MBA students in Singapore decided to get on a plane a week after the tsunami to try to help out in Thailand, and my husband Andrew and I went with them. It was too painful to watch the news reports and to know we were only a short flight away. Once in Phuket, our resourceful students learned of a village up north that needed help. We spent the next day filling up our cars with things we thought survivors might need, and in the evening we distributed what we had in a relief camp that had been built by the Thai military.

We weren't saving lives. The camp was already providing food, tent shelter, and sanitary facilities. But the people in the camps had lost everything. We handed out toiletries for the adults and toys for the kids. After the distribution, we stayed and played soccer with the kids, who were delighted with the new balls we had given them. In the middle of all of this, a Thai relief volunteer walked up to us with an adorable four-year-old girl. "No Mama, no Papa," he told us. I picked her up and snuggled her while she chattered cheerfully in Thai, clearly having a lot she wanted to tell me. After a few minutes I handed her to my husband. We had been discussing adoption for the past year or so, having never had children of our own. I was enthusiastic about adoption; Andrew was less sure. But after a moment with the little girl in his arms, he looked at me and said, "I'd sign the papers for her right here, right now."

Of course it wasn't that simple, and the complete story of how Paris became our daughter is a book in itself. In brief, the connection we felt to Paris convinced us that we should investigate adoption, though we never expected to become her parents. We started talking to adoption agencies about children in Cambodia and Nepal, and Paris stayed in the camp with her grandparents. We visited them periodically in Thailand through the spring of 2005. Then in June, at the belated funeral of Paris's mother—her body finally identified—the grandparents asked us to raise Paris. Months of legal work ensued, but we brought Paris home to Singapore at the end of the year.

Since then, we have visited Paris's grandparents and village frequently to keep her connected with family, friends, culture, and the Thai language. Through these trips we met Sam, a teenage boy in the same village. He was not orphaned by the tsunami, but he did lose his grandfather, some friends and his home. Sam is smart and hard-working and he was keen to find a better educational opportunity. We were very taken with him, and could see that he would put to maximum use any leg up he was given. Over a year ago we offered Sam's parents paid schooling for him at an international school in Singapore, and he joined us just a few months ago.

At the end of some of our Thailand visits, the kids head home to Singapore with my husband Andrew while I stay behind at a hotel to catch up on the writing of this book, trying to counteract some of the obstructions to progress brought about by parenthood.

So here in Thailand, I call Lilly and George to get the answers to a few questions. As the phone rings, I step out onto the patio of my hotel room for better reception and let the door close behind me.

"Damn!" I say to Lilly. "I just locked myself out of my hotel room and I'm in my pajamas!"

Lilly laughs and says, "Well, you're lucky you have your pajamas at least."

I sit down on a beach chair in the hot afternoon sun, deciding to worry about how to get back into my room later.

Lilly and George are used to these phone calls, where I call from some far-off place in the world and ask them to remember some trivial detail from sixty or seventy years ago.

"Remember when George had to go off to the labor battalion, the first time, in late 1942? Do you remember saying goodbye to him?"

"Sure I do. We went to the station."

"Was it just the two of you?"

"No, his mother was there too. And my other boyfriend, George's friend Csányi."

"He was there too?"

"Sure. Why not?"

I manage to get many of the details that I need, and I realize once again how lucky I am that I can have these conversations. Just after I hang up the phone with Lilly, though, I start to wonder why Csányi wasn't also off in a labor battalion.

Lilly, at eighty-seven, must weigh close to what she weighed in early 1945—almost nothing. George has Parkinson's disease and has had a tough couple of years, including spinal surgery that couldn't completely correct a chronic leg-pain problem. They're always happy to hear from me, but they sound more and more tired with every month that passes. Particularly for George, my pop-quiz questions are getting harder and harder to answer.

They no longer live in Miami. Last summer, they moved to the San Francisco Bay area to be near their son, around the same time my parents moved to a large retirement community in central Florida. My dad has since become something of a celebrity there. He has spoken at a Holocaust memorial event, had a front-page spread in the local paper, and is now being invited to talk at every church, synagogue, and school in the area. (He told me yesterday, "This one place that invited me, they want to pay me!") People recognize him on the street, where he is met with the occasional, unexpected hug.

In two weeks, my dad and I will descend on Lilly and George's home from different directions. So I am here in Thailand trying to tackle a tough chapter, the one that follows George from 1939 through 1943. I have George's "Shoah" interview, the interview that he, my dad, Lilly and Oli all did with Steven Spielberg's Survivors of the Shoah Visual History Foundation. I also have transcripts of talks I've had with him, but I'm still somewhat confused. He was in multiple Hungarian labor battalions (forced labor camps for military-age Jewish men), and I have trouble placing what happened where and when.

I have slowly realized that some of this confusion is due to the style in which George answers questions. In the middle of discussing, say, camp X, which provided some degree of safety relative to other places he could have ended up, he will explain how he got there: through luck, his penchant for making quick and risky decisions that paid off, or his ability to befriend someone in power. This will lead him to discuss someone or some situation in camp X minus 1, without it being clear that he has switched focus to the previous camp. With this pattern recognized, things have started to make more sense, and after days of working out the timeline of George's whereabouts, I am finally able to write the chapter. I'll have it drafted in time to take with me to show them. We will sit down together, and I will write notes in the margins. Through this process I will continue to demonstrate to them how much I care about what happened to them, and that I am in awe of how they managed to survive.

George talks about luck every time I interview him, and I am sure that luck must have played a large role in whether one survived the Holocaust. But George was also gutsy. When confronted by the thugs behind the synagogue that night, or when facing other dangers, he was quick to assess the situation, and his gut reactions—often far-fetched ideas that seemed to come into his head from nowhere—were what saved him. He was a daring young man with blond hair falling across his forehead, sharp blue eyes and a quick wit. And out of his halting answers to my questions, from his couch in California where he sits uncomfortably, I do my best to bring that young George back, so that he can remain forever.

Chapter 7

GEORGE

While Oli and Laci had to endure a lot, their difficulties result-
ed from family frictions that gave a romantic Romeo-and-Juliet
quality to their relationship. Lilly and George, on the other
hand, had bigger problems to contend with. Unable to enter
law school in Budapest, and tired of filling capsules with aspirin, George considered his options. Acting on what he would
later describe as a premonition, he moved to Budapest to work
for a family friend who owned an iron factory. There he learned
to operate a lathe, which was a skill that would prove very valuable in the coming years.

George worked in the factory for a year, then returned to
Beregszász when he was called in to join a Hungarian forced-
labor battalion. This was a requirement for Jewish men of military age, and George was twenty-one. Men in the battalions
were often sent off to do difficult work in poor conditions,
and if unlucky, they could be sent to the Russian front. George
wanted to avoid conscription if at all possible, but he had few
options. He turned to his mother's brothers for help. One uncle
was a dentist, and the other was a doctor. They came up with
an idea that they thought was George's best shot at remaining
free: They suggested that he fake a sciatic nerve problem—a
malady that causes terrific pain in the lower back and leg, but
that has no visible symptoms. His uncles explained the afflic-
tion to George, gave him a book about it, and also wrote up a
medical form certifying that he suffered from this debilitating
illness.

The next day, George presented the certificate to the Hungarian officer conducting the physical exams. The officer crumbled the paper in his hand and dropped it into a nearby trash

71

bin. George lost all hope. He was told to lie down on the examination table and, once prone, he was told to raise his legs. He took his big gamble.

"I can't," he said.

A few minutes later, amazed at his luck, he left the building with a one-year deferral in hand. He rushed to the Kleins' house to tell Lilly the good news.

Through most of 1942, things continued to go well for George. He got a job as an apprentice at a law office. In the evenings, he had a second job playing piano in a small band that performed at a local café. The young people of Beregszász danced to the music; the only downside was that George had to watch Lilly dance with one boy after another. All too often, she was paired with his friend Csányi.

In the summer of 1942, George's mother secured his admission to Pázmány Péter, the top law school in Hungary. This was an extraordinary feat, for there were almost no Jewish students at Hungarian universities at that time. George's mother had pulled strings with the former colleagues of her admired husband, Moritz. But George's year-long deferral was coming to an end, and he would soon have to join a labor battalion. He was faced with the challenge of somehow managing to "attend" law school while living and working in a forced labor camp. This would necessitate some fancy footwork. The school required a book of attendance to be signed by the professors of each course George was enrolled in. He knew that he would not be able to attend lectures, but fortunately the teachers rarely kept track of all of their students, so he just needed to get the book signed. He hired someone he knew in Budapest to go to the university at the end of each term and obtain the signatures of the professors. George figured he could find some time to study while in the labor camp. Attending exams would be a bigger problem, but George was determined, and was convinced he would find a way.

During his deferral, George was required to spend between

four and six hours a week training with a Hungarian battalion, marching with a shovel at his shoulder. He had learned the basic military drills and knew how to march in formation. In October, the deferral came to an end, which meant these tedious duties were about to be replaced with real perils. George had learned that the labor battalions could be dangerous, even deadly. As he packed his rucksack with the few possessions he was allowed to bring—some clothing and a blanket—he had little idea what awaited him, or the conditions in which he would be living and working.

The next morning, wearing the yellow armband that signified he was in a Jewish labor battalion, he said his farewells at the train station to Lilly and his mother. (While Lilly claims that Csányi was there as well, George says he was not. Memory is self-serving, as well as selective.) George boarded a train that took him southwest to Püspökladány, a town about 200 kilometers east of Budapest. When he arrived at the camp, he saw that it had once been a horse stable, and he soon found himself among hundreds of young Jewish men from all over the country. This was a distribution camp, meaning that George would remain there until he was assigned to a permanent work camp.

The young men slept on the floor under the blankets they had brought with them from home. With little else to do to fill the time, George became a prolific writer of love letters to Lilly. These letters were censored by a lieutenant from the Hungarian reserve army who became impressed with George's devotion to Lilly. He and George began talking, and before long George was working in his office. Because of this friendship, George was able to secure a rare and valuable favor—a weekend pass to return home.

So, late on a snowy evening in December, six weeks after George left Beregszász, he returned to town. No one knew he was coming, so he walked the kilometer from the station to his home in the dark alone. Approaching his house, he saw light from the front window and his mother sitting in the living room. He stood outside in the cold for some moments, watching her through the glass. It seemed unreal to be standing there, to be home. He entered through the front door and received his mother's surprised embrace. He spent part of the next day with Lilly, then had to board the train back to Püspökladány.

A few days later, the lieutenant called him into his office and said that he had received a letter from a camp near Budapest where pontoons [supports for temporary bridges] were being manufactured. The officials at that camp had requested that the lieutenant send six or seven skilled workers. The lieutenant thought that this would probably be a good place for George to work, particularly given his experience operating a lathe.

That Sunday, together with several other young men, George boarded a train to Budapest, under the charge of a Hungarian soldier responsible for delivering them to the new camp. When they arrived at their destination on the outskirts of the city, they were escorted through the gate into the walled enclosure of a military camp, and then straight to the building where the laborers lived. George was relieved to see bunks with mattresses, and pleased to note that the building was empty, since this suggested that the incumbent laborers were allowed to take leave.

The following day, George began his career as a munitions factory laborer. Work started at 6:00 a.m. and ended at 4:00 p.m. The intervening hours were spent standing at a steel-cutting machine making parts for the pontoons. The food rations were reasonable, but not abundant, and anything sweet, even a small dab of jelly, was coveted.

George was occasionally able to get Sunday passes to go to Budapest. There he stayed with family friends, the Földis, and spent time with Lilly when she was able to visit from Beregszász. All in all, his situation was not terrible, yet dangers loomed constantly. Periodically, boys who worked at the factory were selected and sent to the Russian front, where they presumably fought with as much enthusiasm as Herman had more than two decades earlier. It was clear to George that the probability of survival was meager if you were sent East. Meanwhile, other laborers were occasionally selected to be transferred to different camps. While life was rough for George and his peers, they understood that the work they were doing at the factory was comfortable compared to the hard labor done by most other battalions.

Thus, each day brought the possibility of a shift into much darker circumstances. George kept his head down, did his job, and studied Roman law—required curriculum for the first year of law school—in the outhouse at night. When it was time to take his yearly exams in the spring of 1943, he finagled a one-day leave and sat for his six-hour oral test in front of the examination board of three law professors. He passed.

THE WALK

"I would think he [Herman] was in his 50s, he was a young man and if it wasn't for the fact that he wasn't able to shave during the three days and nights when we were taken to Auschwitz, and his beard came out really white even though his hair was dark. I think that added to his looks, looking older than he actually was."

(Gene "Gabi" Klein, Shoah interview, Survivors of the Shoah Visual History Foundation)

"Later I found out that my brother and he were together and three other young kids, so because he couldn't shave for three and a half days, his beard—you know, he shaved twice a day, he had such a heavy beard. But his beard was kind of grey. You know that next to the four sixteen-year-olds he looked old, and they sent him, you know, to the other side..."

(Lilly Isaacs, Shoah interview, Survivors of the Shoah Visual History Foundation)

Herman turns to the left, and over his shoulder he watches Gabi go off to the right. His son moves further away, and is soon lost from sight, obscured by the men who fill the growing space between them. Together with the other men, Herman rounds the front of the train, where he sees a barbed wire fence and, through the wire, long wooden buildings. He follows those in front of him as they approach the wire and then turn right. He scratches his face and registers the unaccustomed sensation of stubble under his fingers.

Chapter 8
THE WINDOW

The sound of shattering glass woke the whole family. Gabi sat upright in bed, instantly alert. He followed his father, arriving in the living room in time to see Herman shouting through the broken window, "I know who you are!" In the darkness, Gabi could just make out shards of glass as they glinted on the floor. The rest of the family stood motionless. They kept the lights off.

Shocked and scared, Gabi tried to make sense of what had just happened. By this time—1943—his family had lost the ability to protect him from what was going on around them. At fifteen, he was becoming increasingly aware of the threatening developments in town and the world. He still nurtured comforting blind spots, such as the belief that the war was being fought very far away and that what was happening to the Jews elsewhere in Europe could not possibly happen in Beregszász. But this illusion had been harder to hang onto in the preceding months, particularly after a recent event at his school.

Gabi and his classmates had poured into their auditorium for an assembly. School-wide assemblies offered a break from the normal class schedule, and so they were welcome—even if they were often quite boring. Usually a teacher or the school director spoke, and occasionally there was a guest speaker. The large room was noisy, and Gabi and his football teammates made their own contribution to the racket as they took their seats. Settling in, they prepared themselves for an hour or so of daydreaming.

All went quiet when the school director rose and walked to the podium. He explained to the students that a guest speaker was going to talk to them about the war being fought in Europe. He introduced the man who approached the podium as a member of the Hungarian Arrow Cross from Budapest. A sense of dread came over Gabi upon mention of the Arrow Cross, which was the party of the Hungarian Nazis.

The speaker began by addressing the current state of the war in Europe. As he discussed the hardships being faced by many across the continent, he repeatedly returned to the key theme of his speech: the Jews. Wealthy Jews, Jewish bankers, Jewish businessmen were, he told them, at the root of Europe's many problems. Gabi could feel his heart beat hard in his chest, and the fear he saw on the faces of his friends sitting next to him did nothing to assuage his own. Looking around the auditorium at his Jewish and Gentile classmates, he felt for the first time that he and the other Jewish kids were on one side of a divide and the Gentiles were on the other. Mixed in with the fear was anger at being singled out as the speaker blamed the Jews for one problem after another. The Jews caused the war. The Jews caused economic problems. Gabi knew he had done nothing wrong. What did this man think he had done to deserve this? Why was he being picked on just because he had been born into a Jewish family?

The speaker ended his tirade by stating that Europe would be much better off without the Jews. Gabi went through the speaker's logic, piecing things together: Jews caused all the problems, and therefore Europe would be better off without Jews, therefore… Gabi's mind went back to that long-ago overheard kitchen table conversation between his parents and the Polish couple, and their recounting of what they had seen being done to Jews. Their words had appeared incredible at the time, but now suddenly seemed to lie within the realm of possibility.

When the speaker left the podium and the students were dismissed, Gabi and a few of his Jewish friends huddled together. Within their group they expressed more anger than fear: their conversation focused on the unfairness of being singled out in this way. They walked back to class together, aware that their school was a different place than it had been just an hour before. Not much attention had ever been paid to who was Jewish and who was not, and Gabi's friends were both Jewish and Christian. Except for issues of courtship, nobody had seemed to care very much who was from what sort of family. But the assembly speaker had put an end to this innocence, and whether or not one was Jewish took on increasing importance in the months that followed.

Standing in the living room with glass around his feet, Gabi understood that the threat was now more than just words. He watched Lilly as she started to pick up the shattered glass. Like Gabi, Lilly had been trying to persuade herself that her life in Beregszász was safe, even when confronted with strong evidence to the contrary. Some months earlier she had gone to Budapest to visit George, who had managed to get a Saturday leave from his labor battalion. George had taken off the yellow armband that marked him as a Jewish worker, stuffed it into his pocket, and traveled into Budapest to meet Lilly's train. They had spent the day together, and then went to the Földis in the evening. Lilly stayed the night there, while George was obliged to go back to his barracks. The next morning, as Lilly stood on the platform to catch the train back to Beregszász, she saw George running toward her. He had managed to get another short pass to see her off—a sweet surprise for Lilly. She stood with her arm in George's as they watched the trains come and go.

Several tracks away a cattle train pulled into the station. The train was a good distance from them, but Lilly could see small barbed wire openings near the top of the cars. Someone standing nearby on the platform said, "Those are Jews from Italy." Lilly squinted to try to make out shapes in the darkness of the high windows, but the train was too far away. She simply could not imagine it was possible that humans were in those cars where beasts were normally held. With this failure of imagination came a simple and adamant lack of belief.

For both Gabi and Lilly, the brick through the window was a defining moment. It was no longer possible to pretend that they would be continuing to live as they had before. As Gabi knelt down to help Lilly pick up the glass, they both felt the sense of vulnerability that their attacker had intended.

Herman was furious with the young man who had thrown the brick. He had reached the window just in time to see him run off, and he recognized the assailant as a local thug and Nazi sympathizer. In the current situation, he could not count on the protection of the police, which meant that an idiot like this could do what he wanted. It fell to Herman to provide safety for his family in circumstances where he felt increasingly powerless.

During the preceding months, the Jewish laws had been more and more strictly enforced. Herman and Bertha had become increasingly worried about the future. Herman was now no longer able to get merchandise to stock his shop. The Hungarian authorities were still allowing him to keep his store open because he had served for Germany in World War I, but by this time he had very little to sell. The Jewish wholesalers from whom he had previously purchased were no longer in business, and his new suppliers were increasingly under pressure not to sell to Jewish merchants. His shelves and counters were nearly bare.

Lilly had found a creative, if temporary, way of helping some weeks before. One of her best friends, Nora, was married to a police captain named Kelemen, who had been transferred from Beregszász to the nearby town of Munkács. He had been forced to move—partly because he had been perceived as being too good to the Jews in Beregszász. Kelemen was friendly with the Klein family and had learned of Herman's difficulties; together he and Lilly devised a plan. Lilly took the bus to Munkács and met up with Kelemen. Together they visited the large hardware store where Herman used to get his supplies. Kelemen told the owner that he had just married and that his new wife—he placed his hand on Lilly's shoulder—needed to buy goods and supplies for their household. Lilly chose items for their "new home," and Kelemen helped her onto the bus back to Beregszász, her arms loaded with wares for Herman.

This infusion of merchandise helped keep the store going for a while, but as soon as the goods were sold, his shop was nearly empty again.

Herman and Bertha had been living with the *numerus clausus*, the difficulty of maintaining their business, the occasional anti-Semitic verbal abuse, and the general discrimination that had been imposed upon the Jews. The brick through the window was the logical next step on the path they had been sent down, but it still marked a turning point, because it was their first direct experience of physical violence against the Jews. Someone could have been hurt, or even killed.

By the time the family had cleared away the glass from their floor and furniture, the sky was beginning to lighten. Herman walked to the lumberyard and purchased a sheet of plywood for each window that faced the street. The windows were double-paned for extra insulation in the winter, and between each pair of panes he inserted the board that would keep dangerous objects from flying into the house and hurting his family.

RECOLLECTION
(Written 2008 and 2009)

I am on the phone with Oli. Another overseas call to Budapest, but this time I'm in Australia, having just moved with my family to Melbourne. I'm spending a Saturday in my office at Melbourne Business School, working on the chapter about the broken window. I want to know what Oli had been thinking when the family stood in their dark living room after the brick had smashed through the window, but she is too distracted to talk about her memories from sixty-five years ago.

"They wrote on the wall across the street. Hitler, with the Nazi sign."

"Across the street from your house? Where?"

"Here! The apartment block next to mine."

"When?"

"Last week."

This isn't the first time she has told me about the anti-Semitism she has encountered. There were nasty comments overheard on a tram. There was the mother of one of Oli's piano pupils, back when Oli was still giving piano lessons, who—perhaps fooled by Oli's blue eyes—went on at length about all the problems caused by obnoxious Jews.

Nearly a year after Oli told me about what had been written on the wall, I stood with her at the neighboring apartment building. These apartment blocks were built in the Soviet era, and looked it: Oli's immediate neighborhood is made up of worn and depressing concrete buildings.

I told her I was glad that someone had covered up the graffiti, but looking at this photo now, I realize I should have brought paint with me to completely obscure the writing. Oli

really should not have to see such things. She fears a resurgence of European anti-Semitism strong enough to bring harm to her, her children, and her grandchildren. When someone draws a swastika and writes "Adolf Hitler" on a wall across the street from Oli's apartment, it's hard to persuade her that such fears are unfounded.

Chapter 9
THE ARRIVAL OF THE SS

The wooden boards that darkened the living room may have made the house seem safe, but they offered no real protection. As the months passed, stricter laws governing the activities of Jews were enforced and it became almost impossible for Herman to earn a living. He still went to the store every day, but there was still very little business to transact. He sat at his counter, staring at his bare shelves and empty windows.

In early 1944, Germany discovered plans by the Hungarian leadership to follow Italy and defect from the Axis. In response, German troops entered Hungary in the middle of March and started making their way east; soon they would be in Beregszász. Gabi and his Jewish classmates were told at school that these were their last few days at the gymnasium, and a letter was sent home to tell parents their final school date.

By this time, the residents of Beregszász knew that the war had turned against Germany. Home radios had been collected by the Hungarian police, but some people had managed to keep theirs. Herman and other friends would gather at a neighbor's house to listen to the news from the BBC. The reports from London made it clear that the end of the war was in sight. Yet life in Beregszász was still getting worse and worse. Once Gabi's last day of school came, he had very little to do except sit at home waiting for the war to end and his life to return to normal.

One day, two Hungarian gendarmes came to Herman's store and told him to inventory all of his possessions. When he was finished, they put a padlock on the door and said he would be given the store and its contents back when the war was over. Herman was distressed, but not particularly surprised—he had already seen most other Jewish businesses in the town shut down. In anticipation of the closure of his own store, he had selected housewares from his small supply of goods that he knew Lilly and Oli would need when they were married. He had put all of these items into two cases and brought them down the street to the shop where he bought his tobacco. The owner of the shop was a Christian widow of the war from which Herman had returned over twenty years before. He asked her to keep the cases safe for him and his daughters, and trusted that she would.

For the most part, Herman suffered the growing fear and trials of those weeks with his usual grace and style. But cracks in his fortitude were beginning to appear. One evening, as the family settled into dinner, Herman had a small argument with Bertha as she was putting food on the table. In an explosion of anger, he sent a pot of soup crashing to the ground. The rest of the family watched, stunned, as the steaming liquid spread across the floor. Herman left the room.

The first day of April was both Oli's twenty-second birthday and Herman and Bertha's twenty-fifth wedding anniversary. As was tradition, a clandestine meeting with Laci marked Oli's birthday.

Oli's Diary, April 1, 1945:

I remember 1st April last year, it wasn't very calm. We went into the building of the Finance Ministry next to the post office. We were standing in the corridor for a long time and I was in a bad mood. All the changes and problems depressed me. I couldn't be so happy about presents any more although I used to be so delighted to receive even the smallest fancy thing from you.

In spite of the difficulties of that time, Herman still managed to get a gift for Bertha for their anniversary. He gave her a porcelain dessert tray with a collection of small matching dishes. But within days, Bertha carefully re-wrapped the gift and packed it into a wooden crate so that Herman could hide it, along with their other most precious possessions. They were well aware that, under the new German occupation, their valuables might be plundered.

Herman carried the wooden crate down to the cellar, his steps falling heavily on the stairs. He then went out to the shed in the yard to retrieve his shovel. Back in the cellar, he cleared the stacked firewood from the corner, and when the area was bare, he pushed the tip of the shovel into the hard, dense dirt. He dug with great effort, and it took him several days to make a hole large enough for the crate. When he judged that the hole was sufficiently deep, he lowered the wooden box down, replaced the dirt, and smoothed the surface level with the rest of the cellar floor. He covered the corner with the firewood. Weary from the exertion of this grim work, he climbed the stairs, worried about what lay ahead for his family.

The Jews of Beregszász were informed that they were required to wear a yellow star on their clothing. Bertha and her girls sewed them onto the family's clothing and coats. Lilly's was perfect: all the six points were of equal length and equidistant from each other. Her badge did not make her camera shy in the least, and she had her picture taken posing in her black coat and high-heeled shoes.

Gabi was not nearly as sanguine about the new decree. He wore the star with anger and fear, hating that he was marked, along with the other Jews of Beregszász, as separate and apart. When he walked in town, something he did less and less often, the star gave permission for strangers, people who had no knowledge of him, to shout insults. "Crazy Jew! Stupid Jew!" they would yell to him as they passed. There are no photos of Gabi wearing the star.

A few days after this mandate, German soldiers arrived in town and set up their headquarters in the temple and the

schools. They could be seen sitting in the outdoor cafés, drinking their coffees and ignoring the locals—both Jewish and Gentile. Gabi heard of people who were happy that the Germans were there, who had given gifts and proffered invitations. The Jews attempted to keep a low profile, staying indoors except when necessary.

In spite of his parents' cautions, Gabi and a friend ventured into the center of town soon after the Germans were installed. They climbed up the side of a six-foot wall, just high enough to look over and watch the soldiers, taking note of their uniforms and the submachine guns they carried. One soldier saw their heads peering over the top of the wall, and Gabi watched nervously as he approached them. The soldier spoke to the boys in German, making casual conversation, and Gabi used his school German to reply, willing himself to appear at ease in spite of his fear. After a few more exchanges, the soldier continued on his way. The boys waited until he moved a good distance away and had disappeared around the corner before they jumped down, thankful for the wall that had hidden their yellow stars.

The Nazi occupiers called together the Jewish leaders of the community. A committee was formed of about a dozen Jewish men, whose purpose was to convey messages from the Germans to the Jewish population in the town. One of their first tasks was to inform the others that the Nazis were holding hostage sixty Jewish men, prominent members of the community. A ransom of one million *pengő* (about $30,000) would buy their release.

Mr. Meisels, a local attorney, arrived at the Kleins' house that evening and explained the situation to the family. He had been a very good friend of George's father, and the Kleins welcomed him into their home. They did not have enough money to make much of a contribution. Bertha realized that they would have to sell some of their belongings, and gathered together some of their spare linen. She and Oli went out to find Christian neighbors willing to buy from them, two sellers in a hubbub of commerce that was transacted that evening all over Beregszász. Some neighbors had become unfriendly to Jews in recent months, so Oli and Bertha skipped those houses. They did find buyers however, and some gave extra money to help them with the dire situation of the hostages. By the next morning, the entire million *pengő* had been collected and the hostages were released. But there was a casualty: one of the Jewish doctors in town had given himself a lethal injection to escape the Nazi occupation and what he feared would follow.

A few days later, Herman came home in the afternoon looking shaken and upset. He went into the bedroom with Bertha, and Lilly, concerned by his appearance, secretly stood outside the door to listen. Herman told Bertha that someone in town had told him about the way some Jewish women had been searched to ensure they were not carrying valuables. He said that they probed inside the women's vaginas to see if anything was hidden there. He was terrified that this would happen to his daughters, and through his whispered words this terror spread to Lilly, who quietly stepped away from the door.

Mr. Meisel returned about two weeks later bringing more bad news: The following morning the Kleins would have to leave their house and go to the temple for resettlement. They would each be allowed to take one small suitcase. After he left, Herman sat the family down in the living room. He told them that they should not be worried because the English and the Americans were on their way, the Nazis would soon be gone, and the war would be over. It would not be long before they were back home. Gabi was frightened, but his father's assurances calmed him. The family spent the evening sorting their belongings and packing their cases, taking food, blankets and pillows. They set out multiple layers of clothing to wear the next day.

Several weeks before, concerned that the war might force his family to be on the move, Herman had had sturdy hiking boots made for everyone. Izaks, the best shoemaker in town, cobbled the boots. The night before they left the house, Lilly cut a slit in the lining of one of her boots and hid the small engagement ring George had given her when they were fifteen, along with her mother's diamond earrings. Gabi also made his preparations, going through his possessions and deciding what to take with him. He made simple choices, packing his toothbrush and some clothing. He strapped his bar mitzvah watch onto his wrist and went back to join the rest of the family.

After they had done all they could to prepare for the next morning, the family settled in to try to sleep. Eventually, and fitfully, they all slept, but in the middle of the night a tremendous scream woke them. Bertha calmed Herman, but the voice of his nightmares betrayed his fears to his children. As Oli, Lilly, and Gabi lay in the darkness, listening to the echoes of their father's fear, his reassurances of a few hours before evaporated.

Early the next morning, Lilly began packing two additional cases with never-used sheets and table linens. Her marriage trousseau had been in preparation for years; some of the rent from their boarders had been used to buy items from the best linen shop in town. Now, unable to take the trousseau with her and unwilling to leave it behind, the family asked Laci to take these possessions, together with the family photo albums, to his parents' home for safekeeping.

Once her bags were packed, Lilly added extra layers of clothing to what she was wearing. She carefully unwrapped the tissue paper from three precious pairs of nylon stockings that Herman had given her as a gift. While Oli had worn her stockings before for her meetings with Laci, Lilly had left hers enveloped in their protective wrapping. Now, she pulled on one after another until she was wearing all three pairs.

Laci arrived to collect the suitcases. Oli wanted nothing more than to fall into his arms, but she was restrained by her parents' presence. Just as Laci was getting ready to leave with the cases, two Hungarian soldiers came through the front gate and up to the front door. They were accompanied by László Csudaki, a man who had taught geography to both Lilly and Oli in gymnasium. Oli had admired Mr. Csudaki, whose easygoing rapport with the students made him one of her favorite teachers. His presence here in their living room revealed that, like so many others they had trusted, he hated Jews, and he hated them. They watched as Csudaki, his brown hair combed back severely from his forehead, conferred with the soldiers. One of the soldiers called out the names of each member of the family from a list he carried. As he did so, the teacher verified the identity of each person. The soldier then turned to Laci and asked, "Who are you?"

"I'm a friend of the family."

"It is not necessary for you to stay," ordered the soldier.

Oli stood silently as Laci went out the door, through the yard, and into the street with the two heavy cases. A few days before, he had offered to hide her in his house, but she knew that she could not leave her family. She also knew that Laci's parents were no more happy about her being Jewish than her parents were about Laci being Gentile. As Laci disappeared into the street, Oli wanted to run out after him, but it was too late to change her mind.

Laci watched from a distance as the Kleins were ushered out of their home and the soldiers put a padlock on the door. The family placed their suitcases on an open horse-drawn cart and joined other Jews heading toward the temple. They passed their neighbors' homes, seeing fluttering curtains in the windows of some houses and, in others, curious faces peering out at the desolate parade passing through the streets of Beregszász.

THE WALK

"But I remember one thing yet, I still saw the men, and I sent over a comb, somehow, to my father, because I knew he didn't have any, to make sure he had a comb. You know, little did I know that he won't need it long."

(Lilly Isaacs, Shoah interview)

Herman turns to the left, and over his shoulder he watches Gabi go off to the right. His son moves further away, and is soon lost from sight, obscured by the men who fill the growing space between them. Together with the other men, Herman rounds the front of the train, where he sees a barbed wire fence and, through the wire, long wooden buildings. He follows those in front of him as they approach the wire and then turn right. He scratches his face and registers the unaccustomed sensation of stubble under his fingers. In his other hand he turns a comb.

Chapter 10
BARRELS AND BRICKS

Throughout the day, converging streams formed by the Jews of Beregszász reached the grounds of the temple in the town square. Extended families found each other in the courtyard, and when the Kleins arrived, Bertha was anxious to find her parents. She and Lilly found Záli and Toni lying side by side on wooden cots in a temporary hospital that had been constructed under a large tent behind the synagogue. Lilly looked at her grandfather, who seemed to be only barely holding on, and wondered how he would survive if they had to stay there.

There was much talk among family and friends about what was happening and where they might be going. Theories and rumors abounded, but no one was certain of anything. They spent the night crowded in the temple yard, sleeping in beds made from the blankets that each family had brought with them.

The next morning, Csányi, one of Lilly's hopeful suitors, managed to get inside the temple with scrambled eggs and onions. His family's hotel was being used as the SS headquarters, and he had escaped his duties serving the new regime just long enough to bring the Kleins their breakfast. Their neighbor, Mrs. Riha, arrived later in the day bearing freshly baked Easter treats: pastries with poppy seeds and walnuts.

Soon afterwards, everyone in the courtyard was told to gather their belongings and begin walking to a barrel factory across town. Bertha had to leave her parents behind in the makeshift hospital and did not know when she would be able to see them again. Hungarian gendarmes escorted the column of Jews through the town square and down the middle of the street that led away from the temple. Oli noted the crowd's passivity as they followed the gendarmes, like ducklings following their mother, and she felt deeply depressed by her powerlessness. She looked at the passing houses and saw that there were people watching from their windows. Then she saw György Orosz, her Latin teacher and Herman's skating partner, standing solemnly next to his wife on the front steps of their home. As the Kleins passed, he removed his hat and bent in a slight bow, a discreet show of respect to his departing neighbors.

After an hour's walk, they arrived at the factory. Families set to work creating living spaces among the rows of open-sided roofed structures in which lumber was usually stored. Blankets were hung to create temporary walls and a semblance of privacy. Again, small clusters formed for discussion about the potential meanings of this change in circumstance. Gabi spent the evening lying on his blanket listening to his parents discussing with others the possibilities of what would happen next.

The days in the barrel factory passed like months for Gabi. There was nothing to do except sit around, wait and wonder. And they were hungry. There was some food to eat, but not much, and Gabi's stomach was constantly sore and rumbling.

One night they awoke to the sound of Hungarian gendarmes calling everyone to emerge from their blanketed sleeping areas. They passed from family to family, shining their flashlights on the half-awake faces and demanding at gunpoint that valuables be surrendered into the buckets they carried. They made it clear that they would shoot anyone who held anything back. Lilly thought about the jewelry hidden in her shoes as she watched a mother pull earrings from the ears of her crying baby. When the gendarmes approached the Kleins, Oli and Lilly removed the Timex watches from their wrists, gifts received years ago from Uncle Manny during his visit from America. Gabi thought about trying to hide his own watch, but when the men turned to him and he stared at the gun barrel pointed at his face, he reached with unsteady fingers under his sleeve and slowly undid the strap. His most precious possession disappeared into the bucket of treasures.

The gendarmes moved on to the next family. Gabi passed back under the hanging blanket, shaking from the fright of the gun, furious that these men should have the right to steal from him. The watch was supposed to have been his for his whole life, and he had owned it for only three years. He sat down on the dirty wooden floor and dropped his head into his hands.

A few days later, the gendarmes came into the factory and began assembling a group of about ten young women. Lilly was ordered to join them. As Herman and Bertha looked on in terror, their daughter was boarded onto the back of a truck. They watched the truck disappear, imagining the worst: that their daughter had been taken to "service" the officers. The wait for her return seemed interminable. When the truck finally came back in the early evening, the family rushed out to meet her, all of them relieved when they saw her smile. Lilly and the other women had spent the day scrubbing floors. They had been put to work cleaning the confiscated home of Oli's best friend, which was now being readied for use as a military headquarters.

After staying in the barrel factory for about a week, everyone was once again told to gather their belongings. They were then marched to a brick factory a few hours away. The factory was a large operation with multiple buildings, including sheds for drying and storing bricks. As was the case at the barrel factory, the sheds were open-sided, so once again, the families hung blankets and set up their temporary homes.

Over the following days, the population of the ghetto soared as more of the Beregszász Jews were rounded up, and those from neighboring towns and villages began arriving as well. Again rumors circulated about what might happen next, ranging from the positive—they would soon be allowed to return home and resume their lives—to the negative—they would be sent somewhere east to work. But for the most part, those in the brick factory inhabited the realm of the unknown, and the only thing to be done was to wait. Gabi clung to the optimistic alternative, hoping that maybe all this craziness would blow over—they would be able to go back to their house, he would be able to return to school, and his father would resume his work at the store.

Laci knew the daughter of Mr. Kont, the caretaker of the factory. By telling the gendarmes that she was his girlfriend, he was able to gain access to the ghetto and bring the Kleins food, books and magazines to help combat the boredom of their internment. He also brought them the bad news that their house had been ransacked and there was an empty hole in the cellar where the crate had been buried.

For Oli, Laci's visits were the one thing she had to look forward to, and she treasured her moments with him. He was able to visit almost every day, but one afternoon, about two weeks after they'd arrived at the brick factory, Laci told Oli that he would not be able to come the next day because he was delivering a furnace to a customer out of town. He promised to visit the day after.

Oli's Diary, January 23, 1945:

When we said goodbye in the brick factory on Saturday afternoon, on 12 May 1944, you said that you'd come at 4 on Monday. When I went in the barracks to my Mum, I felt something very strange, I felt that I would not see you for a long time. I rushed to the gate of the ghetto wanting to see you but you were already far away. I turned back downcast. My heart was breaking and why?

The following morning, Gabi awoke to the sound of German guards shouting. The Hungarian guards translated—"Get up! Get ready to go!"—but Gabi understood the German and was terrified by the presence of the SS. Even though the Hungarian guards had been terrible and stolen his watch, there had still always been a sense that nothing too awful would happen to them under their own countrymen. The Germans were a whole different story. The stiff and shining uniforms, the orders barked in German, the sudden shift in the dull but familiar rhythms of the ghetto were all signs of an unwelcome change.

The Hungarian guards, machine guns in hand, ordered everyone to take all of their belongings and go immediately to one of the main buildings in the factory. The SS had the Hungarian guards assure everyone that they were simply being resettled, that everything would be all right and that families would stay together. The men would work and return to their families each evening, and they would all come back home after the war. The Kleins hurried to gather their things, and once again they all put on multiple layers of clothing. Clutching their cases and bundles, they were herded with the others through the ghetto.

As they turned the corner of a large factory building, they could see a clearing and a train standing empty on the tracks. They were told to leave all of their belongings on the ground. Herman quickly pulled some bread from one of the cases and had Bertha, Gabi and his sisters stuff the pieces in their pockets. At this point, the men and women were separated. The women were sent toward the train, while the men remained in the clearing and watched them go. Gabi marveled at the ingeniousness of the setup: as people approached the building, they would not see the clearing, the train and the discarded cases until they rounded the corner—and by then it was too late. The stripping of possessions was inconsistent with the calming promise of a return to some semblance of normalcy and a re-settled family life. And now, surrounded by men with machine guns, what could possibly be done about their circumstances?

Lilly studied the train. The cattle cars, the tiny barbed-wire windows—the train that she had seen in Budapest filled with Italian Jews was here, waiting for them. Lilly went with Bertha, Oli, and the other women around the far side of the train, where they were instructed to climb up into the empty cattle cars. In the crowded car, they were ordered to strip naked. Lilly then lived the reality of the nightmare she had heard outside of her parents' room just a few weeks before. Once the searches were over, each woman was allowed to put on one layer of clothes. The rest had to be left behind.

When the women arrived back at the clearing, they saw the men undressing. They rejoined their families and stood staring at their shoes, averting their eyes from the naked flesh of their fathers, uncles, brothers and friends. Guards passed among the men, inspecting them and their belongings for valuables. After what felt like an eternity, the men were ordered to dress. Everyone was then told to form one long line and march to the far side of the train. The Kleins were near the front of the line, which stopped at the first car at the rear of the train. The guards started counting people and pointing them to the car.

The line moved forward. A guard pointed to Herman and said, "Seventy-seven." Then he pointed to Bertha: "Seventy-eight." Lilly was seventy-nine, and Oli was eighty. As Gabi started to follow his sisters, the guard said, "No! Number one, next car." Horrified, Gabi realized that he was about to be separated from his family. As he followed the order, Lilly and Oli turned and saw Gabi walking to the right, heading for the doorway of the next car. They alerted their parents ahead of them, but there was nothing to be done, and the family was forced to find the last inches of space remaining in the car. As Gabi approached the doorway to his own car, he saw the backs of his sisters disappearing into the darkness. A guard wrote the number "80" in large writing on the side of the car.

RECOLLECTION
(Written 2001 and 2007)

It has always been very difficult to get agreement on the timing of events, so this time I have come prepared. I place a stack of Microsoft Outlook monthly calendar printouts on Lilly's dining room table. It turns out that you can go back a long way in Outlook, so I have the months from 1938 through 1945.

The three siblings take their seats around the table. Behind Lilly, wooden shelves with glass doors encase artifacts from their childhood. I spot the silver container with a hinged lid that houses the *etrog*—a large species of lemon—that is held in the left hand during prayers on the Jewish holiday of Sukkot. There are other treasures as well, all saved in the suitcases Laci took from the house on the morning the family was taken away. Mixed in among these precious possessions are photos of Lilly and George's four grandkids: toothless smiles among smuggled heirlooms.

As I turn on my video camera, Oli looks at the calendar pages in front of her. "I've come all the way from Budapest for an examination?" she asks. I tell her that I don't think it will take too long, and she gives me her Eastern-European, elderly aunt "whatever you say" nod. I know she finds some of my questions tedious, but I also know she is pleased that I am writing their story. I think what puzzles her is my need for exactitude and the many detailed queries it entails. She is impatient for me to finish, often reminding me that if I want her to see it completed before she dies, I don't have much time left. Lilly, meanwhile, enjoys being interviewed. She likes to talk about her past, and she is happy to have an interested listener. And my dad is always game, in keeping with his usual enthusiasm for things. I count on him in these discussions because he seems to understand my questions, sees where I am heading, and can keep Lilly focused if she wanders away from the question at hand. The three of them get on well, but they are also happy to disagree with one another. I encourage disagreement, because the one who answers a question first is not necessarily the most accurate.

We start by working through various events in the late 1930s and early 1940s, and first run into trouble with when the SS arrived in Beregszász. It is hard to track down exactly when the Germans entered the town. Germany officially occupied Hungary on March 19, 1944, but the SS did not arrive in Beregszász right away. I discover that April 1, 1944, which was both Oli's birthday and Herman and Bertha's anniversary, works well as a reference point for other events, but estimates of the passage of days and weeks are still murky. I use this anchor to try to pin down when the family was evicted from their home.

Jill (to Oli): Your parents' anniversary and your birthday were on April 1. When do you think the SS came?

Oli: Very soon after that.

Jill: Next week?

Oli: Maybe two weeks later.

[…]

Jill: How long after the SS arrived, in the middle of April, did you actually have to leave your house?

Lilly: I would say about the end of April.

Jill: After they collected money?

Oli: Yes.

Jill: How much longer were you in the house?

Oli: Two weeks.

Lilly: Yes, a couple of weeks.

I continue the interview, soon approaching another issue that puzzles me, which is the date they left for Auschwitz. Based on Oli's diary, I know that it was around mid-May, but I want to try to pin down the exact date. While Hungarian Jews had been taken to camps before then, the first trains of the systematic mass deportation of Hungarian Jews arrived in Auschwitz in mid-May, which means my family members were deported early in the process.[1] I know that their area of Hungary was the first in which Jews were rounded up for mass deportation, and that their brick factory ghetto was one of the major gathering stations in the area. Hugo Gryn, the survivor and memoirist from Beregszász, believed he was on the last transport from the brick factory, and he reported seeing other trains arriving and leaving. My dad, however, never saw any trains in the ghetto before the one that took him and his family away. All of this suggests that they may have been on one of the very first trains to arrive in Auschwitz.

Dad: The question is, "When did we leave on the train? What was the date?"

Oli: It was Sunday.

Dad: Fifteenth May.

Jill: That's a Monday.

Oli: I know Laci came on a Friday to bring some food and newspapers, and he told me, "I'll come back to see you on Sunday."

This does not jibe with what Oli wrote in her diary. She wrote, "When we said goodbye in the brick factory on Saturday afternoon, on 12 May 1944, you said that you would

---

1. Two trains of Hungarian Jews apparently arrived in Auschwitz on May 2, but they were not part of the mass deportation of Hungarian Jews. [Lawrence Rees, *Auschwitz: A New History* (Public Affairs, 2005)].

come at 4 on Monday." Normally, I would give precedence to Oli's diary because it was written so much closer to the actual events (though even that was a full eight months after they were taken to Auschwitz). But Oli gets either the date or the days of the week wrong, saying that the twelfth was a Saturday, when actually it was a Friday. In a taped interview I conducted in 1997, however, Oli refers to seeing Laci on Friday and to his promise to see her on Sunday. Moreover, she says specifically that they left the ghetto on Saturday, which would have been the thirteenth. So my best guess is that she said goodbye to Laci on the afternoon of Friday, May 12 and the trains departed on the thirteenth.

If that Saturday is counted as a full day in the three days on the train—Lilly and my dad recall being taken to the train in the morning, and they all recall a three-day train ride—that covers the days of Saturday, Sunday, and Monday, suggesting they reached Auschwitz late on the fifteenth or early on the sixteenth. I know they arrived at night, because my dad remembers it being dark, while Oli states in her diary that the train stood all night in the dark after their arrival.

Auschwitz Chronicle: 1939-1945, a detailed index of events at the camp based on eyewitness testimonies, says the very first trains of the Hungarian deportation arrived on May 16.[2] As Herman and his family probably arrived no later than the sixteenth, this suggests that they were on one of these trains, and that the trains arrived after midnight.

I wrote the text above in 2007. In 2009, I was working in my office at Melbourne Business School in Australia, when I received an email from my cousin Tom, Lilly and George's son. His email read: "Hey! Check this out!!! Pretty amazing."

---

2. Danuta Czech, *Auschwitz Chronicle: 1939-1945* (New York: Henry Holt & Co, 1997), 627.

Attached to his email were Lilly's Auschwitz documents, which had been forwarded to him by the United States Holocaust Memorial Museum.

The date "15.5.44" jumped out at me. According to this document, Lilly's arrival date in Auschwitz was a day before *Auschwitz Chronicle* says the first trains of Hungarian transports arrived. It is possible that the eyewitnesses got the date wrong; it is also possible that Lilly's document, which includes later dates as well, was not created at the time of arrival, and is in error about the date. Or it is possible that the first of the three trains arrived late on the fifteenth but was offloaded on the sixteenth, which would reconcile the two dates and fit with the family's recollections. (While it is possible that more than one train arrived that night, no one in my family recalls seeing another train at the arrival ramp.)

Around 430,000 Hungarian Jews were systematically deported to Auschwitz in the spring and summer of 1944. Based on the numbers quoted in *Auschwitz Chronicle*, these victims probably filled more than a hundred trains. I think it is almost certain that my father, my aunts and my grandparents were in the first group of trains to arrive. It is possible, even likely, that they were on the very first train of all.

Chapter 11
ALONE

Gabi approached the doorway to the train. He looked up at the two small, narrow windows crisscrossed with barbed wire on either side of the entrance, climbed onto the metal rungs of the short ladder, then pulled himself inside. There were two barrels in the middle of the car: one was filled with water; the other was empty. Gabi turned to his left, sat down near the door with his back to the wall, and watched as others took their places. He recognized many of the people who entered the car, but there was no one from his family—no cousins or grandparents—nor any close friends. He felt a hollowness in his chest, along with a growing panic, and as each person crowded into the car, his fear and loneliness became sharper. He wanted to be sitting with his father, to have his mother and his sisters next to him. Up to this point they had endured everything together. Gabi had believed it when they had been told that families would remain intact. He had never imagined until this moment that he would be forced to face any of this alone.

The car became increasingly, unbearably, crowded as more people climbed up through the entrance. They packed in tighter and tighter around him, pressing up against his body from all sides. He brought his knees up to his chest to make himself as small as possible. Once the last of the eighty people managed to squeeze in, the doors were closed from the outside. Gabi heard the bolt sliding into the latch.

And then they waited. The train didn't move for hours. The still air grew hotter and more oppressive, the small windows inadequate for effective ventilation.

Then a shot was fired, startling everyone, and the train finally began to move. In the adjoining car, Herman, Bertha, and the girls were still standing, because it was not possible for everyone in the car to sit. Beyond their own discomfort and panic, they were all distraught that Gabi was not with them. Herman spoke to the girls, saying he wanted them to remember something very important. He told them their Uncle Manny's address in Scranton, and made them practice repeating it over and over again until he was sure they had it memorized. Lilly and Oli did not want to think about why they might need this knowledge, but they did what their father asked.

By the next morning, the water barrel was empty in Gabi's car. The sun heated the roof and penetrated the small windows, making the eighty cramped inhabitants more and more thirsty. The stench was almost intolerable. The barrel for excrement was filling fast; some who had taken ill were vomiting. Gabi's only respite came when he managed to sleep for a few short hours here and there. But he never slept for very long—the nightmare of the car, the suffocating heat and his mounting thirst constantly tugged him back to wakefulness.

Occasionally, someone would be hoisted up to the small window to look out and report back to the others. Because of his small size, Gabi was often chosen for this role. Once the scene was described, the occupants of the car would debate where they were and where they were going.

Every now and then the train would stop, the doors would open, and the prisoners would be instructed to pour the barrel of waste outside. Air that in normal circumstances would have been considered rancid and foul was inhaled gratefully. No one was allowed leave the car, so they had to squeeze in even tighter, allowing the barrel to be dragged to the doorway. As the doors were closed again, the guards repeated the same mantra: When they arrived, all would be well. As long as they were willing to work hard, all would be well.

Huddled in their own car, Lilly, Oli, Bertha and Herman envisioned a future based on these promises. Bertha would stay at home, while Herman, the girls and Gabi went to work. They imagined Bertha cooking for them, and the whole family gathering for dinner in the evening. They wouldn't be in their own home, or even their own town, and they would have to work hard, but they would be together. They could live this way until the war was over, until they could return to Beregszász.

Lilly sometimes talked with her friend Imre Neuvelt, who was also in the car. They stood together under the narrow window, and he occasionally lifted Lilly up so she could look out and catch some of the cool air. They considered whether it would be possible to squeeze through the opening and escape, but it was clear that neither would fit.

When Lilly looked out at one of the stops, she realized that she recognized the place. They were in Aunt Lenke and Uncle Csányi's town, where she had spent summers helping in the pharmacy. She saw a young woman in the distance and recognized her friend Zsuzsu, the daughter of a local doctor. She shouted to her through the small window, pleading for some water. Zsuzsu ran away and returned a few minutes later with a bucket, but a guard stopped her as she approached. The train began to move. The thought of cool water being so close, yet unattainable, caused Lilly to weep.

Exhausted from standing for hours, they eventually found a way to sit down between each other's outspread legs. As Oli sat down in front of Herman, she felt her father pull her back against his chest and squeeze his arms tight around her. With that gesture, Oli understood, he was forgiving her for loving Laci.

Eight months later, she described their journey in her diary:

Oli's Diary, January 23, 1945:

We were jolting in the train for three days and nights and we had one piece of dry bread. In Jegenyemihály a railwayman promised that he would write to you. Did he really do it? Everything I had was left at home but I had some of your pictures with me. The pictures reflecting our happiness in Tiszaborkút. The farther the train took me the sadder I got, we didn't know where we were being taken or how long the journey would last. At Kassa we were taken over by the Germans and after leaving the border of the country the train was winding among bare rocky mountains, along unknown rivers, through long and frightening tunnels.

By the third day, Gabi was nearly crazy with thirst. His throat burned and his head felt as if it would split in two. Others had lost control entirely, and the car was filled with their screams and pleas for water. A teenage boy sitting nearby told Gabi that he had watched someone drink a baby's urine. Some people prayed; others lost consciousness. Late that night, the train stopped for the last time. Someone was hoisted up to the window and he reported to the others that he could see bright lights and wire fences. They sat in the dark for hours.

The doors were opened suddenly. Screams in German of "Out! Out! Fast!" assailed them. Gabi got up with difficulty—every muscle and joint in his body was aching from the journey—and looked through the open door of the car at the scene outside. None of it made any sense. He jumped down from the train into what appeared to be a different world. There were blinding lights, shouting SS officers, machine guns and huge barking dogs. He saw seemingly endless barbed-wire fences punctuated by tall lampposts, and above this, guard towers. It was as bright as day. Skinny men in blue-and-white-striped uniforms pulled people out of the car. He heard one whisper to several young women, "Give the children to the old people," but he could not work out why he would say such a thing.

The same sights assaulted the rest of the family as they left their car. A Polish prisoner in striped clothing spoke to Bertha in urgent Yiddish. He instructed her to say she was younger than she was, while the girls should say that they were older than they were. Bertha translated this to her daughters. They heard other men telling women to give their children to their mothers, that they would see them again in the evening. Lilly watched her neighbor, Erzsébet, hand her infant over to her mother, Fáncsi. Other women refused to let their children out of their arms. George's mother, leaving another car far down the tracks, heard the same instructions and took the young child of a friend into her arms.

Gabi heard his name shouted through the noise and panic of the people around him. He ran over to his family and they all embraced. Oli realized that, incongruously to the point of absurdity, she could hear an orchestra playing. Just audible over the din of the crowd, the shouts of the SS and the barking of the dogs was a man's beautiful voice singing "O Sole Mio." The men in the blue stripes continued to unload the train. Those who had died, those who were unconscious, and those who were simply too ill to move were carried unceremoniously from the cars.

The SS officers shouted that the men and women must stand in separate lines in rows of five. Herman began to say goodbye to Bertha and his girls, but Lilly interrupted, urging him not to say goodbye, that they would see him very soon. As everyone moved into position, Herman took a spot in the middle of a row with Gabi to his right. The men soon began to move forward, ahead of the women. Lilly could see the back of her father's head; his hair was in disarray. He was normally fastidious about grooming. She pulled a comb from her pocket and slipped out of line. She called over to Gabi, handed the comb to the boy on his right, and told her brother to pass it to their father. Gabi gave the comb to Herman, saying that Lilly had sent it.

The men continued moving while the women waited. Suddenly, Lilly saw Csányi Donat—George's rival for her affection—appear at her side. He asked if she would allow him to kiss her. Lilly looked into his face and considered his question. Perhaps because of the shock she was in, perhaps because of her mother's presence, or possibly out of deference to George, she said no. Csányi ducked quickly away and rejoined his row in the men's procession.

As the men moved toward the front of the train, the sky began to brighten, with the promise of a warm spring day. Gabi saw barracks with families outside: mothers, fathers and children all together. There were flowers growing by the sides of the buildings. He felt calmed by what he saw. True, there were prisoners behind barbed wire, but at least families seemed to be together and natural beauty was cultivated.

In addition to Herman, Gabi's row included three boys about his own age that he knew from home—one to his right and two to the left of his father. Looking up at Herman, he realized that he had never seen his father unshaven before. A few rows ahead of them, Gabi saw that some men were being sent to the right and some to the left, with older men going to the left. Before he could ponder the meaning of this, his row reached the head of the line. They faced a group of immaculately dressed SS officers, their uniforms perfectly pressed and shoes spotless and shining. An officer directly in front of them held a riding crop in his white-gloved hand. He gave the row a cursory glance, and then pointed the crop at Herman, indicating that he should go to the left. He motioned to the others in the row to go to the right.

There was no time to speak—distance opened between them before they could grasp what was happening—but Gabi and Herman looked into each other's eyes as they realized they were being separated. Gabi could not understand why he was being sent in a different direction from his father; he did not want to leave him, but there was no alternative. He assumed that this was a temporary separation, a matter of processing and categorization, and that they would soon be back together.

Gabi followed those in front of him. Looking around, he saw in the distance several old people, men and women in civilian clothes, being chased and beaten by SS officers. He was unable to grasp what was happening. *Who would beat old people?* He could not make sense of it, but the thin precipice of hope on which he'd been standing began to shift beneath his feet. He kept walking, and tried not to think.

The women meanwhile continued to stand in place. Lilly looked down at the ground and noticed coins and paper money lying in the dirt. She wondered what they were doing there, why no one considered them valuable enough to pick up. It was another feature of this perplexing world, another reversal of the way people usually behaved and the way life usually worked. Her mind was clouded, beset by thirst, hunger, fear and disbelief.

Somehow, Bertha was still holding a beige enamel pitcher that they had brought from home. She hoped to find water to fill it. A couple of men in stripes approached them, and one poured some coffee into the pitcher. Bertha shared it with Lilly and Oli, providing some relief for their desperate thirst. They saved the rest for Herman and Gabi, but they did not know where they had gone. Then they were moving forward, so Bertha gave the remaining coffee to an elderly woman who seemed about to collapse.

Their row of five consisted of Bertha, with Lilly and Oli to her right, and their distant cousins Irenke and Arenke next to them. Up ahead, they could see people being sent in different directions; old women and mothers with babies and young children were moving off to the left. The Klein women felt panic at the thought of separation. When they approached the SS officer, he gave the row a brief look. Lilly took her mother's arm and said to him in German, "Mutter."

He sent the entire row to the right.

THE WALK

"We were going for three days and three nights from our hometown. The only thing we had in our car was two drums, one was with water and one was for human waste. There was absolutely no food, there were sick people, there were old people, there were babies. We were crammed basically like sardines, people crying, older people, sick people dying. As I understood, my grandparents actually died on the way to Auschwitz in the car."

(Gene "Gabi" Klein, Shoah interview)

Long columns of those who during the selection had been chosen for the walk to the gas chambers struggled along the dusty roads, exhausted and in low spirits…[1]

---

1. Filip Müller, *Auschwitz Inferno: Testimony of a Sonderkommando* (London: Routledge & Kegan Paul, 1979), 61.

Herman turns to the left, and over his shoulder he watches Gabi go off to the right. His son moves further away, and is soon lost from sight, obscured by the men who fill the growing space between them. Together with the other men, Herman rounds the front of the train, where he sees a barbed wire fence and, through the wire, long wooden buildings. He follows those in front of him as they approach the wire and then turn right. He scratches his face and registers the unaccustomed sensation of stubble under his fingers. In his other hand he turns a comb.

After three days of being unable to move, his muscles and joints ache and disobey. After three days of constant motion, the dusty ground under his feet seems to shift. He is tremendously thirsty. He struggles to keep pace with those around him who are also struggling to keep pace.

Chapter 12
NUMBERS

Gabi and those around him walked through the camp, urged on by the guards with their dogs and guns. Eventually they came to a stop in an open area surrounded by fences. There were signs everywhere that warned in German: "Caution! Electric Fence—Danger to Life!" Gabi's German skills from school were coming in handy, but this warning was a long way from the courteous conversations he had practiced in class. He and his friends desperately tried to make sense of their surroundings, all wondering what would happen next.

Women began entering at the far side of the clearing, and Gabi heard Lilly call to him. She asked where their father was, and Gabi waved in the direction Herman had gone when they were separated. The men and boys were again told to line up in rows of five. This time they marched to an open area in front of a large, red brick building, where guards ordered them to undress. Gabi bundled his clothes, laid the pile on the ground in front of him, then stared at his shirt, trousers and shoes lying in the dirt. It struck him that these were his final possessions, his last connection to his former life. His home was gone. His family, his life, everything that was part of him was gone. In every direction, all he could see were hundreds of naked men, and hundreds of piles of clothes and shoes.

Guards ordered them along a walkway toward the building, outside of which prisoners in striped uniforms stood, razors in hand. When it was his turn, one of the barbers roughly shaved Gabi's head and entire body. Then Gabi followed the others through the doors of the building and into a room where showerheads hung from the ceiling. When the water was turned on, they opened their mouths, gulping down as much as they could before they were ordered to move on.

As they left the shower room, other prisoners sprayed a foul-smelling disinfectant powder onto their bodies. The next room had piles of striped uniforms on the floor. Gabi first had to grab a cap, then a pair of striped pants and a shirt, quickly holding the garments up to see if they would fit. Then there were shoes—wooden clogs made with tattered blue-and-white-striped cloth. It was almost impossible in the mayhem to find shoes that fit. Next was a pile of string and wire, either of which was to be used as a belt. Finally, they were told to pull a cup, bowl and spoon from bins containing aluminum and enamel kitchenware. As Gabi dressed, he saw that his shirt was actually a jacket with pockets at the hips. Standing in line, copying the others, he slipped the handle of the mug through his string belt, placed his spoon into his pocket, and tucked his plate inside his shirt.

Eventually Gabi reached a table where an SS officer was seated. The officer asked for his name, found him on a list, then asked him for his hometown and birth date, which he wrote next to his name. The officer then asked for his prisoner number, but Gabi was not sure what he meant. He followed the officer's eyes and looked down at his chest where he saw a number on his uniform next to a yellow triangle. He read the number to the officer, who wrote it down.

The induction process over, Gabi marched with the others through the camp, past row upon row of barracks. He was having trouble thinking straight. It seemed that he was always a step behind. Just when he had begun to understand that he was no longer in his home, he was on a train. Before he could understand the train, he was in this camp. Now he was in a uniform; his hair was gone; he was a prisoner; he had become a number. What was going to happen next before he had time to come to grips with this?

Entering one of the barracks, Gabi saw men lying on triple tiers of wooden platforms that lined the room on both sides. A stove stood at each end of the room, and a knee-high bench ran through the center between them. The room was crowded with prisoners. Some looked like skeletons. Gabi spotted two good friends from home, János and Tibor. Comparing their experiences, they realized they had come into the camp on the same transport, but in different cars. They spent the next several hours together talking and resting. It was a tremendous relief for Gabi to be with these friends, and he felt his loneliness lift slightly.

The men around them started leaving the barracks. The boys followed. They joined a single-file line outside, which Gabi realized was a food line. He was hungry and very thirsty, and he waited with great anticipation. One prisoner handed him a piece of dark bread, then another ladled a thin, brown, watery liquid into his bowl. A foul smell assailed Gabi's nostrils and he jerked his head away. He forced himself to take a sip, but violently spat it out on the ground. He told his friends that he'd rather starve than eat it, and handed them the bowl. Less discriminating than Gabi, they drank it willingly. Gabi then examined the bread. It was hard and dense, and it seemed that sawdust was a key ingredient. This he ate.

Later, after they had gone back inside, a prisoner in charge of the barracks barked for them to get into their beds. Gabi and his friends found a place together on the middle tier of one of the wooden bunks. The surface was sprinkled with a thin layer of straw. The boys imitated the more experienced prisoners and lay with their heads toward the aisle and feet to the wall. They tried to find a comfortable position, but one did not exist. The lights were turned off. The finality of darkness made it clear to Gabi that there would be no reunion with his father that day. Whatever had taken Herman in a different direction could mean a lasting separation.

This barracks filled with men and adolescent boys was nothing like the family setting Gabi had seen through the fences earlier that day. As his eyes adjusted to the dark and made out the shadows around him, Gabi felt lost. Though exhausted, he could not sleep, and instead stared wide-eyed into the blackness ahead of him. János and Tibor were not sleeping either, so the three boys began to make plans: they would find a way to escape. In whispers they pointed out weaknesses in the security of the camp they had already noticed, vulnerabilities they could exploit. And once clear of the camp, they would make their way to Switzerland, where they could live until the war was over. "Stay focused, stay observant," they told each other. Together they would find a way to get free. Finally, shrouded in a determination that began to dissipate in the silence, they fell asleep.

The women's journey through the day had been equally terrifying. After the selection by the side of the train, Lilly, Oli and Bertha followed the other women through the gates to the camp. The music that Oli had heard when she got off the train was louder now, and soon she spotted the orchestra on her right. As she walked by, she stared at the musicians, unable to make sense of what they were doing here amidst the barbed wire, electric fences, and the wooden barracks.

As the women entered a clearing, Lilly was the first to spot Gabi in the distance, talking with a few of his friends. They expected to see Herman nearby, but there was no sign of him. Lilly called to Gabi, who waved back to her. She shouted a question about her father, and Gabi motioned that Herman was somewhere behind them, back where they had come from. Bertha and her daughters—so relieved to still be together—realized then that Herman and Gabi had been separated.

The men soon moved on, but the women stayed in the clearing for a very long time. Finally, they were marched into another open area in front of a brick building, where they were told to strip off all of their clothes, leave them on the ground, and hold on to their shoes. Women prisoners in striped dresses sorted through their clothing. One put Lilly's stockings in her pocket, then picked up Lilly's dress from the ground and put it to one side.

An SS officer walked down the row, ordering the women to drop their jewelry into a bucket and to surrender their shoes. Lilly thought about her picture of George, the ring he had given her, and her mother's diamond earrings in the lining of the sole of her shoe. She dreaded parting with these final treasured possessions. She set about trying to remove the pearl earrings that she was wearing, which had been a high school graduation gift from her parents. The earrings had miraculously escaped the notice of the Hungarian gendarmes in the ghetto, but not the inspection of this SS officer. It had been months, if not years, since she had taken them out, and they would not budge. The officer became impatient and pulled a pair of pliers from his pocket. He struggled to wrench the earrings free, yanking painfully at Lilly's ears, and finally ripped them out. By this time, the women around Lilly had relinquished their shoes, but, distracted by the earrings, the SS officer failed to notice that Lilly and Oli still held on to theirs.

Lilly wrote to her father in her diary months later, describing their initiation at Auschwitz:

Lilly's Diary, December 26, 1944:

We were going in one by one in a row to a large room where they shaved off our hair completely. I will never forget that feeling when I had to sit down on a chair naked. The German soldiers were standing around and were kicking with their black boots the brown, black and golden blond bunches of hair. A Jewish prisoner got to my hair, and within minutes my beautiful long hair was on my naked shoulders and on the floor. I was crying, but then I couldn't really understand why I was crying so terribly. Then I saw my mother, also bald, and she was crying when she saw what happened to me. I told her not to be upset about it, and then I saw Oli, the bald head to the left. She looked like a little boy. They took us to a shower room, and we were looking at each other laughing. It was so comical to see our friends and people we knew bald. Hot water came from the showerheads, so we got washed, and afterward we went into another room where we got grey shift dresses like long shirts, made of stiff cotton. Now, after eight months, that is still the one and only dress we have. They gave us men's socks, all kinds of men's and women's underwear.... We were laughing when we saw those fantastic, ridiculous underwear. Instead of laughing, we should have been screaming.

When they were in the showers, Bertha was worried that their shoes would be taken from them when they got out, so she asked Lilly for the diamonds. Lilly dug the earrings out from the lining of her shoe, and Bertha placed them into her mouth. She kept them there, under her tongue, through the rest of their processing into the camp. Oli later wrote to Laci about her first hours in Auschwitz in her diary:

Oli's Diary, January 22, 1945:

Each German soldier saw us and we couldn't even feel ashamed. Our hair was cut bald, our clothes were taken, all we had left were our shoes. I hid your picture there, so I managed to take it with me. We were given coarse grey clothes and together with several hundreds of other persons we went on escorted by a German soldier. Wire fences, bare and hard ground, no birds, no flowers, sinister looking people. Identical green wooden barracks, what are you hiding?

Lilly described this same trip from the showers to their barracks:

Lilly's Diary, Dec 26, 1944:

We got some terribly bitter liquid to drink, then we had to stand, five in a row, and started out on the same road that took us to the bath. The soldiers with dogs were always next to us. In the front of a barrack we saw our men standing, and you must have been among them, Daddy. I can imagine how you must have felt to see us with our hair cut off and in those grey dresses. We were very cold. The spring wind was blowing, and our heads were very cold. We passed lots of barracks where the men were, then we got to the lager [prison] for women.

As they walked, they saw, above the trees, a large chimney from which smoke was rising. Lilly assumed that their clothes were being burned. But the air had a sickening, greasy smell, which puzzled her. When they reached the barracks in the women's camp, they discovered many women already crowded into the center aisle between the wooden tiers of bunks. Lilly, Oli and Bertha found George's aunt Margda and her daughter, Anikó, who had arrived with them on the train. They all huddled together, wondering what was coming next.

Through the commotion, Lilly heard a woman calling, "Is there anyone here from Beregszász?" Lilly called back, and her cousin Violet wove her way through the crowd toward them. They all embraced, and Violet, who had been living in Budapest, explained that she had been arrested at a train station in the city. She had already been in Auschwitz for several months and had been assigned the task of tattooing arriving prisoners. Lilly, Oli and Bertha had their prisoner numbers on their uniforms only, but Violet explained that most arriving prisoners had their numbers tattooed on their forearm.[1]

After a while, Violet took Lilly and Oli aside. She explained that any women who were not with them after the selection were already dead, and that all children and old people were

---

1. Some prisoners at Auschwitz were designated (unbeknownst to them) "depot prisoners," which meant that they would only be in Auschwitz temporarily before being transferred to other camps. These prisoners were not tattooed.

killed with a poisonous gas. The SS officer sent people to the right or left, deciding who to kill immediately and who to preserve for slave labor. Young women with children were also gassed, she told them, which explained why the prisoners at the train told women to give their children to older relatives. Violet also told them that the bodies of those who were killed were burned in the crematoria, producing the smoke that came from chimneys.

Lilly and Oli knew that they could not tell their mother about this. They hadn't seen Bertha's parents since the temple in Beregszász. The rest of Bertha's family—siblings, nieces and nephews—had not been rounded up with them, and they had not been together in the brick factory. If Bertha's family followed them here, her parents and young nieces and nephews would be killed. How could they possibly tell their mother this? It was almost impossible to believe it themselves. Other prisoners were apparently spreading the same news, because screams and cries broke out from groups of women around the barracks.

Someone began shouting that everyone needed to get into the bunks. Violet explained that this was the barracks capo, one of the veteran prisoners who ran affairs for the SS, and that they should be obeyed at all costs. Their capo was a young woman from Poland. Everyone immediately scrambled onto the wooden planks. The higher tiers seemed to be the best, since it was warmer near the ceiling, and Lilly and Oli managed to secure a place there for Bertha. They then joined three other young women on the lowest bunk, just above the filthy floor. It was impossible to change position or to roll over without all five moving together.

Though they were exhausted, it was difficult to surrender to sleep. There was too much to try to take in. Violet's words reverberated in their minds as they grappled with thoughts of the slaughter of so many people who had arrived on the train with them—family members, friends and children that they would never see again. Surely it couldn't be true?

RECOLLECTION

My father and his sisters vividly remember their first hours in Auschwitz. Most memoirists, too, recount in detail the initiation process in the camp: the shaving, the shower, the uniforms, and the tattooing. Memoirists, by definition, write with the benefit of hindsight. When they recount their experiences, they know the most important truth of the camps, a truth of which they were unaware at the time: that many of the arriving prisoners went through a very different process, culminating in shower rooms that turned out to be gas chambers. All these writers, in their own ways, thus reflect on the power of the SS officer they confronted at the moment of selection, the pointing of a finger or the flick of a riding crop deciding the fate of the people who passed before him.

I have read dozens of these memoirs, yet it is Lilly's succinct encapsulation that sticks with me:

> "And then they chased us into a shower, and we were the lucky ones. We got the water."
>
> (Lilly Isaacs, Shoah interview)

Chapter 13

SOUP, SOAP AND SMOKE

Shouts woke Gabi early on his first morning as a prisoner in Auschwitz: "Get up! Get out!"

Moments before, Gabi had imagined he was home in his own bed, wrapped in his sheets and blankets, waking for a day of school. This fantasy dissipated quickly, reality brought home to him by the hardness of the wood beneath him, the pain in his stomach, the thirst in his throat, the press of the other bodies against his own, and the noise.

Gabi, Tibor and János joined the flow of prisoners exiting the barracks. It was still dark, but bright lights illuminated the area, and they could see prisoners from the surrounding barracks pouring into a central clearing. Capos swung clubs and cursed at them. As Gabi ran with the others to line up in rows of five, he saw two bodies tangled in the wire fence. It was clear that they had deliberately run straight into the fence. He could not comprehend why they would give up their lives. Without doubt, they were all living in some sort of man-made hell, yet Gabi could not understand why anyone would take their own life rather than carry on.

The new arrivals mixed with the prisoners from other barracks, some of whom looked like they had been in the camp for a long time: their tattered uniforms hung loosely from narrow frames, their fingers were bony and their faces gaunt. "Hats off!" shouted the young SS officer standing before them. They all yanked their caps from their heads and slapped them against their thighs. "Hats on!" They put their caps back on. This was repeated dozens of times until they could all execute the maneuver with the precise timing and exact snapping sound mandated by the officer. Gabi shivered in the cold and darkness of the early morning. "Stand up straight," whispered a prisoner behind him in Yiddish. "Look strong." Gabi spoke little Yiddish, but he understood. Though he did not know why he was being given this advice, he did as he was told. He squared his shoulders and looked straight ahead.

They stood for hours as they were counted, and then counted again, and then counted again. The sun rose. It began to rain. Still they stood at attention. The shock of the day before was beginning to wear off, and standing there in his ragged uniform with water dripping down his face, Gabi began to grasp his new reality. He thought to himself: *I do not have a home. I do not have a family. I am in this prison called Auschwitz, with tens of thousands of other prisoners. I do not have a name. I am only a number.* Slowly, with unwelcome clarity, he came to see that the escape plans made the night before were childish and silly.

The officer, having conferred with his superiors, was finally satisfied with the count, and the capos shouted, "Dismissed!"

The women, too, were standing at roll call before sunrise being counted by SS guards, some male, though most were female. Each time a guard passed, she pointed her riding crop at a couple of prisoners and ordered them to leave the ranks. Lilly, Oli and Bertha stood together in their row, feeling the cold of the early morning air. When they were finally dismissed, they followed the others back to their barracks. Shortly afterward, the prisoners lined up outside for their morning meal. There was no food, only a strange, bitter drink whose only redeeming feature was that it was very hot; the rising steam warmed their faces and the cups warmed their hands.

After that, they were led to the nearby latrine. On the way, Lilly noticed a pile next to one of the barracks. She assumed at first that it was wood, but as they got closer she realized she was looking at a pile of bodies, skeletal women stacked one on top of the other. Although Lilly knew what she was seeing, she could not process what was in front of her. In this state of disbelief, she entered the latrine. The water was cold and there was no soap. The women splashed water on their faces and dried themselves using their dresses.

This was their morning routine. There was little to do afterwards except to feel the ache of their empty stomachs and try to suppress their fears about the rest of the family and what lay ahead. They were not put to work, so each day took an eternity to pass. Sleep continued to be a challenge, as they were usually stuck in uncomfortable positions, unable to move. Their bunk was so crowded that Lilly and Oli sometimes elected to sleep on the concrete floor, in spite of the rats that sometimes scuttled across them. The start of each new day brought with it both a feeling of relief that the night was ending and anticipation of the hunger and deprivation that the day would bring.

During the morning roll calls, women were chosen and taken away. Lilly, Oli and Bertha cared about nothing more than staying together, so these selections were a daily threat. SS guards would call people out of the ranks, sometimes randomly, sometimes by virtue of some shared characteristic or profession. During a morning selection a few days after their arrival, an officer called for all redheads to step forward. George's aunt Margda stepped out of her row, a scarf wrapped around her red hair. Anikó followed her mother, asking their capo if she could go, too. The capo told her to stay put and not to go with her mother, but she pleaded with the officer guarding the selected women. "The more the merrier," he said, and allowed her to join her mother. Lilly had no idea where they were being taken, but the next day she saw another prisoner wearing Margda's scarf.

It seemed that older women were more likely to be chosen in the selections, which worried Lilly and Oli. Due to the harsh conditions, Bertha was looking years beyond her true age. She had trouble holding herself at attention through the long hours of roll call. Every morning her daughters did their best to help her look youthful; they even managed to scavenge a red polka-dot scarf to cover her grey hair. Still, each morning was a trial of her strength and endurance.

After years in the camps, the Polish capos became harsh and sadistic. Beatings were frequent, and violence was often random. The prisoners learned quickly that it was a good idea to do whatever they were told and to stay clear of the capos whenever possible. Yet sometimes a capo would go out of her way to help, doing her best in nearly impossible circumstances. One night Lilly lay in her bunk listening to the screams of a young prisoner going through labor as she gave birth in the barracks. As soon as the baby was born, Lilly saw their capo rush out the door carrying the newborn, ignoring the mother's cries. Word spread the next morning that the capo had taken the baby to the latrine and killed her there. Had the baby been left with the mother, both mother and daughter would have been in the crematorium by morning.

Breaking any of the rules could have harsh consequences. One night Oli desperately needed to use the toilet. They were only allowed to go to the latrines once a day, in the mornings just after roll call, but she knew she could not wait until then. She snuck out of the barracks and made her way to the latrine, moving quickly and quietly in the night. When she had almost made it back to her barracks, a female SS guard stepped into her path. She wore an elegant nightgown and carried a heavy wooden stick. She screamed at Oli for being outside, and when Oli tried to explain why she was there, the guard raised the stick and brought it down onto her shoulder. Oli fled into the barracks to Lilly and her mother. Fortunately, the blow didn't cause serious injury. But for the next two days, Oli continued to feel the repercussions of the simple need to use a toilet.

On Lilly's twenty-fourth birthday—May 24, 1944—she made her way with Oli and Bertha out to roll call. As they were arranging themselves in their row, their capo pushed Bertha.

"Don't push my mother!" Lilly yelled. "Push me!"

The capo grabbed Lilly's arm and dragged her back inside the barracks. She slapped Lilly hard on the face. Lilly was stunned; she had never been hit before. The capo continued to hit her, while berating her for having the audacity to complain.

"You still have a mother. I haven't had a mother for years! I haven't had parents or any family for years!" she yelled, striking Lilly again and again.

Finally, exhausted, she allowed Lilly back outside. Lilly returned to the roll call bruised and bleeding, and took her place again beside her worried mother, thinking that this must be about the worst birthday that a person could have.

A few days later, all of the women were handed postcards. Lilly looked at the card in her hand and saw that the return address was a town in Germany. They were instructed to write on the cards that they were fine, and being treated well. Lilly thought hard about where to send the card. She wanted it to reach George, but was unsure where he was. Then she had an idea: she could write to the Földis in Budapest, at the house she had stayed in when George had weekend passes from the labor camp. George was most likely still seeing the Földis, and would get the card the next time he visited. With the small pencil she had been given, she wrote what she was told to write: things were wonderful and all was well. They worked during the day while mother stayed home to cook. They were all in good health and in good care. She hoped George would see through the obvious lies. At least he would know she was alive. Oli wrote similar falsehoods to Laci, wishing desperately that she could tell him what was really happening to her.

It felt to Gabi as though his first two weeks in Auschwitz were spent waiting for roll call to end. They had to stand in their rows of five before dawn every morning, again in the early evening, and occasionally in the middle of the night. Sometimes they stood for hours in downpours of chilly spring rain. In between roll calls, Gabi slept, or talked with his friends. He gathered what information he could from those who had been in the camp longer, and who knew more about what was going on.

On his second day, he had approached a Polish prisoner who had clearly been in the camp for a while. Gabi asked him in German why his father and others had been sent to one side and he had been sent to the other. The prisoner took him outside the barracks and pointed to the sky, where Gabi could see the top of a smokestack spewing ashes and smoke. The wind brought some of the ashes to them; white flakes blew by their faces like snow. "See that smoke?" the man asked, pointing at the tower. "That is them. They have all been killed."

The matter-of-fact way in which the prisoner said this struck Gabi dumb, and he was sure that the man must have misunderstood. It took some time for him to comprehend what the man was saying. He could not believe it possible that so many people were being killed, and even though the prisoner seemed very confident, Gabi decided that he must be mistaken. Given the chaos of their arrival and the vastness of Auschwitz, Gabi doubted the man's certainty about the fate of his father. Surely it was impossible to know for sure who had gone where, in which case it must be possible his father was simply in another part of the camp.

On that second day in Auschwitz Gabi drank his soup. Disgusting though the meal was, hunger outweighed repulsion. The meager rations did little to quell the pain in his gut, the stone-like emptiness that he carried with him. The prisoners received a piece of bread in the morning—the same dense, sawdust-filled mixture they'd been given the first day—along with some sort of ersatz coffee. In the late afternoon they would wait for their evening meal, watching for the two prisoners carrying a large cauldron hanging from a pole balanced on their shoulders. At mealtimes, some prisoners would try to get in line first, though it was a risky strategy. If the prisoner serving the soup failed to ladle it from the bottom of the pot, one would receive only a thin liquid. Gabi tended to favor the middle of the line, when the pot was less full and he felt he was more likely to receive a tiny piece of carrot or beet. He and his friends ate their soup and bread on the ground outside the barracks, but afterwards they were still starving. It was difficult to think of anything but hunger and food.

The morning selections were terrifying. Gabi learned why the new arrivals were told by the more experienced prisoners to stand straight and to look strong. At each roll call, the SS selected the weakest prisoners and sent them to the gas chambers. Even a dejected look on a man's face was enough to single him out for selection. While the main purpose of the selection was to kill off those incapable of working, the SS sometimes appeared to be playing games with them, asking for men from a specific profession, such as musicians or doctors. Some would raise their hands—perhaps thinking that they would be able to work in their own field—only to be sent with the weakest prisoners to the gas chamber. Gabi learned from what he saw and decided the best option was never to volunteer for anything. The optimal strategy for staying alive, he realized, was to be unnoticed, to blend into the background.

One day at morning roll call, hundreds of prisoners were selected, and Gabi watched with dread as the SS officer scanned his row and then pointed to him. He was reassured by the fact that the many prisoners who were being chosen were in relatively good physical condition. They were not the weak and downtrodden usually sent to be gassed. Those who had been selected re-formed into rows of five and were ordered to march toward the gate. They walked for about half an hour until they reached a railroad station, at which point they were handed over to Ukrainian guards who ordered them onto a train. Gabi was relieved that the car was not as crowded as the one he arrived in a few weeks before. They were able to sit down, with some space between them. But then a Ukrainian guard carrying a machine gun climbed up and ordered everyone to move away from him as he set his stool down in the middle of the car. He bent over and drew a large circle with chalk around him. Sitting cross-legged in the center, he told his prisoners that if anyone crossed the line he would shoot him. Gabi did not doubt that he was telling the truth.

Oli's Diary, January 13, 1944:

They beat us and they were very rude. Our food was little and bad, we starved a lot. We were constantly dazed and couldn't think normally. No wonder, after seeing the corpses dumped on each other and the flaming chimney of the crematory. We lived in this horror for six weeks, standing in the rain and wind for hours, dreading we'd be separated. The camp was huge and unfortunately we couldn't learn anything about Dad and Gabika. People were brought here from all over the world and they had to live this horrible life.

What Oli really wanted was soap. She hated that she couldn't wash properly, abhorred the layer of grime she wore on her skin. She imagined how good it would feel to have a real shower with hot water and soap, and to be able to take all the time she needed to wash. She knew that hot water and a chance to bathe leisurely were unobtainable, but she also knew that some women had managed to acquire soap inside the camp. During one evening meal, Oli saw a chance to get some for herself. Sitting like gold at the bottom of her soup was a small piece of bacon—something to barter. Plans formed immediately in her mind.

Later that night, she slipped out of her barracks and headed to another block in search of a trading partner. Her route there led past a chimney shooting flames high into the sky. The sickening smell was intense and, as she looked up at the sparks and flames, she understood—at a deeper level than she had before—what was happening in this place. When she entered the barracks, she asked if anyone had soap they would like to exchange for bacon, and she quickly found someone. With her small piece of soap in hand, she made her way back, this time avoiding the stick-wielding SS guard in the fancy nightgown. The next morning in the latrine, Oli, along with Lilly and Bertha, savored the small luxury. The hardships of the day were easier to bear with fresh faces and clean hands.

One morning, as they were being counted, a large number of women were selected for work at another camp. For several weeks the three had survived these selections intact, but it was a roll of the dice each time an SS officer peered at them. Now they watched as an officer worked his way toward them, pointing to women along the way, making unknown calculations according to mysterious rules. Lilly froze in terror when the officer pointed to her, and her panic increased as he passed over Oli and Bertha.

She stepped out of her row and joined the other women standing in a group, waiting to be taken away. Next to her was her cousin Irenke, now in tears. She was devastated to be separated from her sister, Arenka, who was standing in the front row, not far from their group. Lilly edged her way to the fringe of her group closest to Arenka. The two women made eye contact and understood each other instantly. Both turned to watch the officer, and as soon as he looked the other way, they quickly swapped places. Lilly's heart raced as she stood in Arenka's former spot, convinced that they were about to be found out. If they were caught, she would at best be sent away with the others, and at worst be beaten or killed. The officer methodically continued to select women until he had his quota. Irenke and Arenka held on to each other as the group reassembled into rows of five and marched away. When they were finally dismissed, Lilly embraced her mother and sister.

A few days later, in early July, the women were settling into the barracks in the evening when their capo announced that many prisoners were going to be sent to another camp. An evening roll call was held. They were counted off en masse and told they would be taking a shower before leaving Auschwitz. By this time they had learned what "showers" meant for many at Auschwitz, and the women were petrified as they marched to the bathhouse. They felt some relief when they stopped at the same building they had bathed in when they'd arrived, but it wasn't until the water started to fall that they were sure they were not about to be killed. They were made to hurry through the shower, then dress in their grey dresses again. Finally, they were rushed back to the train tracks where they had arrived six weeks before, and loaded on to cattle cars. Many of the women who had been selected for transport were from Beregszász, and all dreaded another arduous ride of unknown duration to an unknown destination. But at least they were leaving Auschwitz alive.

THE WALK

The long line of old men moved and walked silently behind the truck carrying the sick and disabled people....
Even from a distance, the howling of dogs, screams from
sentries, shots and the puffing of a departing locomotive
generated an atmosphere of fear.

*(From the memoir of John Wiernicki, a captured Polish resistance
fighter, who secretly observed the processing of Hungarian prisoners as the trains arrived on the Birkenau unloading ramps)*[1]

---

1. Wiernicki, John, *War in the Shadow of Auschwitz: Memoirs of a Polish Resistance
Fighter and Survivor of the Death Camps* (Religion, Theology, and the Holocaust)
(Syracuse University Press, 2001), 159.

Herman turns to the left, and over his shoulder he watches Gabi go off to the right. His son moves further away, and is soon lost from sight, obscured by the men who fill the growing space between them. Together with the other older men, Herman rounds the front of the train, where he sees a barbed wire fence and, through the wire, long wooden buildings. He follows those in front of him as they approach the wire and then turn right. He scratches his face and registers the unaccustomed sensation of stubble under his fingers. In his other hand he turns a comb.

After three days of being unable to move, his muscles and joints ache and disobey. After three days of constant motion, the dusty ground under his feet seems to shift. He is tremendously thirsty. He struggles to keep pace with those around him who are also struggling to keep pace. He wants to stop and rest, but the dogs and machine guns deny him this choice.

RECOLLECTION
(Written 2011)

In writing this book I have faced three big challenges. The first is a constant desire for greater detail. Even when an event seems well described in an interview, I always find detail lacking when I actually try to write about it. Oli told me years ago about getting hit by the SS officer for going to the latrine at night, but when I draft a few paragraphs describing this incident, I find that I have more questions than facts. Was everyone asleep when she sneaked out? What part of her was struck? What was she struck with? So I call Oli, reminding myself again how lucky I am that I can just pick up the phone and talk to her, reminding myself also that I'd better get this book finished soon, unless I want to be left with questions and no one to ask.

Oli and I discuss Lilly and George for a little while. George is in the final stages of Parkinson's disease and Lilly is absolutely devastated by his illness. Then I get to my questions. I find out that the others weren't asleep when she left the barracks, and she was hit in the back. I forget to ask her what she was hit with. (I really should list all of my questions before I call, but I always think I'll remember everything.) So, I email my dad:

Hi - talked to Oli to ask her a few questions about Auschwitz for the book. I have a few more questions that I either forgot to ask or she had trouble with the English. Could you call and ask her:

1) they were in the camp with sisters, Arenka and Ireke. Did they know them from home or did they meet them in the camp?

2) Also, she told me about getting hit by an SS guard for leaving the barracks one evening. What did she hit her with - a stick or a whip (riding crop)?

3) It's unclear to me when they first saw the flames from the crematorium. Lilly says their barracks were very near the chimneys (which fits with the map I have - the women's camp was close to

it), and so even on the first night they saw flames. But Oli says she first saw the flames when she snuck out to trade a piece of meat for soap in another barracks one night. Can you ask her about this?

Thanks,
Love you!

He emails back:

Hi Jilly, I talked to Oli yesterday, and here are the answers: They were together with Arenka and Irenke in Auschwitz [they were 2nd or 3rd cousins to us] but they were sent to other slave labor facilities from Auschwitz. Oli said she was going to the toilet during the night [which was not allowed] and when she came back to her barracks, an ss female guard, screamed at her and hit her really hard on her shoulder [oli said it was a good thing she wasn't shot] The crematorium was not visible from their barracks, but when she went pretty far to exchange a piece of bacon, which she found in her soup, for a piece of soap, she could see the chimney and the flames really well. Oli sounded good, but she can't get over the situation with Lilly and George. By the way Oli was hit by the guard with a heavy stick. Love to you all, Dad

This helps clear up a few things. But, as mentioned, Lilly, Oli and my dad often remember things differently. When I spoke with Oli, I asked about Irenke and Arenka. I had drafted a couple of paragraphs about them, and I was trying to get more detail about who was standing where and how difficult it was to swap places, and Oli told me that *she* swapped with Arenka, not Lilly. I told Oli that Lilly remembered that it was she who swapped, but Oli says that she took Arenke's place.

I go back to the paragraph about the swap and try to figure out what to do. Lilly has told me this story multiple times, and this is the first time I've heard it from Oli, so I'm inclined to go with Lilly's version. Still, to be more certain I call Lilly. I tell her what Oli told me, but Lilly is adamant that she was the one who swapped. Lilly is even able to describe the thoughts she had about possible punishments if she were caught. So I go with Lilly's version, and go back to my draft to add Lilly's worries about punishment. I also fix Irenke's name based on the spelling Lilly gave me. ("Don't the sisters have really similar names?" I ask. "Not really," she says.)

There is also the matter of the uniforms. My dad's email is inconsistent with what Lilly has said in the diary and other earlier interviews. I decide to stick with my earlier sources.

One major discrepancy took years to resolve. Lilly and Oli both remember the strip search occurring before they left the ghetto, and in particular that the men had to get undressed in the clearing before they got on the train. My father, when I interviewed him in the late 1990s, had no such recollection. This was a puzzle, because having to strip naked in front of your family and friends seems like an event that would lodge firmly in memory. I asked him about it several more times over the years, but he couldn't remember a search or the men having to stand naked in the clearing; they went straight to the train, leaving their luggage on the way. He said that he was pretty sure he would have remembered getting searched and having to undress if it had happened, but thought that maybe he was so out of it at the time that he wasn't processing what was going on.

Was it possible that my dad was in such a state of shock that he didn't form a strong memory of the incident? Or, were Lilly and Oli mistaken about the men having to stand naked? Oli does mention the scene in her diary, which was written within a year of the event: "There were men standing in the courtyard of the brick factory naked, at the mercy of our policemen." Thus, my inclination is to go with the recollections of Oli and Lilly.

Then, in 2004, I found a further clue. While driving in France, I was playing an old taped interview I had done with my dad for a term paper in college, back in 1981. I hadn't listened to the tape in many years. As I drove through the winding streets of Fontainebleau in a drizzling rain, I heard my dad describe the morning when they were taken to the trains, and in this description he says, ". . . they searched everybody. They took everything you had away, all the suitcases, personal belongings away. They searched you to see that you didn't have any valuables . . ." He doesn't say that they had to get undressed for the search, but he does recall a search. The next time I talked to him, I told him about the tape, and he was surprised, but he also said that he thought that his recollections in 1981 were much more likely to be correct than what he could remember so many years later.

The third challenge I face is perhaps the most complex of all: it has to do with when they came to understand what the business of Auschwitz really was. This is murky territory for a number of reasons. Once someone knew what was happening, it probably became difficult to remember the more naïve and innocent time beforehand—later knowledge might color earlier memories. Further, "knowing" can happen at multiple levels. Auschwitz was full of deceptions to keep arriving prisoners calm. The orchestra, the gardens, the families living together were all an illusion carefully concocted to give the impression that things were not as horrible as they actually were. (The family camp that my father saw served an additional purpose: these Czech families were kept together in relatively nice quarters in case of Red Cross inspections.)

But the deception could not continue for long: new arrivals quickly came into contact with veteran prisoners who knew much more about what was really taking place in the camp. Both my dad and his sisters learned from these prisoners that the selections upon their arrival determined life and death. My dad seemed to learn early on that being selected during roll call typically meant death, while Lilly and Oli did not seem to know this.

From a safe and distant vantage point, I imagine that when my dad learned about the meaning of the first selection upon arrival, it would have been pretty clear that Herman had been killed. When I asked him when he realized that his father had died, he said he pretty much knew the second day, when he talked to the Polish prisoner. But he has only said this recently. Years ago, he used to say that he didn't know where his dad was, and that he only really knew Herman was dead after liberation. I think that, at least early on, my dad probably held on to the ambiguities available to him—imperfect communication between prisoners who spoke different languages, the chaos of their arrival, and the sheer incomprehensibility of killing on that massive scale—to allow himself to believe that his father might still be alive. That's what I would have done.

For Lilly and Oli, it was easier to imagine that both Herman and Gabi were alive, though the fact that they saw Gabi after the selections without Herman was a strong indication that their father had been killed. But they had even more ambiguity to cushion them, because it was quite possible that the men had been split into different groups after selection. Lilly has always told me that she believed Herman would survive— he was so robust and fit. It was Gabi she worried about; he was so young and skinny, and Lilly thought that he would not be able to withstand the hardships of the camps. She addressed her diary to her father, assuming—or at least hoping—that he would read it when they were back together again after the war.

Lilly and Oli, despite their very similar experiences in the camps, seem to have realized at different times that mass killings were occurring in Auschwitz. Lilly dates her realization to their first night, when Violet told them what was happening. Oli, on the other hand, told me that she didn't really grasp it until the night she went to trade her bacon for the soap and walked near one of the chimneys. That this comprehension might develop slowly is hardly surprising. How else could one come to understand the unfathomable business of Auschwitz? Perhaps the men my father saw on the fence that first morning suffered from an unfortunate perceptiveness, while those new arrivals standing at roll call had managed to suspend themselves in disbelief.

Chapter 14
MERCY

In the late afternoon, Gabi's train stopped at a station and the doors were opened. The air that filled the car was not the air of Auschwitz; it was cool and scented with pine. Gabi jumped down to the station platform and found that he was in the mountains. Steep forested slopes rose up on all sides.

The prisoners lined up and were counted, and then were ordered to march. Gabi had no idea how long they would be walking, but it only took an hour to reach the entrance of their new camp. As they stood to be counted again, Gabi noticed that the posts holding up the fences didn't have the electric terminals that made the fences at Auschwitz so deadly. Each prisoner was handed a blanket and then sent toward the kitchen building. As they walked, Gabi smelled something he had not known for many weeks: fish. At home, Gabi had never cared much for fish; now, he salivated at the thought of such a meal.

Once in line, the prisoners untied their metal cups from their belts. Each was given a piece of bread and a cup of fish soup, which they ate outside while sitting on the ground. Gabi felt more optimistic than he had since entering the cattle car that took him from Beregszász. Perhaps the world was coming into balance again. As they ate, the prisoners wondered at their good fortune, at this positive turn of events. Decent food, their own blanket—luxuries. When Gabi said to another inmate, "This is heaven!" he was expressing a profound truth about the relative nature of suffering. Their loss of freedom, the absence of family and home, the filth they were eating, were indeed heavenly when contrasted to the world of Auschwitz.

After they had finished, the prisoners were taken to their quarters: round, tent-like huts made from thin plywood and arranged in a ten-by-ten grid. Each housed about twenty prisoners. Gabi crouched down to enter his assigned cabin through the small opening. There was a stove in the middle of the hut that vented through a central chimney. The prisoners spread out on the straw floor like spokes in a wheel, feet toward the stove.

Gabi was awakened before dawn by the shouts of his new capo. Everyone rushed out to get their breakfast, but after the unanticipated fish soup of the previous evening, breakfast was a disappointment—chicory coffee and a slice of bread. Perhaps, Gabi thought, they alternated between better and worse food, or maybe dinners were superior to the breakfasts. The prisoners lined up outside for roll call, with each capo responsible for his own row of ten tents. One thing that was clearly no different between here and Auschwitz was the incessant counting. They stood forever in rows, five people to a row.

A short man they had seen the night before approached their capo. He was a German prisoner and the head capo of the camp. He collected the count of prisoners from each capo and reported the total to an SS officer. Then he addressed the crowd. He told them they were in a camp called Wolfsberg, and that they would be divided into work parties building railroads and roads. They were expected to work hard and to do what they were told.

The prisoners were counted off as they walked in their rows toward the camp gates. Gabi was one of a group of fifty that was marched to a railroad-building site. They were told that their job was to carry steel rails, about twenty meters in length, up to near the end of the tracks. Other work parties delivered the wood ties, and these were then joined to the rails by prisoners swinging large, heavy mallets. Ahead of the newly laid tracks, the largest and strongest inmates operated machines that pounded the earth, compressing the gravel into a level bed for the next set of rails.

Gabi worked in a team of three. Because he was the shortest, he took the middle of the rail. Together, they hoisted the metal onto their shoulders. Gabi was not at all sure he would be able to walk, but he took his first step without falling down, and then the next and the next. Step by step they made it through the first delivery. Gabi soon realized that the middle was a good place to be, because more weight was borne by the men at either end. Still, the weight on his shoulder was tremendous, and it shifted dramatically depending on whether he was on flat ground, at the top of a hill, or in a dip below the other two men. Sometimes his small frame bore the bulk of it. At other times he had to hold the rail up with his hands in order to keep it at the same height as his team members, and this was much harder than using his shoulder.

The edges of the rails were sharp, and after a while his shoulder began to bleed. On the next trip, he switched to the other shoulder, but before long both shoulders were bloody. Gabi was barely able to keep going. He tried not to think beyond that day. He was already developing one of his basic survival strategies: "One day at a time; just get through this one day." A brief break at lunchtime was the only rest from the day's toil. The prisoners had a few short minutes to eat a tin bowl filled with watery soup and a small piece of bread. They ate quickly and then returned to their labors. When the capo finally announced the end of the day's work, Gabi almost collapsed from exhaustion. Only the thought of food, the anticipation of a meal like the one from the night before, kept him going through the march back to camp. But when Gabi watched his bowl fill with a brown, watery muck, just like an Auschwitz supper, he knew for sure that he was still in hell. He wondered what hopes would get him through the next day.

Still—one day at a time—Gabi survived his first weeks in Wolfsberg. Gradually, he learned about the workings of the camp, which appeared to have been built just prior to their arrival. While they were among the first occupants, other transports soon followed. Gabi guessed that the small group of prisoners already there when he arrived had built the camp. Now the population was around 2,000.

The capos' huts were located at the end of every ten rows of tents, near the "parade ground" where roll call took place. A young boy also resided in each of these huts. It was common knowledge in the camp that these young prisoners, who were about fourteen years old, were kept as the property of the capos, to be used as desired. The children appeared to be well fed, at least in comparison to the ordinary prisoners. The capos themselves were very robust. They wore clean uniforms and real shoes, rather than canvas clogs. They also tended to beat prisoners as a matter of course. Some capos did so in a measured way, doing just enough to demonstrate to the SS officers that they could be tough and should be kept in their privileged position. Others went beyond the call of duty and enjoyed exercising their brutal responsibility. The capo for Gabi's row of tents was an older Polish Jew who was less zealous about punishment, and Gabi managed to avoid his beatings.

Sunday was a day of some relief. The guards were off duty for the most part, which meant a respite for the prisoners. Some inmates were so exhausted that they slept through the day, conserving their energy in preparation for the next week's labor. Many of the younger prisoners, however, spent the day talking with others who shared their language. Gabi often spoke with the Mermelstein brothers from Beregszász, who were a bit older than him. New acquaintances were gradually brought into the circle, and Gabi was heartened by their camaraderie. Their conversations, which at first were about family and food, eventually became mostly about food and food alone. The descriptions they created for each other could be tasted by the tongue, held in the mouth, chewed between the teeth and inhaled through the nostrils. The only thing in their current lives that came even close to their imagined meals, hoped for daily but rarely realized, was when the kitchen worker dipped the ladle to the bottom of the soup cauldron and dredged up a piece of vegetable or, even more rarely, a tiny morsel of meat. It was a thrilling moment; an instant when eating, in a tiny way, acquired the character of remembered meals from home.

As the weeks passed, Gabi's family became more and more distant in his mind. At first, he was jealous of those who were in the camp with a father, a brother or an uncle. Family members provided support for each other, as well as a connection to their past life. With time, though, Gabi learned that being with family could also be a curse. When a father died, the son was likely to give up. When one of the Mermelstein brothers died, the other soon followed. The will to live was so entangled with family that, after a relative's death, the surviving son, uncle, nephew or brother was often unable to go on. Gabi came to feel fortunate that he had only himself to depend on and to care about. Still, the companionship he felt with the other boys and young men, and their Sunday conversations filled with complaints, stories and remembrances of dinner tables at home, helped sustain him through the week.

When he first saw people die at the camp, it had shocked him, and he worried about his own ability to stay alive and retain his sanity. But he soon became numb to these losses. People died from starvation, from disease, from work-related accidents. Someone he spoke to one day could be dead the next. Sights that in his earlier life would have been terrifying became commonplace.

The summer passed, one day at a time, and by August Gabi was wearing down. He had become more used to the daily toil, the lifting and the fatigue, but it wasn't getting any easier. The muscles he would have been building through such exertion were lost to the lack of calories to build them—the fish soup disappeared after their welcome meal, never to return. He did find some relief in occasional work details that weren't as difficult as hauling the rails, such as digging holes and spreading gravel. All of it was hard work, but nothing was as arduous as carrying the metal rails that tore the flesh of his shoulders.

For all of his parents' and sisters' attempts to fatten him up when he was at home, being skinny seemed to have a survival advantage. Prisoners who were overweight at the start did not last long. Used to consuming much more than the meager portions allotted, they lost weight quickly and soon died. Gabi's caloric requirements were better suited to the available rations, but he was still hungry all the time, desperate for more food. Little by little, he was wasting away.

As he continued to lose weight and felt himself becoming weaker, Gabi began to fear that he too would soon be just another body in striped pajamas carried from a tent. Yet he was determined not to die. He saw his struggle to survive as a battle he was fighting with the SS. If he gave in, if he surrendered his life, then the bastards would win. He did not want to give them this victory. If he stayed alive, then he won. He was also resolute about returning home to his family. He worried about what would happen if his mother and sisters came home and he didn't. This concern got him up off the cold ground every morning with his mind set on making it through another day. But mental fortitude could take him only so far. The inescapable physical reality of calories consumed versus calories burned had its own inevitable consequence. So too did the changing of seasons: the summer was ending, the days were turning cooler, and soon there would be snow, cold and darkness.

One of Gabi's survival strategies was to blend into the background and make himself as inconspicuous as possible. This way he was less likely to be singled out for a beating by a capo, or to be struck by a rifle butt because he wasn't doing his work. The selections at Auschwitz and his first months at Wolfsberg taught him to avoid calling attention to himself, and certainly never to volunteer for anything. He broke this rule only twice: once in Wolfsberg, and again in another camp a few months later.

The first instance occurred one morning late in the summer during roll call. An SS sergeant walked up to Gabi's section and yelled, "Which one of you young inmates speaks German?"

Acting purely on instinct, Gabi raised his hand high into the air. As he realized what he was doing, he reasoned with himself that the officer was unlikely to pull out a single prisoner for execution. Selections usually gathered dozens, or even hundreds, and in any case, Gabi hadn't experienced selections since Auschwitz. Work, starvation and disease did the job of culling the weaker prisoners from the ranks. Gabi followed the officer, and as he neared the camp entrance he saw a man waiting for him in a long leather coat. Gabi panicked. *What have I gotten myself into?* The man had the dark and neatly dressed look of a Gestapo officer, and Gabi was sure he had made a very bad decision.

The man asked Gabi if he spoke German, and when Gabi said that he did, the man introduced himself as Herr Fürst. He was a civilian engineer who needed an assistant for his work. He explained that his job was to conduct a survey for a new road to be built through the forest, and he wanted someone to help carry the equipment and stand with the surveying rod while he took measurements. Gabi immediately understood that this job would be much easier than his usual daily toil, and when they walked together into the woods and started their work it became clear to Gabi that the risk he had taken had paid off.

Throughout the day they made their way slowly through the forest. Herr Fürst would place his tripod among the underbrush and point in the direction that he wanted Gabi to walk. After a few steps, Gabi would turn and slowly walk backward as the engineer called out, "Go… go… go… stop!" Gabi would then turn the side of his stick with the numbers on it toward Herr Fürst, who would look through his scope and make some notes. They repeated this routine until it was time for Herr Fürst to have lunch, during which Gabi ate with a nearby work crew. After lunch, they continued their work until it was time for Gabi to be taken to where he would meet up with the rest of the work crew for the march back to camp.

Near the end of the second day, as they headed back toward the camp, Herr Fürst told Gabi, "I can see what a horrible situation you are in, and I want to do something to help you." Gabi was dumbfounded. He wondered how it was possible that this German cared anything at all about him or his situation. Herr Fürst went on to say that he couldn't help him outright because of the SS guards, but that he could obtain some food for him. He explained that there was a barracks in the woods, where he ate his lunch with the SS officers, and where he had hidden some food in a corner, under a bench. The building was empty in the late afternoon. They would get there half an hour early so that Gabi would have time to eat, and then they would go to meet his work party. As they neared the perimeter of the camp, Herr Fürst indicated the barracks. Gabi left him. The building was dark and empty, and Gabi hurried to the far corner and looked under the bench. *Chicken! Rice!*

For the two extraordinary weeks that he worked with the engineer, Gabi supplemented his daily intake of stale bread and watery soup with food from the SS kitchen. He feasted on foods that he had not tasted for months: beef, chicken, milk. In the dark corner of the mess hall, he quickly drank all of the liquids, took some bites of the food and put the rest in his pockets. Sometimes there was so much food that he shared with his young friends once he was back in his hut, putting real flavors and calories in their mouths in place of their Sunday fantasies.

As the days passed, he grew sturdier. The boost to his well-being was more than physical: the fact that this German cared about him, and was willing to take great personal risks to feed him, restored some of Gabi's faith in other people. Working in the forest with the engineer, he could forget for a while that he was a concentration camp inmate. He was not a prisoner, torn from his home and family. Instead, he was on one of the camping trips that he used to take with the boy scouts. He was taking a walk in the woods.

RECOLLECTION

I have watched my father talk to audiences about his Holocaust experiences many times. Almost every time, I have learned something new: sometimes an incident I didn't know about, and sometimes just a small detail. He holds up well during these talks, even though the events he is speaking about are very distressing. As soon as he is done, he bounces back to his usual good humor and wants to discuss dinner plans.

When he was in Wolfsberg as a sixteen-year-old prisoner, he knew full well that being assigned to work with Herr Fürst was a tremendous stroke of luck. But it took some time for him to realize just how pivotal a role his benefactor had played. After my father was liberated and could better weigh the impact various events had had on his ability to survive, he credited Herr Fürst with saving his life.

In every speech he gives about his camp experiences, my dad tells the story of the civilian German engineer in the long leather coat. My father speaks of the cattle cars, the cruelty of the SS officers and the murderous selections without flinching. Decades after their final walk in the forest, it is the kindness shown to him by one man that forces him to stop speaking, lower his eyes and weep.

Chapter 15
BRICKS AND BOMBS

Lilly, Oli and Bertha rode on the train for three days. It was not quite the nightmare of the ride from Beregszász to Auschwitz; the car was less crowded and they could sit. They had bread and water, and once again, a barrel as a toilet. Two soldiers accompanied them inside the car, which added to the embarrassment of having to use the barrel.

Many of the women on the train were from Beregszász, and they speculated about their new, unknown destination with both hope and trepidation. Where they were headed surely had to be better than where they had come from. It seemed impossible to imagine a place more horrific than Auschwitz, but then it had also been impossible to envision Auschwitz when they had first left Beregszász. Perhaps there was a worse place, and they just lacked the imagination to conjure it.

Occasionally the train stopped and they were given more bread and water. The guards always jumped down from the train during these stops, but the prisoners of course enjoyed no such freedom.

At one stop, the women could see city buildings, impressive in their ornate beauty; after some discussion, they decided that they must be in Dresden. The open door of their wooden box framed an outside world in which life continued as normal. They were tormented by the fact that, beyond the tracks, people were going to sidewalk cafés, to shops and to movies. People were going home to their families at the end of the day. All of this normality had existed while they were locked behind electric fences and barbed wire.

After three days, they arrived at their destination, which they would learn was a town called Gelsenkirchen in northern Germany. They were marched from the train to a camp, and along the way saw destruction unlike any they had seen before. Gelsenkirchen had been heavily bombed, with the result that the streets were cratered and filled with rubble. Grim residents—mostly women—grey with dirt and plaster dust, regarded them with vague curiosity. A bombed-out petroleum refinery came into view, a few of its vast chimneys and huge tanks still standing.

Their barracks in the new camp were huge military tents, with accommodations similar to those in Auschwitz. As in Auschwitz, there were tiers of wooden shelves that would serve as their uncomfortable beds, but here at least there were blankets and straw for bedding. Fewer women had to fit into the allotted space, so sleeping would be much more comfortable. They were each given a plate and a spoon, and then—to their astonishment—they received the extraordinary luxury of a toothbrush: one to be shared among three women. As they collected their provisions, Oli, Lilly and Bertha couldn't wait for the moment when they could finally brush nearly two months of residue from their teeth.

Soon a barrel of soup arrived and they were told to serve themselves. They took turns hungrily scooping a bowlful from the container. That night, for the first time in weeks, it was possible to change position without the cooperation of every bunkmate. Further evidence of improved conditions was provided the next morning when they received farina and milk for breakfast, a delicacy compared to the fare at Auschwitz. And they didn't have to rush while in the washroom; they could wash their bodies and brush their teeth.

But they had been sent there to work, and they all wondered what they would have to do and how hard the labor would be. Lilly, Oli and Bertha hoped that whatever their work was, they would be able to do it together. That first morning, as they stood to be counted, they learned that all of the women would be helping to clear the rubble from the bombed petroleum refinery they had passed the day before.

They were marched back to the refinery, and immediately saw that they were to be part of a massive work effort. Hundreds of men were laboring at the site. Some of them were German workers, but most were prisoners of war from various countries—mainly Czechs, Italians and Belgians. The women were taken to a wall that had crumbled and told to remove the rubble. As they stared at the large chunks of concrete, they wondered how they could possibly lift the larger pieces. They worked for eight hours, their muscles aching and their hands scraped and cut by the rough material. One SS guard entertained himself by pouring water onto the porous chunks of concrete carried by the women who passed him, then laughing as they stumbled from the increased weight.

When the rubble had been cleared, the women were moved to a new task, collecting bricks from the destroyed refinery and removing residual clumps of mortar. They sat on the ground, using hammers to chip away at the hard grey paste. Lilly became quite adept at this job, discovering the exact angle and force necessary to detach the residue. With one blow, the mortar would shatter and the brick would be clean. She worked quickly and efficiently, much faster than the others. One of the guards overseeing their labor noticed Lilly's facility, and called over one of his colleagues to point out her talent for brick cleaning. They both laughed. Lilly didn't care that they were making fun of her. She took pride in doing things well, even if she was a slave doing a menial task.

There were kindnesses as well. Some of the German workers and foreign prisoners of war noticed the desperate situation the women were in—their gaunt faces and ragged uniforms—and found ways to help them, providing them with small gifts. Many of the guards were older Wehrmacht soldiers who had been brought in to guard the camps while their younger SS counterparts were sent to war. Some of these men were relaxed and even sociable toward the prisoners. Oli thought that the man who guarded the area of their barracks, who she guessed to be in his forties, looked strikingly like her father. Oli would often exchange pleasantries with him when they passed each other. Seeing him made her miss her father terribly, but it helped her to share a few words with this man, and to be treated as a human being. Sometimes when they passed, he would hand her a small parcel, usually containing a special food treat that she could share with her sister and mother.

The bricks the women prepared were used to begin reconstruction of the refinery. When they ran out, new bricks were shipped in on boats via a nearby river. The women had to unload the bricks from the hull of the boat and transport them to the worksite. They formed a line and tossed the bricks from one to another, two at a time. The work was tiring and dangerous, frequently resulting in injured hands and bruised feet.

The weeks went by—long days of labor followed by camaraderie in the tents in the evening. Their paltry portions of food were occasionally supplemented by the generosity of the men they worked with, but the women were still hungry all the time. They were also infested with lice, which caused them to itch constantly. Oli had developed sores on her back, and Lilly and Bertha tried to give her some of their food to help her heal, but Oli wanted her mother to get any extra rations. Bertha would refuse in turn, and so there were constant struggles between them.

It was a difficult life, but it was orders of magnitude better than Auschwitz. They could imagine carrying on this way until the end of the war. In fact, the most immediate danger they faced was not from their German guards, but from the Allies. By early September, air-raid sirens were sounding frequently and the prisoners had no access to any kind of shelter beyond their tents. The bombings might signal a hastening of the war's end, but they were still terrifying. No bombs had fallen near them yet, but every day the women witnessed first hand the destruction that had previously been brought to the town. And now that the refinery was rebuilt, it was once more a target, with their camp not far away.

On the evening of September 10, 1944, the air-raid sirens blared, and the women saw flashes on the horizon, closer than ever before. Lying in their bunks that night, trying to sleep, they heard explosions in the distance. The next morning was quiet and, as usual, Lilly, Oli and Bertha were brought to the river to move the bricks from the boat. Many boats traveled the river, and this morning the river traffic was busy. Lilly heard a shout and turned around just as a woman standing on the deck of a small boat tossed something into the air. Bertha picked up the onion that landed at her feet, feeling its dry skin in her hand. The three of them decided they would share it at dinner that night; Lilly could almost taste the onion on her tongue.

That evening, they ate in their barracks, saving the onion for last. As they swallowed their first mouthfuls of soup, the air-raid sirens blasted again. Knowing there was little they could do to make themselves safer, they stayed where they were and continued to eat. Suddenly, planes roared low overhead and, seconds later, a bomb exploded with an ear-splitting blast just outside their tent. The three women instinctively threw themselves to the floor. As more explosions shook the ground, they panicked and ran outside. A gated fence separated them from an open field, and the Wehrmacht guard who reminded Oli of her father hurried to open the gate so they could all rush through. Screaming, they ran into the meadow, where they formed huddled masses in the tall grass, their arms covering their heads.

Lilly, Oli and Bertha lay next to each other as bombs fell all around them. The noise—the explosions, the planes and the screaming—were overwhelming. Lilly thought about the onion still in the tent, regretting that they had not eaten it earlier. A plane flew over them, so close that she could make out the soldiers who were spraying them with machine-gun fire. It occurred to Lilly that, with their shaved heads and grey uniforms, the prisoners were probably indistinguishable from soldiers.

Grass was burning, and the dirt being blown into the sky landed on them like a heavy rain. And then they heard the thud of a bomb hitting the ground right next to them. They shut their eyes, and waited for the explosion to follow. Seconds passed. Disbelievingly, they opened their eyes and stared at a silent shell resting in the dirt a few feet from where they lay. "If we live through this, and we get back home, can I marry Laci?" Oli asked her mother. Bertha's reply was instantaneous: "No."

Eventually the explosions stopped, the planes disappeared, and the noise of the engines was replaced by the screaming of the injured and the wails of the bereaved. Lilly, Bertha, and Oli stood up and found themselves in a field of carnage. Body parts lay scattered around them. Prisoners who were able moved through the field looking for loved ones and friends. Oli saw a mother wailing, holding the severed head of her daughter. Lilly recognized a distinctive grey shoe still on the foot of a dismembered leg. "Kati," she said softly to herself. As they heard the planes circling back, Oli, Lilly, Bertha and the other survivors staggered into their torn tents, doing their best to help the injured. They expected more women to enter the tent behind them; their absence was evidence of how many lay dead outside. Cries of pain and grief filled the barracks.

Oli realized that she had been holding her spoon when the bombing started, and that she had taken it with her when she ran out of the tent. Though she hated to go back to the field, a spoon was a very valuable possession and, if lost, would not be replaced. It was getting dark, but there was still enough light to see; she found her spoon in the dirt where she had lain with her sister and mother. As Oli picked it up, she heard a cry. Following the sound, she found Ráhel, a young woman from Beregszász, her legs terribly burned. Oli dropped to her knees next to her. Ráhel was beside herself with pain as Oli slipped her arms underneath her body and, struggling to stand, managed to lift her from the ground. She stumbled back to the barracks and placed the injured woman on a bunk together with other casualties. Among them, Oli spotted Marika, a teenage girl who had lived across the street from Bertha's parents' house. Her wounds were awful, and it was clear that she would not live much longer. Oli sat with her deep into the night, holding her hand until her suffering ended.

Roll call the next morning revealed the surviving women standing in dirty, bloody rags. Blankets were distributed and the SS officers ordered them to collect the bodies in the field. For a few moments the prisoners stood motionless, dreading the idea of having to witness the carnage a second time. But of course there was no choice: the SS trained their guns on them and hustled them out through the gate.

In the meadow, surrounded by so much slaughter, it was hard to comprehend how anyone had survived. The ground was littered with bodies splayed in grotesque, awkward positions, blood-soaked and sometimes in pieces. The prisoners spent the day in a merciful trance, loading their blankets with the bodies, and parts of bodies, that they found on the scorched and cratered ground. They dragged the blankets to the edge of the field, where a group of Italian POWs had created a funeral pyre. The stench of burning flesh seared their nostrils. By the end of the day, over 200 bodies had been collected and burned.

A light snow fell that evening, portending what would prove to be a very long, cold winter. Air-raid sirens sounded once more, but many of the women were no longer even capable of fear. At one point the next day, bombers flew low over them, and they all dropped down onto the cold, snow-dusted ground. The planes passed, but no bombs fell.

The half-rebuilt refinery had once again been completely destroyed, and the Germans recognized it was fruitless to start over. Within a few days of the bombings, the women learned that they were to be transported to a new camp. Once again they were marched to the station and crowded into cattle-car wagons for yet another journey. There was relief at leaving Gelsenkirchen after the horror of the preceding days. They rode for hours until the train stopped and the doors opened, revealing their new surroundings. Oli wrote to Laci about these events in her diary:

Oli's Diary, January 23, 1944:

There was a terrible bombing on 11th September after 6 o'clock, followed by two others. I don't want to write about it, and I'm grateful to God that he protected us. I pray to him that he be with us in the future and we do not experience another bombing. I would like to tell you about it all when I am at home. Would to God this wish of mine came true. I will tell you everything in detail, then I would like to erase it from my memory.

Thank God we left this place (unfortunately only few of us) and were brought here to Sömmerda, Thüringia on 19th September. The land is beautiful, full of green trees, colorful flowers, lots of smiling children in the street. It is a summer resort. The camp is at the end of the town, consisting of wooden barracks with washbasins and toilets. Everybody has their own bed, there are three one above the other. Unfortunately we have only one blanket, which is not enough.

At their new camp the women received new dresses with grey-blue stripes. These uniforms were heavier than the old ones, offering a bit more protection against the cold. Each woman was given a piece of cloth, on which they had to write their prisoner identification number, and a yellow star, which they were ordered to sew onto the front of their uniforms.

The act of discarding their bloodstained grey dresses and putting on their new uniforms was a tangible symbol that they had left the ordeal of Gelsenkirchen behind. In the barracks, the women were delighted to find that they could each have their own bunk. Some of the young women fought over blankets and straw, but Lilly, Oli and Bertha couldn't be bothered; they found a column of three empty beds and climbed in for the night.

They assembled the next day at dawn outside their barracks and were told they would be working in a munitions factory—the Rheinmetall-Borsig factory in the town of Sömmerda. The women were divided into a day shift and a night shift, and half of them were immediately marched out of the camp to the factory. To Oli, Lilly and Bertha's relief, they were all assigned to the same shift, and as part of the night shift, they were told they would start work that evening.

At dusk, they began walking to the factory, escorted by their guards. Because the pavement was forbidden to prisoners, the women walked in the street. Graffiti on the walls that they passed proclaimed: "Death to Jews." While it was liberating simply to walk through a town after so many months, it was also painful in the same way that their glimpse of Dresden had been. Lilly and Oli found it difficult to accept the normality of the domestic scenes they observed through the open windows of the homes they passed. White curtains swayed in the evening breeze, and families could be seen sharing their evening meals. For Oli, this reminder of ordinary life was a knife in her gut, making the loneliness for her father and her brother almost unbearable. On the other side of the lace curtains, mothers, fathers, sisters and brothers were talking, laughing and eating. Here on the street, there was cruelty, suffering and misery. The two worlds almost touched and the propinquity brought tears to her eyes.

For Lilly, the sight of the families eating magnified her own hunger. The prisoners had been fed little that day, and she envied the full dinner plates on the tables she passed. She remembered how, at home, she would leave the noodles at the bottom of her chicken soup, disliking their taste and texture. Now she wanted all of those noodles back; she would give anything for a bowl of her mother's chicken soup, filled with noodles. But seeing the food on the tables was not nearly as painful as observing the families sitting and talking together, safe from harm. Like Oli, she desperately wanted to feel that human warmth, that forgotten feeling of being exactly where she belonged.

At the edge of town, the lights of the huge munitions factory lit the sky. The women were escorted through the entrance into a long, narrow room, where they were assigned to work at various stations. Bertha and Oli were part of a group instructed to sit along both sides of a long table near the entrance to the hall. Lilly proceeded with the others toward the far end of the room, passing more tables, equipment and an extensive conveyer belt along the way. Eventually she was seated in front of a scale at her own small table.

Their tasks were explained to them. The women at Oli and Bertha's table were taught to make gunpowder parcels by placing an exact amount of powder into tiny nylon sacks. They then placed these on a conveyor belt that carried them to the next group, whose job was to press each pouch into the wide end of a bullet casing. These, in turn, went to women who operated machines that assembled the wide and the pointed ends of the casings. Lilly's job was to weigh the bullets to ensure that they were precisely the correct weight for their caliber. She then passed them to a workstation where small machines turned the bullets while workers used a small paintbrush to cover the seam of the casing with a colored sealant. Different colors indicated different calibers. Finally, yet another group of women packed the finished bullets into wooden boxes and labeled them to indicate what type they were.

The women were all closely supervised to prevent sabotage. An SS officer paced the floor, watching their hands as they worked. They were expected to move fast, repeating their motions at a tiring pace. Lilly had to keep her eyes on the scale at all times. The shift lasted for twelve hours. There were a few breaks, during which Lilly could rejoin her sister and mother, but these passed quickly.

They worked their shift six days a week, with Sunday a day off. Much of this free day was spent trying to get clean: washing uniforms with the small pieces of soap they were given and picking lice off one another. They itched and scratched incessantly. While these weekly cleanings brought a small measure of relief, nothing truly eased the discomfort caused by the lice.

Between them, the women had managed to scavenge a needle or two, and they found creative ways to make their uniforms more attractive. They tore off the bottom of dresses that were too long, then pulled out the loose strings for thread. They sewed new hems, and used the extra cloth for belts or headbands. Some of the women had remarkable seamstress skills, and Oli and Lilly followed their example to make their own dresses more "fashionable" as well. Oli used the excess cloth from her dress to make a bonnet, which both protected her head from the cold and rain, and hid her unruly newly-grown hair. As the women sewed and cleaned, the talk was of food. They shared recipes, described their favorite dishes and imagined what they would eat first once they got back home.

The weeks passed this way: six days of hard work at the factory and a seventh day of rest. On Friday evenings at sundown, just before they left for work, the women turned on the one light in their barracks, and gathered to recite the *Shabbat* prayer. As their voices joined together and reverberated against the wooden walls and rafters, they each entered their own world of memory, recalling previous lives when they had sat safe in their own homes, ready to enjoy the meal that marked the start of their Sabbath.

Sömmerda offered a bit more independence than the previous camps. The prisoners were still counted when they left for work, and again when they returned, but they no longer had to endure the extended roll calls that had marked their routine in the past. Outside of work hours they were generally left to do as they liked. Their Wehrmacht guards treated them with relative kindness. The SS guards at the factory were vicious, however, and any suspicious behavior brought a severe beating.

Some of the foremen who helped run the factory were friendly and helpful; others were harsh and cruel. The French POWs who worked the day shift occasionally left notes of encouragement or scraps of newspaper for the women on the night shift to find. In this way the women learned about the progress of the war. Now and then the POWs even left them food. Oli befriended a Ukrainian woman during a shift change, a forced laborer who worked the day shift packing gunpowder. The woman sometimes left bread for her, and occasionally even a vegetable. To reciprocate, Oli left a few cigarettes that had been given to her by an older German man who worked in the factory.

Although the prisoners were now fed regular meals, portions remained small and had little nutritional value. However, Bertha and her daughters were fortunate to have friends among the kitchen staff—a pair of sisters about five years older than Lilly whose parents had been close friends of Bertha and Herman back home. Whenever Börzi or Puti saw Bertha and her daughters reach the front of the dinner line, they would dip their ladle to the bottom of the pot in order to serve up a heartier soup.

Occasionally at mealtime the women received a little pat of margarine with their bread ration. Lilly was astounded to see some of the older women smear the margarine on their faces as a moisturizer! Even here in Hitler's camps, where they were barely subsisting, there were women who thought about their attractiveness and wanted to retain their youthful appearance. Lilly and Oli always ate their margarine, too young to be concerned by wrinkles, and unwilling to forgo the nutrition afforded by the small amount of fat. Bertha would try to persuade one of her daughters to take hers, but Lilly and Oli would insist that their mother eat it herself.

The weather grew colder. They were now well into the autumn of 1944, and the women's striped dresses—and the single blanket they had when they slept—were not enough to keep them warm. Even though the factory work was tedious and exhausting, they were grateful to be working inside, as opposed to the outdoor work they had performed at the previous camp. As winter closed in, they were finally given some warm clothes to augment their uniform: trousers, wooden shoes, men's long underwear and a coat. Once again they had to sew their number onto their clothes, this time onto the back of the coats.

Oli received a light-yellow coat and as she began to sew her numerical identity—12900—onto the back, she wondered about the woman who had worn this coat before. Was she still alive? The coat might keep her warm, but its history chilled her. Sewing the last stitches into her patch, she realized that the purpose of the prison number was not to warn the citizens of Sömmerda about who she was. Its purpose was to tell her that she was a person of no worth and no significance. The dark, wet walks to and from the factory in a stranger's yellow coat, branded with a number, were a twice-daily reminder of her place in the world.

THE WALK

While there is no way to know for sure whether Herman went to Crematorium II or III, he would have been closest to II after the selection, and I would guess that prisoners were sent on the most direct route. In any case, Crematoria II and III were nearly mirror images of one another, and what Herman would have seen and experienced would have been very similar, regardless of which one he entered.

I use aerial photos of the camp taken in 1944 to see Herman's likely route in more detail. The SS blew up the crematoria when they evacuated the camp in January 1945, so present-day photos don't show everything that was there. But there are descriptions of what the crematoria compounds looked like:

Situated behind the fences surrounding the Birkenau barracks, the crematoria constituted a separate complex of
installations of mass extermination. Crematoria II and III
had their own barbed-wire fences. Two gates led to the
Crematorium II compound and one to Crematorium III.
Trees and bushes planted all around functioned as a natural screen, or "green belt" [*Grüngürtel*] that hid them from
view by unauthorized persons—above all the prisoners
who lived in adjoining barracks.[1]

1. Franciszek Piper, "Gas Chambers and Crematoria" in *Anatomy of the Auschwitz Death Camp*, 166.

Herman turns to the left, and over his shoulder he watches
Gabi go off to the right. His son moves further away, and
is soon lost from sight, obscured by the men who fill the
growing space between them. Together with the other older
men, Herman rounds the front of the train, where he sees
a barbed wire fence and, through the wire, long wooden
buildings. He follows those in front of him as they approach
the wire and then turn right. He scratches his face and
registers the unaccustomed sensation of stubble under
his fingers. In his other hand he turns a comb.

After three days of being unable to move, his muscles
and joints ache and disobey. After three days of constant
motion, the dusty ground under his feet seems to shift.
He is tremendously thirsty. He struggles to keep pace with
those around him who are also struggling to keep pace.
He wants to stop and rest, but the dogs and machine guns
deny him this choice.

A row of trees appears on his left, lining the fence. Shortly
afterwards, he and the others turn left through a gate in
the fence. Ahead of him, Herman sees a brick building with
a large, tall chimney.

Chapter 16
TWO HUNDRED AND ONE

In the early autumn of 1944, with his engineer benefactor gone, Gabi was back to the privations of camp life. Every morning started the same way: awakening to the shouts of the capo, running outside into the cold pre-dawn air, then standing five to a row to be counted. On many mornings there were fewer standing than there had been the night before. Prisoners carried those who had died to the tent entrances, where they were tallied. When roll call was finished, the bodies were put in wheelbarrows and taken out of the camp. Gabi was glad that he didn't have that abysmal job, even though his own duties were not easy. Now he was no longer carrying rails; instead, he was digging ditches into hard, rocky ground and breaking up stones with a pickaxe. The tools were heavy and the work was dangerous.

At every roll call, the younger, smaller prisoners stood in the front rows so that they would be visible to the SS officers and capos. Gabi always stood next to Dániel, a sixteen-year-old boy he had befriended. Dániel, who had a harelip, managed to maintain a consistently optimistic outlook; Gabi wondered whether dealing with disfigurement had somehow helped his attitude. In any case, his positive view on life matched Gabi's own and Gabi felt stronger in Dániel's presence. They made a good team. Work parties were counted off by rows, so the two of them were usually assigned to the same group and could march side by side to the worksite. Open conversation was forbidden, but they could whisper to each other when no one was watching, and their companionship helped ease the monotony of the long walks to and from work.

The worksite was a cacophony of machine noise, metal hitting stone and the shouts of capos. Gabi worked near men who operated gasoline-powered equipment that pounded the earth flat for roads. Gabi was too small to handle the heavy machines, which probably weighed more than he did. Sometimes he had the job of raking the earth before it was pounded, which was a respite from the more difficult labor of swinging the pickaxe. The site was slippery, muddy, and treacherous—so much so that prisoners often died in accidents. Unstable, narrow-rail wagons, pulled by a small locomotive, were filled with dirt by prisoners standing on both sides of the rails. Debris spread unevenly could topple the wagon and kill the prisoners on the heavier side. A poorly aimed pickaxe could pierce a foot in flimsy clogs. Stones were constantly flying through the air, striking anyone in range. Occupational dangers aside, some prisoners simply died from exhaustion and starvation, the conditions of everyday camp life taking their lethal toll. When a prisoner died, he still had to be brought back to the camp at the end of the day to be counted in the evening roll call. Two large prisoners would pick their dead colleague up under the arms and drag him back down the long road to the camp. The dead were replaced with prisoners brought in from other camps.

The encroaching winter made the workdays shorter, but also made the earth harder and the hours more difficult to endure: the thin uniforms offered little resistance to the cold wind and the incessant rain. The walk back to camp was impossibly exhausting after the day's work, with the increasing cold only adding to their misery. It was this growing cold, more than the chronic hunger, that became the biggest threat to their continued existence. Gabi and his fellow captives wondered if it was even possible to survive a winter up in these mountains, under these conditions, wearing nothing but rags. When they finally entered the camp gates under a dark sky, there was yet another roll call to undergo, after which they would each again receive a cup of insipid soup and a piece of bread. After eating, they dragged themselves to their tents and collapsed into another night's sleep, during which their bodies struggled to recoup enough strength to make it through another punishing day.

Accompanying them always—at work, during roll call, and in their bunks at night—was the unrelenting itch caused by the lice that crawled on their skin, on their uniforms and in their shoes. Some prisoners were so infested that their body hair actually shimmered. The camp officials also disliked the lice, not because they cared about the prisoners' comfort, but because lice brought the risk of typhoid, and the administration did not want to lose their workforce to an epidemic. And so, one morning at roll call, the SS organized a massive cleaning of the inmates and the camp.

The prisoners were divided into two large groups and told that they were being taken to shower in the nearby city. But as they marched out of the camp, Gabi was apprehensive; there was no way of knowing where they were really going. After a short walk, however, they did indeed arrive at a bathhouse.

The prisoners were split into smaller groups for their showers. Gabi's group was eventually taken into a dressing room, still lined up in rows. They were told to leave their jackets, pants and hats in a pile in front of them with their number facing up. Men with disinfectant worked their way through the rows of uniforms, spraying each pile. Before entering the shower room, Gabi and the others were completely shaved and then sprayed with the foul-smelling disinfectant, human skin and clothing receiving the same treatment. The chemicals stung and burned any open wound. But then something wonderful happened: each of them was handed a small sliver of soap.

Gabi entered the warm, humid air of the shower room. Standing beneath a shower he felt the extraordinary sensation of hot water falling onto his head, down his back and onto his legs. It had been six months since he had felt warm water on his body. In the camp latrines, water sprayed out of a faucet; he could wash his hands and face in the morning and after work, but the water was freezing, there was no soap and time was short. Now he savored each drop as he lathered himself and the filth on his body washed away. The man next to him was working hard to scrape off the lice eggs that clung to his thigh in a large, shiny pool. Gabi would have happily stood there for hours, but of course the order to leave came much too soon, and the prisoners were sent dripping into the cold air outside the bathhouse. It was a bright day; Gabi felt warm sunlight on his face and shoulders. He and his companions were then marched around the building and back to the dressing room, where they found their clothes covered in a powdery residue.

After all of the groups had been processed, they marched back to camp. Soldiers formed a line through the center of the camp so that the newly cleaned prisoners would not mingle with those who hadn't yet gone to the bathhouse. Gabi waited with the others until their tents had been disinfected and the remaining half of the prisoners were marched out. It was a relief to feel clean, but the reprieve from the lice was short. In their crowded and unsanitary conditions, the prisoners were infested again within days.

Interruptions to the daily routine were rare, and most were not as pleasant as the trip to the bathhouse. One evening when they returned to the camp at the end of their workday, the prisoners saw two rows of SS guards facing each another in the roll call area. This, they knew, was not a good sign. One of the SS officers announced that all prisoners were to be punished because one had complained to a civilian engineer about the horrible conditions in the camp. Remembering Herr Fürst, Gabi was sorry that the unlucky prisoner hadn't found someone with the same compassion for his suffering.

The officer instructed the prisoners to run between the two rows of guards, who held an assortment of weapons in their hands—pieces of lumber, metal pipes, whips and rubber hoses. Gabi watched as the inmates ahead of him made their way through the vicious gauntlet. Soon it would be his turn, with Dániel behind him. It was critical to keep moving as fast as possible. The slower prisoners—some of whom had hardly made it back to camp that day—were struck again and again. Those who fell were beaten relentlessly. Gabi saw that there would be no avoiding the blows, but they could at least be minimized. He covered his head with his arms and ran as fast as he could. A blow landed on his back, his legs and his head, but he managed to keep going and make it past the guards. He looked back and saw Dániel emerging behind him, still standing.

Gabi was furious. He was used to the grind, to the basic inhumanity of his daily treatment, and even to incidents of capos or guards beating a prisoner for some imagined or minor offense. But this was senseless, systematic brutality that the guards treated as sport. He saw the bloodied men around him—some of whom had been badly battered—and tried to bring meaning to what he saw. There was none to be found. Gabi ran to his tent, where he inventoried his injuries. He was bruised in several places, but he wasn't bleeding, and he knew he was lucky to have fared much better than many of his fellow prisoners.

The days grew darker and more frigid, and the fear that he would freeze to death grew with each degree the temperature declined. So it was a blessing when, one morning during roll call, two trucks drove through the gates and stopped near the prisoners. The back was opened and several inmates were ordered to unload the contents—heavy winter coats and sturdy shoes. Row by row, the prisoners were ordered to line up and take one coat and one pair of shoes from the respective piles. Gabi knew, of course, that these were almost certainly the belongings of people who had been killed. Red targets were painted on the backs of some, while others had a large square of blue-and-white stripes sewn on the back.

Gabi spotted a dark herringbone coat in the pile and pulled it out. It was heavy and three-quarter length. On the back, a target had been painted with a broad brush; the paint had run down in several places leaving red streams that ended near the hem. Caring not at all about aesthetics, he slipped it on and immediately felt the cold wind abate. Then he discarded his worn-out clogs and pulled on a pair of boots. They fit well enough, with the tops coming to just above his ankles.

Their winter coats made the walk to and from the worksite much more bearable, and the shoes provided needed protection as well. Gabi and the other prisoners wore their coats constantly: at nighttime they slept in them, with their feet toward the pot-bellied stove in the center of the tent. As the days continued to get colder, the relentless rain turned to snow. The prisoners had no gloves, socks or underwear, so the icy weather penetrated to the bone. Snow also made the already treacherous worksite even more hazardous, with prisoners slipping and falling as they did their jobs.

Rumors began circulating that there would soon be a selection to take some of the prisoners to work in a factory. The factory, they heard, would be heated. A couple of days later, as the inmates lined up in the dark for morning roll call, the guards announced that the youngest among them would be transferred to another camp for factory work. Gabi figured that they wanted to keep the older, larger prisoners for the more physically demanding building jobs, but that they could spare the smaller ones.

First those born in 1930 were told to form a separate group, then those born in 1929. Dániel and Gabi lined up in the 1928 group, with Dániel several boys ahead of Gabi. Groups born in 1927 and 1926 were also formed. A guard started counting off the 1930 line, with another guard walking behind him and writing down each prisoner's identification number. They then continued with the 1929s. Gabi had no idea how many they were taking, and he waited nervously for the guard to get to him. The counting progressed to the line of 1928s, and continued past Dániel to the boy standing in front of Gabi, who was number 200. Gabi held his breath, waiting to hear the number 201 spoken by the guard. Instead, the commanding officer shouted, "Stop!" Gabi and Dániel exchanged desperate glances as the order was given that all those who had been counted off should proceed to the camp gates.

There were other friends and relatives separated and Gabi saw that someone in the younger group wanted to stay. As Dániel moved away with his group, Gabi—whose usual strategy in the camps was always to remain unnoticed—left his line and approached an SS sergeant.

Trembling, Gabi asked, "Can I go with that group, because my friend is there?"

The sergeant walked over to the commanding officer, and the two men briefly conversed. Gabi saw the sergeant point toward him and heard him say, "That prisoner wants to go," but could not hear the officer's reply. The sergeant returned and told Gabi that they had the number they needed and no one else could go. With a last bit of courage that Gabi could hardly believe he possessed, he asked the sergeant if it would be possible to switch with someone who wanted to stay. "Absolutely not! No switching allowed!" the sergeant told him. Gabi knew the battle was lost. He returned to his group and watched Dániel go with the other boys to the entrance of the camp. The gates opened and they were marched out in their rows of five, leaving Gabi bitterly disappointed not to be included and saddened by the loss of his friend.

There was nothing to do but carry on, but the walks to and from work were lonely and left Gabi lost in his own thoughts during the journey. The end of the year was approaching—though Gabi had no idea of the exact date—and he often wondered how much longer the war would go on, and what 1945 would bring.

One evening after another exhausting day, they were counted—as usual—as they walked through the gates. Then they lined up for evening roll call. They watched the guard who had counted them at the gates approach an officer, but instead of the usual quick report of the tally, the two conversed at length.

The roll call counting began, and then was repeated again and again. Someone was missing. A search party of guards went out to find the missing prisoner, while everyone remained in their rows in the icy night. Finally, several guards marched their bloodied prisoner back into camp. They had clearly already exacted punishment. But there was more to come.

While everyone stood watching, the guards painted a bull's-eye on the back of his striped shirt. An officer announced that attempted escapes would be severely punished and Gabi was sure he was about to witness a shooting. Instead of guns, however, a group of guards picked up lengths of wood and began beating their captive. Gabi expected them to beat him to death, but they stopped while the prisoner was still alive, though just barely.

Late in the evening, the prisoners were finally dismissed, permitted to eat their small rations and to catch the few hours of sleep that remained. By the next day, word had gotten around that the prisoner hadn't actually tried to escape; he had merely made the mistake of falling asleep. He was the driver of one of the narrow-gauge locomotives that pulled the wagons full of dirt and rocks from the building sites. He had lost his battle against sleep, failed to wake when the workday was finished, and none of the guards had noticed him.

Near the end of the year, there was a dramatic overnight change at the camp. Most of the regular SS guards disappeared, replaced by one-time Wehrmacht guards who had recently been inducted into the SS: the dark-green cloth of their uniform jackets still bore the outline of the eagle insignia on the chest above the right pocket, and the two horizontal bars on each lapel had been replaced with the insignia of the SS. The arduous work, starvation and exposure to the cold continued, but the atmosphere in the camp was different. The Wehrmacht guards weren't exactly friendly, but the older men lacked the inherent brutality of the SS, and there was a noticeable reduction in beatings and random violence. The inmates guessed—correctly as it turns out—that the SS guards had been redeployed to the front lines where they were needed to fight. They saw this as an auspicious sign. Perhaps, Gabi hoped, the war really would be over soon.

RECOLLECTION
(Written 2011)

George died three weeks ago. He was ninety-one and advanced Parkinson's disease had rendered him immobile. He left us during an afternoon nap, with Lilly sleeping beside him. His children, Tom and Debby, were with them.

I got the call—which I had been expecting for weeks—while riding the tram to work in Melbourne. As we crossed the Yarra River downtown, I was reading an e-mail from the *Journal of Consumer Research*, where my co-author, Tina Lowrey, and I were hoping to publish a paper about gift-giving and other forms of help among prisoners in the Nazi concentration camps. Our first version of the paper had only just kept us in the game, with the editor stating, "I'm allowing you to come back with a new version of the paper, but I'm not encouraging it." Harsh as that sounds, it was actually good news, given the stature of the journal and its extremely high rejection rate. We worked on revising the paper for eighteen months and had recently resubmitted it. As I read through the new decision by the editor, I saw that we were now on more solid ground—more revision was necessary, but there was clear hope for publication. While reading the reviews and thinking about how much work still lay ahead of us, I received a call. "Blocked." This often signals an overseas call from my parents, so as I accepted the call I was bracing myself, and when I heard my dad's voice, I knew.

As it happened, my father and I were one day away from flying to California for our twice-annual visit with Lilly and George, so the timing, at least, was somewhat fortunate. I was relieved that my father would not have to make a separate trip for the funeral, and that I would be there in time for it, given the Jewish tradition of quick burial.

I arrived on the same morning as my parents. Zack—Tom and Tom's wife Angela's eighteen-year-old son—was waiting for me at the BART station in East Oakland. As I descended the escalator from the platform, he saw me and waved, flashing the signature smile that helped get him voted "student most likely to lose all his money in his divorce settlements" by his classmates. It is now a tradition that my visits begin with a meal at Cactus, a Mexican restaurant across the street from the station. As we ate, Zack told me about his summer plans. His high school graduation was the day after George's service; it would be a welcome look to the future after we had gotten through the funeral.

The next morning, I was with Lilly in her bedroom. So far, she had held up better than we had expected—crying, yes, but also demonstrating the same toughness that had helped her to survive the Holocaust. As often happened when I visited, Lilly was rummaging through a drawer, telling me she had something for me. I was helping her dig when I saw a document. The date 1944 jumped out at me:

> *April 1, 1944. The most awful day in our city. We had to collect 1 million pengő. Poor, miserable Jews, to keep them from killing us.*

"Lilly, what's this?"

"That's the diary that Sari wrote in the camps. I made her the diary and traded it for a piece of bread. Her grandson Ben sent this translation to me."

I kept reading:

> *... April the 5th of last year. We started wearing the yellow star. The first day of Pesach was on the 9th. I don't think I can properly convey the feeling of sadness, of fearful days. The German motorcade noises, the locked gates at night, every day new orders, whispers ...*

The disorderly packing on Monday, Tuesday, Wednesday, and Thursday of the restlessness, complexity and horror. 40-year-old households had to be squeezed into a few backpacks. No wonder it was hard . . .

April 20, 1944. Our first day in the ghetto. We are in the courtyard of the synagogue. 100 people are housed in one hall.

May 17th. 94 of us were in one wagon; no windows. Some air filtered through a crack. Often, especially during the day we thought we will choke to death.

I put the pages in order and found the opening paragraphs. Sari started writing her diary just before liberation. She begins her story in the spring of 1944, and the diary provides dates for certain key events in Beregszász. As I have already explained, my father and my aunts were unable to recall the specific timing of every event when we worked through the calendar pages for the spring of 1944. I had sought out these dates without success, in the end having to accept a certain vagueness with regard to some of the events recounted in Chapter 9.

It is historical fact that the Germans occupied Hungary on March 19, 1944, but I could find no evidence of exactly when they rolled into Beregszász, or whether the yellow stars had to be worn before, or only after, they arrived. The date of the yellow star *decree* for Hungarian Jews appears to have been March 31, 1944, but I found it impossible to discover exactly when the Jews of Beregszász were ordered to comply with it. Sari's diary provides a date: April 5, 1944. She might have misremembered this, of course, but she was recollecting major events in her life only a year afterward, which leads me to give her evidence weight. Her recollection of the Germans coming in just around Passover is also consistent with the reports of Hugo Gryn and Aranka Siegal, both memoirists from Beregszász. As mentioned above, Rabbi Gryn recalled the Germans being on the same train he took home from school in Debrecen for the holiday. Ms. Siegal places the arrival of the Germans a couple of days before Passover.

The only detail in Sari's diary that does not jibe with other accounts is that she says hostages were taken on April 1, which would have been several days *before* the Germans arrived. Gryn, Lilly and Oli all recall the hostages being taken after the SS arrived, and the accounts of survivors from other towns in the area also describe hostage-taking as one of the first actions of the arriving Germans. Other than this discrepancy, Sari's dates are consistent with the order of events, as well as the intervals between them, that I suggest in Chapter 9.

During the week I spent with Lilly, I thought about the fact that I had so far written only one of the two chapters that would focus on George. Chapter 7, about him going off to the labor camp, had been written long ago, but the chapter about the second half of his war experiences was still only a set of notes and interview transcripts. I knew I had enough information to tell the story, but I also had to accept that some details would now be lacking. There are many questions that I should have asked him.

I'm not sure when it became clear to me that George would no longer be able to tell me his stories. On one of my trips back, he could, a little at a time, during his strongest moments; the next trip, he couldn't. Even on those final visits, when he could still talk a little, I worried that I was burdening him by bringing up his past. But he always seemed to appreciate my interest and to want to share his wartime stories to the extent he was able. His later war experiences, the parts I was still asking about, included some amazing risk taking and deception, of which George was very proud. Yet he also always made a point of reminding me that luck had played a critical role in every step of his survival.

We buried George under a deep blue sky at a beautiful

cemetery. After the Rabbi said the prayers, we each shoveled dirt on George's casket, as dictated by tradition. As I took my turn, I thought of his bravery throughout the Holocaust, and his ingenuity and creativity in tight circumstances. I thought of how he always spoke about the events of his past with humor, with wonder at the luck that befell him along the way, and with a characteristic lack of bitterness.

But with my final shovelful of dirt, I also remembered the last time he mentioned his past to me. He was imprisoned by his disease and rarely spoke. I had been asking Lilly some questions about painful events that had happened to her and George. When she left the room, I heard George speak two words that I had never heard him say before.

"I'm angry."

"About what they did to you during the war?"

He gave the slightest of nods, and said, "Yes."

"I don't blame you," I replied.

Chapter 17
PAPERS AND FABRICATIONS

George crouched in a stairway as bullets flew overhead. German soldiers dropped dead in the street, caught by Soviet gunfire. He had survived over two years in labor camps—years when he could have been sent at any time to die on the Russian front—only to have the front come to him.

George had stayed in the camp on the outskirts of Budapest for almost a year and a half—from late 1942 until the middle of 1944. The days were long and the work, manufacturing pontoons, was hard, but George still knew that he had it pretty good compared to those in other labor battalions. He had heard awful stories from young men who had transferred into his camp. And as the war progressed, more and more men were sent from the labor camps to the front, from which no one ever seemed to return. Food was scarce and he was often hungry, but he wasn't starving. He was friendly with the lieutenant who ran the camp—a short man they nicknamed Pufi—so he was able to get occasional passes to visit the Földi family in Budapest.

The German invasion in March 1944 did not directly affect George, but it did make him very concerned for his family and Lilly's family in Beregszász. When he received a letter from his mother telling him that Jews in the area were being rounded up, concern turned to worry and fear. He managed to get a phone call through to his mother at the family hotel that she ran, telling her that he would try to get a pass to come home. "Stay where you are," she insisted. "Do not come home under any circumstances." George followed his mother's instructions, but he became increasingly anxious about what was happening in Beregszász.

Then he heard nothing. There were no letters from Lilly or from his mother. This silence kept him up at night and was always with him while he worked. After two months without news from home, he finally heard from Lilly. During one of his visits to the Földis, the couple presented him with the postcard she had sent him at their address. He read Lilly's words over and over. She said that they were all well and that they were working during the day while Bertha stayed home to cook for them. George was relieved to hear some news, but he did not trust the optimistic tone of the card. He knew from his own experience that people who were forced to work for the Third Reich were rarely well taken care of, and he had a hard time believing that Jews would have been transported from Beregszász so that they could enjoy a nice, quiet life somewhere else.

Aerial bombings of Budapest and the surrounding areas started in April and were increasingly frequent by mid-summer. American and British bombers could be seen regularly in the sky from George's camp just north of the city. The camp was next to an artillery compound, so he knew they were a likely target. Every day and every night brought the threat of Allied bombs.

At six o'clock one summer morning, when the 300 prisoners were preparing to start work, the lieutenant gathered them together and asked if any of them knew how to work with cement. George had never used cement in his life—he hardly even knew what it was—but his hand shot up. This might be a chance to move somewhere safer, away from the bombings. A few hours later he was riding in a train with about a dozen other volunteers, all of whom were as ignorant about building materials as he was. They were thankful to be traveling north, but the ride was short: they had only traveled about ten kilometers when the train stopped in a town called Budakalász.

The men were put to work right away. They found themselves in an empty building where they were supposed to put in a cement floor. Fortunately, they were not alone. Seasoned Hungarian workers intuited the meaning of the new arrivals' perplexed and worried faces, and quickly taught them how to mix and lay the cement. With their help, the young prisoners were able to fake their way through their first day.

They slept in a facility next to a building where German soldiers were housed. The Russian lines were getting closer and the German troops had been pulling back. At night, George and his fellow prisoners could see Budapest being bombed in the distance: bright flashes of light signaled the destruction of the city. They knew that the bombs could easily have been falling on them, and they were grateful for their distant vantage point. At the same time, of course, they feared for those they had left behind in the camp.

Their skills as cement workers grew as the weeks and months went by. Then, in October 1944, there was startling news: Miklós Horthy, the Hungarian head of state, had resigned and the government was in chaos. It seemed to George and his companions that this could be an opportunity. They had stayed put in the past because they could be shot for being found anywhere else without a pass. But an escape would not be difficult, and in the current disarray they guessed they could make their way to Budapest unchallenged.

They slipped out of the camp later that day, traveling south along the tracks until they eventually reached the city. Their plan was to cross the Danube from the Buda to the Pest side, then make their way east. But when they reached the river they saw that the nearest bridge was guarded by German guns. At the next bridge they saw the same thing, and again at the next; every bridge was defended, making it impossible to cross. They learned that the Arrow Cross (Hungarian Nazi Party) leader, Ferenc Szálasi, had taken control of the government. It was now late at night, the Nazi party was in charge, they were clearly not free, and they could be shot at any time as escapees. Their hopes of freedom were crushed, but their more immediate problem was how to get to safety.

They headed north, retracing their steps, but they doubted they could make it all the way back to camp without getting caught. Then they realized that they were in the vicinity of their previous camp—the pontoon factory—and that perhaps they could find shelter there. After some discussion, they sent a message to their old lieutenant, Pufi, providing their location and asking him to send help. The men waited anxiously, not knowing if Pufi would rescue them or if German soldiers would find them first. Eventually, two covered trucks appeared on the road. To their immense relief, the driver of the first truck told them that Pufi had sent the vehicles.

They stayed under Pufi's protection for a few days, but then all the prisoners were on the move. Budapest was now surrounded by Soviet troops, and the factory was dangerously close to the front lines. The prisoners were moved to a high school in the city. No information was provided, but they all suspected that they were about to be sent to fight against the Russians. George knew that this would be almost certain death.

That night, as soon as it was dark, he cautiously approached the fence that surrounded the school. Then, when no one was looking, he climbed the fence, jumped down and fled. As he ran, he was amazed that he had managed to escape without being seen. But he knew he was still in great danger, and he had not thought much beyond scaling the fence. He slowed his pace and began to walk. At a street corner, he looked up into the window of a streetcar and was amazed to see the face of a friend from Beregszász, Leo. Leo saw him, and motioned with his eyes down the street. George ran to the next stop, where Leo emerged from the car. They said little at first, with Leo leading the way to somewhere they could talk: a nearly empty movie theatre where they sat far from the others. They conversed for a long time, exchanging stories of their wartime activities. Leo was Jewish, but clearly well connected in the city. He told George that he was living in a "safe house" and that George was welcome to join him there.[1]

1. "Safe houses" had been set up in Budapest by Raoul Wallenberg and other diplomats to protect Jews who still remained in the city. Wallenberg declared these

At the safe house George was able to get fake papers, including a document showing that he worked for the Red Cross. Yet he wasn't comfortable staying there; the house did not in fact feel safe to him, and he worried that the SS would raid it. George realized that he would need a stamp on some of his documents, so he carved a likeness of the required seal into the heel of his shoe and stamped his papers. Another piece of identification presented him as a sixteen-year-old gentile. With his blond hair and blue eyes, he did not look Jewish, and he also looked very young. This was fortunate: anyone in their mid-twenties would arouse suspicion on the streets because almost all young men were serving in the Hungarian military.

After four days at the house, George thanked Leo for all of his help, and struck out on his own to live as a gentile, false documents in hand. He worked for several weeks at a temporary job in a cheese factory in the suburbs, making smoked cheese—one more addition to his growing list of strange occupations. He traveled as little as possible. Streetcars were sometimes stopped by German soldiers who, if they suspected a man of being Jewish, would order him to drop his pants. Circumcision had become a death sentence. Jews were regularly rounded up, taken to the Danube and killed, their bodies left to float in the river. One night, George was on a stationary streetcar when he saw German soldiers through the windows. He held his breath as they approached, and felt extremely lucky when his car began to move and the soldiers surrounded the one behind him.

When his job at the cheese factory ended, George found work in an iron factory and lodging in a room in a townhouse nearby. The shelling continued; it was clearly a matter of days,

---

properties to be "extraterritorial buildings" protected by Swedish diplomatic immunity, and those who stayed there were given various documents, including protective passports and passes, as well as Red Cross documents. Unfortunately, safe houses were sometimes still raided by the Arrow Cross Party.
<http://www.wallenberg.umich.edu/heroism.html; http://www.ushmm.org/wlc/en/article.php?ModuleId=10005211>, both accessed February 13, 2013).

or weeks at most, before the Soviets broke through the German ring around the city. In the meantime, the last weeks of 1944 were bitterly cold, and there was little food to eat. One day, George saw people hacking pieces of meat from a dead horse that lay frozen in the street. Another day, at work, one of George's co-workers managed to obtain a pig, which was butchered into sections, with a lottery conducted for each piece. George was thrilled to win the neck, which was full of fat, ignoring the traditional edicts for living a kosher life. The meat lasted for days.

Eventually, the Soviets broke through the German lines—and George found himself huddled under a stairway in the middle of a firefight. The Soviets advanced rapidly down the road while German soldiers retreated or were killed. The battle moved past quickly, leaving George in liberated territory, under Soviet rule.

The Soviet army immediately established a headquarters in a building close to where George had been hiding, and called for all Hungarian males aged fifteen to sixty to report. When the men had assembled, a Russian major ordered them all to line up and get ready to march. They were being moved to a holding facility. George could hardly believe that, within hours of being liberated, he was about to be put in another camp. Certain that the major was Jewish, George left the line and approached him. When the major confirmed that he was indeed a Jew, George explained that he too was Jewish, and requested that the major please not send him with the others.

The major interrupted: "You son of a bitch, these are Stalin's orders and you have to go!" Then his voice softened somewhat and he added that George shouldn't worry, that nothing would happen to him. There was still street fighting nearby, he told George, and he had been ordered to move the men away from the battle lines.

They marched well into the night, traveling approximately ten kilometers. George knew that many of the men with him were Hungarian Nazis; he felt they deserved whatever was coming to them. He also knew that he had to convince his captors that he had been a victim and not a persecutor. When they arrived at their destination, they were taken down to a cellar where a Ukrainian lieutenant was processing the prisoners. He asked George for his identification papers, and as George handed him the documents, he told the lieutenant that he was Jewish. Without warning the lieutenant slapped George across the face with remarkable force. In the eyes of this lieutenant, it was worse to be a Jew than a Hungarian Nazi. George was ordered to follow the others, and as he staggered behind them, he touched his burning cheek, felt the wetness of blood and dumbly contemplated his red fingers. He had survived the Germans, only to fall into the hands of a new group of anti-Semites.

After processing, they were all moved to a holding area, where George was crammed into a small space with about 2,000 other Hungarian men. They learned that they would soon be sent to Soviet camps. George studied his surroundings carefully, assessing the opportunities for escape, but there were Russian sentries everywhere, watching the prisoners carefully.

Soon after daybreak, another Russian major stood before them and called everyone to attention. In perfect German he asked, "Who among you has a Red Cross certificate?" George raised his hand and shouted that he had one. About six other young men did the same. The major scanned the crowd and announced, "You people can go." The lucky few worked their way to the entrance, where they were allowed to pass. Outside they conferred with one another. They were all Jewish, and had largely come by their Red Cross papers the same way George had. One knew of a home where several Jewish families had been hiding before the Soviets arrived. There was a four o'clock curfew in effect, after which anyone on the streets would be shot, so they had to get to the house quickly. They made their way back to Budapest, through the freezing streets, and reached the house ahead of the curfew.

The home was crowded, filled largely with Jewish women and girls. Shortly after the men arrived, a group of Soviet soldiers appeared at the door and pushed their way into the house. They took stock of the inhabitants, but did nothing else, saying that they would check back that night. Several hours later the soldiers returned. When they entered the house, they pointed their rifles at George and the other men, ordering them to stand against the wall. One of the soldiers remained with the men, while the rest took the screaming women into other rooms. They raped the women repeatedly and left in the morning.

It was clear that they all had to get out of the house and find other shelter; the soldiers would undoubtedly return. George decided to make his way to the old Czech embassy. He was not the only person to have this idea. When he arrived, he saw a crowd of people, including several young men from Beregszász. After conferring, George and the other Beregszász residents decided they would try to make their way home. This was a journey of over three hundred kilometers, and they had no idea how they would get there. They had a little money among them, so they started at the train station, where they were able to catch a train going east. But the train only took them so far. They traveled for days, making some of the journey on foot, trudging through snow and fighting off the blustery cold. Finally, as they approached Beregszász, they met a man with a sleigh. They arrived home at last, gliding behind two horses that breathed a damp mist into the freezing air.

THE WALK

In the crematorium yard, the SS men told the prisoners that they would undergo a disinfection that consisted of delousing and bathing.[1]

---

1. Franciszek Piper, op. cit., 169.

Herman turns to the left, and over his shoulder he watches Gabi go off to the right. His son moves further away, and is soon lost from sight, obscured by the men who fill the growing space between them. Together with the other older men, Herman rounds the front of the train, where he sees a barbed wire fence and, through the wire, long wooden buildings. He follows those in front of him as they approach the wire and then turn right. He scratches his face and registers the unaccustomed sensation of stubble under his fingers. In his other hand he turns a comb.

After three days of being unable to move, his muscles and joints ache and disobey. After three days of constant motion, the dusty ground under his feet seems to shift. He is tremendously thirsty. He struggles to keep pace with those around him who are also struggling to keep pace. He wants to stop and rest, but the dogs and machine guns deny him this choice.

A row of trees appears on his left, lining the fence. Shortly afterwards, he and the others turn left through a gate in the fence. Ahead of him, Herman sees a brick building with a large, tall chimney. As they enter the yard in front of the building, an SS guard shouts to them that they will soon have a shower and be disinfected. Herman anticipates the water that will finally quench his thirst.

Chapter 18
BEARING WITNESS

In December 1944, the freezing rains that had been falling on Sömmerda turned to snow. In addition to the relentless hunger that continued to plague them, Bertha, Lilly and Oli now endured a constant struggle against the wet and cold. The single blanket each had received upon arrival could not combat the winter temperatures, and their feet were painful and numb. The shoes that Herman had made for them were long gone; they wore wooden clogs that provided no warmth. The winter clothes they had been given helped, but walking was still a challenge without gloves, socks or decent underwear, and the hard soles of the clogs slipped and scraped along the street.

It was not just the bitter cold that made the walk to and from the factory depressing. As the women marched in the streets, townspeople would often stop and stare. Oli hated the thought of what passersby must see when they looked at her. Children would point and stick out their tongues. When soldiers passed, some would curse at them and say vicious things, sometimes so nasty that the women—though hardened by repeated degradation—were surprised at their harshness. From time to time, Hitler youth, with neatly pressed uniforms and ugly smiles, heckled them. The words were hurtful, but the women had come to expect it. So it was a shock when one day an elderly German man intervened. "Don't laugh at them!" he shouted. "There is nothing for them to be ashamed of. It is not their shame, it is our shame!"

The boys stopped and stared at the old man, then exchanged glances, uncertain of what to do next. The women continued walking, and the perplexed boys straggled off in the opposite direction. A single act of courage would not end the malevolence, but Oli was uplifted by this old man who had been bold enough to defend them. One kind heart could be priceless, in contrast to the malice all around her.

One evening at work, Lilly was thinking, as she often did, that she would love to be able to write about what she was experiencing. She had always liked to write poems when she was at home, and there was so much that she wanted to write about now. She had no paper or pencil, but as she watched the women at the neighboring table label a carton of bullets, she had an idea: perhaps the small labels that they glued to the boxes could be used as writing paper. In the morning, as the workers prepared to leave the factory at the end of their shift, Lilly eyed the books of labels on the table. She took her time preparing her station for the next shift, and made sure she was the last to leave. Then she walked to the boxing area, quietly tore some of the labels from a booklet, and slipped them into her pocket. The next night, using a pencil borrowed from the boxing station, she left a note for the French POWs, requesting a pencil of her own. A few evenings later she arrived at her table and found they had obliged.

Back in her barracks after the night's shift, Lilly was able to write for the first time since she composed the fake postcards in Auschwitz. She wrote in tiny letters to use as little paper as possible. There was a lot that she wanted to say, and she thought that writing every day might help her cope with her confined life. This gave her another idea: if she could collect enough labels—a little bit at a time so no one would notice they were missing—she could eventually gather enough pages to make a diary.

Every night at the factory Lilly stole a few labels during breaks, and again at the end of her shift. With the ingenuity that had become a hallmark of the women at Sömmerda, Lilly created her diary. She retrieved an empty label booklet from the trash and used it to make a front and back cover. Then she borrowed a paintbrush and some blue, yellow and red paint from the table where the bullets were sealed. She hoped that no one would miss the materials, and trusted that the POWs wouldn't make a fuss even if they did notice.

Later that day, she decorated the cover in her barracks. First, she painted a large, red rectangle on both the front and the back. When the paint had dried, she dipped the brush into the blue pot and wrote *"Apukám neked irom"* ("I wrote this for you, Dad") on the front. On the back she wrote *"Anyu"* ("Mother") in the top left corner, *"Apu"* ("Father") in the top right, "Oli" in the bottom left, and "Lilly" in the bottom right. In the center she painted "Gabi." Around the edges she drew tiny blue and yellow flowers. Then she carefully added curved lines connecting the flowers, linking them in a chain that provided the cover's border.

With a borrowed needle and a thread pulled from her dress, she sewed the cover and labels together. When the little booklet was completed, she wrote her first entry:

Lilly's Diary, December 10, 1944:

Daddy dear, this can't be true that I am here sitting on the top "ledge"—under me Mother is trying to rest—and Oli tries to toast a piece of bread on a miserably dirty iron stove. This has to be a horrible nightmare and I am just telling you this—like a story I used to tell you, when I read a book and told you what it was about. I wasn't—not for a minute—afraid in that cattle car which took us to Birkenau, that they would kill us. I imagined that they are taking us somewhere where Mother will be cooking for us—where all of us will be working. Unfortunately it didn't turn out this way.

It was terrible when we found out that Gabi wasn't in the same wagon. When we arrived and our little dear brother was coming out of the next wagon—we hardly had time to kiss each other. We had to stand separated from the men and in that moment I realized that they will separate us from them. I remember telling you, Daddy, just "we shouldn't say good-bye."

*Where did I get the strength—how come I didn't even have
any sense at least to kiss you, or Gabi either?*

Lilly went on to tell her father all that had happened to
them since they were separated. Writing to him made her feel
as though he was there with her, sharing in her experiences,
seeing what she was seeing.

She worried incessantly about her father and Gabi. The fact
that Herman had been a prisoner during World War I gave
her hope that he would be able to persevere now. She pictured
Gabi with him, and refused to give up the idea that her father
and brother had been reunited on their first day at Auschwitz.
Gabi had been so thin that she couldn't imagine how he could
lose weight and still survive, but he did have youth on his side.
Herman, though sturdy and vigorous, was in late middle age.
Writing to her father reinforced her belief that he and Gabi
were still alive, out there somewhere, suffering as she and Oli
and Bertha were. And when the end of the war finally came—
which would be soon, if the news passed along by the French
POWs could be believed—they would all be reunited.

The end of the year was coming. Nineteen forty-four, a
year that seemed to have lasted a lifetime, would soon be over.
The women began to speak of Christmas and how they might
celebrate. While Christmas was not a religious holiday for
them, it had always been a central part of winter in Beregszász,
where Jews frequently celebrated with their Christian neighbors. Knowing how much Oli would like having a diary of her
own, Lilly continued to steal labels from the factory, a few at a
time, in order to be able to give her sister a diary for Christmas.

Lilly had other plans as well. She enlisted the help of her
friend Anni Pauk, a musician from Budapest with a beautiful
singing voice. Lilly and Anni surreptitiously dug up two small
shrubs near the barracks and brought them inside. Everyone
pooled their resources to provide rudimentary decorations for
the makeshift Christmas trees.

A four-day closure of the factory for Christmas was announced. The women cleaned and mended their uniforms and prepared for the holiday. On Christmas Eve, Lilly gave Oli the diary she had made for her. It had a blue cover with red and white decorations. Oli's formal name, Olga, was printed in the center in white. Oli gently flipped through the small empty pages, thinking about all the things she could finally tell Laci. She would give him the diary when she returned home, so he could read about all that had happened to her. After the others had gone to sleep, Oli wrote:

Oli's Diary, December 24, 1944:

You were waiting for me in the "Sága" confectionery with your friend, Pista. You were sitting with your back to me when I entered, then you looked back smiling and we shook hands happily for the first time after long weeks. Later we met again and the three of us spent Christmas Eve together. That was when you gave me the nicest book I'd ever read, "Gone with the Wind."

It was nice like all Christmases and it is gone, gone like all the other wonderful days spent with you.

I'm spending the Christmas of 1944 alone in this bleak and bare hall. People have gone to sleep, there is silence everywhere. I'm sitting alone and thinking about where you are now and what you are doing when everybody is together with their loved ones. What are you feeling now when everybody is joyfully celebrating Christmas Eve? I wish this evening brought happiness to everyone, and our small family and the two of us could meet. If only I could be with you now, feel the gentle touch of your soft hand and tell you everything I went through. I would tell you that when I had the biggest problems and I was in danger I always heard your words of encouragement, trusted God and hoped that everything would turn out fine.

WE GOT THE WATER

This is what I am doing now on this December night, asking God to look down on us, wishing that the sun will rise again and brighten up our modest, quiet life.

On Christmas morning, the women stood around the trees singing holiday songs, after which Anni gave a short concert. Lilly stood with her mother, her sister, and her good friend Éva, as Anni's extraordinary voice filled the barracks, reverberating up through the rafters, across the tiered bunks and against the wooden walls. For a few brief minutes, their place of suffering became a magnificent concert hall. Guards stood in the doorway and listened. Anni concluded her performance with "Ave Maria," and tears ran down the women's faces as they thought of their families and loved ones. Each of them was wondering where she would be in a year's time; each was hoping to be far from where she stood now.

That evening, Oli and Bertha went to visit Estika, another girl from Beregszász, in the "infirmary."[1] Estika was very ill with a heart ailment. Even back in Beregszász, the young girl had always been sickly. Her friends were amazed that she had managed to stay alive this long. Yet it was becoming increasingly apparent that she would never leave the infirmary. When they arrived at her bunk that day, Estika's older sister, Judi, was already beside her. Estika's body was swollen, her legs twice their normal size. After a while, Bertha went back to the barracks to sleep, but Oli and Judi stayed with Estika through the night, holding her hands and giving her quiet words of encouragement. The next night, they were at her side once again when she died. She was sixteen.

Air raids came to Sömmerda that same day. Memories of the bombing of Gelsenkirchen were still fresh in all their

---

1. Concentration camps generally did have infirmaries, though equipment and supplies were minimal or entirely absent. Rather than provide adequate medical care, the hospital system allowed the SS to weed out weak prisoners. While some were able to recover in the infirmary and return to the normal camp routine, most died there.

minds, and Lilly desperately wished her father could be there to calm her fears:

Lilly's Diary, December 27, 1944:

There is an air raid. I am so afraid every time I hear it. How good it would be to hold your strong hand and be together with Gabi—maybe I wouldn't be so terrified as I always am. But I can't help being afraid—I would like to live yet and see you Mother–Dad–Oli–Gabi—all of us—together, smiling and happy.

God be with us and help us! Dad, Gabi my darling where are you? It is possible that you are also near the sirens—and you are afraid just like us—and somehow I feel you couldn't care about anything anymore—only to be together. Just once more, please God just one more time we should be together all of us. It is not possible Daddy that we couldn't be together just like we used to be—happily. The sirens stopped. The planes left. We really deserve to be together.

On the last day of the year, the women were handed post-cards and told to write to their loved ones. As she had done in Auschwitz, Oli wrote to Laci, while Lilly and Bertha wrote to Herman and Gabi in the hope that the cards might reach them wherever they were.

At midnight on New Year's Eve, Lilly and Oli did the best they could to celebrate their mother's January 1 birthday. For days, they had bartered, foraged and used their creative skills to come up with gifts that would ostensibly be given by each family member. In Gabi's name, they presented Bertha with an apple, and from Herman she received a pair of slippers. Oli gave her mother a pin she had fashioned, along with some "petit fours" she had concocted from their rations. Lilly gave Bertha a book she had made entitled *Lager Literature* ("Prison Literature"), a collection of her writings. They tried to be cheerful, but of course it was impossible to overlook the fact that Herman and Gabi were present in name only.

Lilly was finding it increasingly difficult to cope. She had put a great deal of energy into the planning of the holidays and her mother's birthday, but now that these were over, she felt the weight of her circumstances. The hard, long nights at work, the air raids and the relentless cold seemed permanent and unending. Icicles hung from the ceilings inside their barracks, and the floor was wet and muddy.

Lilly's Diary, January 8, 1945:

Daddy dear,

I am so sad and so hopeless. Outside it is snowing and the news is very bad. Somehow I never have seen this situation so very hopeless as it is now. Here in the lagers is the truth. In other words, we are really suffering. It would be so, so much easier if I could write to you more often—even if shorter letters—it somehow makes me feel better. Oh, if I only could get from you and Gabi just one short postcard—but I really don't believe that is going to happen.

Oli was able to find some consolation through her diary.

Oli's Diary, January 11, 1945:

It's 1.30 am, all the machines of the factory have stopped, it's quiet and we're having a thirty-minute break. The workers are relaxing, leaning their heads on the table, soon falling asleep. Some people are eating the remains of their food, and are talking. It's nice and quiet, which is quite rare. It's so good to be alone now, it's so very good to be with you. There are grey machines around me in this unfriendly hall, everything is cold and icy, but after a few seconds everything becomes distant and I feel warmth spreading all over me. I'm with you, near you now and when I wake up

*from my daydreams and return to the horrible reality of
the present, the memories are very painful.*

The month of January was filled with air raids. The planes
overhead and the explosions in the distance caused the women
to be constantly on edge.

Oli's Diary, January 22, 1945:

*I've read what I've written so far and somehow I find
it empty, it's not at all like my writings at home but you
know, Laci, there is not one single tranquil moment
in my life at the moment. We are fighting for our life
and I don't know if there will be someone to eat the
sandwich I eagerly prepare for snack. I can't plan five
minutes in advance, as human life here can be taken
in a moment. I'd like to live a quiet life, I wish so much
to describe everything to you the way I'd like to.*

Oli did a lot of her writing on the sly, sometimes when
she was supposed to be working. Her supervisor often left the
area, and the women used the opportunity to slow down or
even stop altogether to rest. At these times, Oli could slip out
her diary and write a few lines. While Oli had mixed feelings
about her supervisor, she was struck by how much his hands
resembled Laci's. Occasionally, he would lean on the table as he
spoke to Oli, resting his hands on the edge. His neat, trim nails
made her think of her meetings with Laci in the confectionary
after they first met. Oli remembered how, in the warm café,
she had admired his hands as they rested on the table near his
coffee. She was embarrassed that her nails were less well kept
than Laci's; after all, she was a pianist, while he spent his days
building and installing stoves. Now, in the factory, she welcomed this connection to her past, just as she had appreciated
the Wehrmacht guard in Gelsenkirchen who looked so much
like her father.

Whenever she could, Oli would help her fellow inmates by taking on the work of the older and weaker prisoners at her table. This contrasted with the behavior of some of the other women, particularly several girls in their late teens who appeared to be driven solely by selfishness and their own need for food. But it wasn't just the young. During the distribution of lunch, Oli would often see women pleading for larger portions. Some, she knew, had been successful and well off before the war: a middle-aged opera singer who had traveled the world, wives of doctors and lawyers. All of them had been brought to their knees by hunger and deprivation. She prayed for them.

Oli also tried to help her mother as much as possible. She and Lilly made arrangements for Bertha to skip work whenever she was feeling unwell. Bertha had often had medical problems before the camps: she had undergone several surgeries, including one to remove her gallbladder, and she had always needed to take various medications. In spite of this, she was faring amazingly well. Like everyone else, she had lost a lot of weight, but then she had started off with a bit extra. Still, her girls worried about her, and they always wanted to give her some of their food. Of course, she refused. She wanted them to eat, especially Oli who was so thin.

With two more months of winter still facing them, Oli and Lilly knew that they had to do something to keep their spirits up. Though they lived at the edge of complete despair, it wasn't in either of their natures to succumb, no matter how grim their lives had become. Writing helped, and they discovered that reading their work to their friends tended to lift everyone's spirits. Oli and Lilly decided that the camp needed a newspaper.

The POWs obligingly provided some full sheets of paper for the enterprise. Work in the factory had slacked off, so Oli and Lilly found plenty of time to write. They managed to find humor in their surroundings and their circumstances, and they particularly enjoyed making fun of their guards. Others were invited to submit poems, while their friend Lyca helped write articles. The first edition of the "Grey Papers"—named for their dim and faded dresses—would be ready in a few weeks.

Meanwhile, Oli's writing continued to help her cope with her circumstances:

Oli's Diary, January 31, 1945:

I'm strong having a more intense inner life than ever. I always adapt to the situation not wishing for more than I have. I am pleased with what I have, the food or the cold do not make me miserable. During one of the breaks I wrote a poem, it's not the best but I will write it down. What I would like to express with this poem is that my moral strength is partly inspired by You.

Crowd shuffling in sludgy mud
I'm going with them
I'm shivering with cold
My hands are stiff, I'm freezing.
There are no stars in the sky
And I'm so sad and gloomy.

While we are going bent and cold,
Dragging ourselves to the factory,
Several painful thoughts flash through my mind.
How long will this fight, this miserable life last?
Why are there so many tormented, humiliated spirits?
And the question is always there: how long shall I live?

Then in the murmuring crowd
I suddenly hear a nice, low and kind voice
It's familiar in this strange world.
Once I heard it on a Saturday,
It was May and lilacs were blooming in the ghetto yard
Where we were standing crying and very sad.

Your voice was crystal-clear music
A soft Chopin melody.
And you were talking to me dear Laci!
You encouraged me not to lose heart,

As you will always stand by me
No one can ever make us part.

But if Fate will ever separate us
I shouldn't be scared, your hand will still be
holding mine.
And I will be with you in my thoughts.
It gives me strength, cherishes hope
It's my consolation in difficult moments
It's a reassuring song on sleepless nights.

I can hear this voice when I'm hungry,
When I'm trembling with the cold wind
When I darn something with stiff fingers.
I'm grateful to God to have given Him to me
And his voice escorts me on my trying way
It's gospel and glorious divine inspiration.

The start of February brought a spring-like break in the cold weather, but also another painful reminder of their situation. In some unfathomable place, Gabi was about to turn seventeen. Bertha had never before been away from her son on his birthday. She had no idea what was happening to him or how much he was suffering. They walked to work through the melting snow on the evening of February 1, hoping that the warmer weather would last. At midnight, as February 2 began, Bertha, Oli and Lilly silently wished Gabi a happy birthday. Later, when she was back in her bunk, Lilly wrote in her diary, "I am thinking of you my dear Gabi today."

Chapter 19
ANGELS AND HONEY

Gabi had lost track of the days and was unaware of when exactly his birthday occurred, but it is possible that he celebrated it by marching from one camp to another. Sometime in early- to mid-February he and the other prisoners were evacuated from Wolfsberg and marched to a new camp, called Schotterwerk. He was lucky to be walking at all.

January in Wolfsberg had been freezing, with a wind that blew through the mountains and cut through the prisoners' clothing as they worked. It was often hard to see on the worksite due to fog and falling snow, making their labor even more difficult and treacherous. The only consolation of that month was that the prisoners began to hear the distant sound of artillery, suggesting that the front was getting closer.

For months Gabi had been lucky, unscathed by injuries while others suffered the accidents—great and small—that were inevitable in their work. Luck rarely lasts forever, though, and one snow-filled day his came to an end. At first it seemed like a minor accident of little consequence. His workgroup had been ordered to widen a recently dug ditch. While Gabi was down in the trench, swinging his pickaxe into the rocky earth, he struck a particularly hard blow, causing a large clump of dirt to fly into the air and strike him in the thigh. Embedded in the soil was a length of rusty barbed wire, a piece of which went through his trousers and penetrated his skin. A small bloody patch appeared on the striped cloth. He pulled the fragment out and inspected the wound. It did not look serious. He continued working so as to avoid any repercussions from the capos, and had largely forgotten the injury by the end of the workday.

Two days later, however, his thigh started to swell. He was reluctant to go to the infirmary, because he was unsure whether he would get his food ration if he didn't work. Worse, many prisoners who were admitted never came out again. So he went out to work in spite of the pain. Every time he moved, he was in agony from the chafing of his trousers against the injury. Two days later, the wound was the size of a tennis ball, the stretched skin hot and painful. Gabi knew he no longer had a choice: he had to get whatever help was available from the camp infirmary, regardless of the risks.

The next morning he got permission to go to the Rivier, as the camp infirmary was known. A small cadre of inmate doctors staffed the wooden barracks. The two in charge were from Greece, both in their early forties. One of them examined Gabi's leg, his kindness and concern evident. He explained in broken German that if the wound weren't drained, Gabi would die of infection.

The doctor picked up a rusty razor blade. The pain was sharp as the blade pierced his skin, but Gabi felt immediate relief as the pus began to drain and the tension eased. The doctor quickly and efficiently squeezed the wound to get the remaining fluid out. When he was finished, he sprinkled the area with white powder and applied a paper bandage. He told Gabi that he could stay in the infirmary for a few days while he healed. Gabi gingerly climbed up into bunk number 57, the space that had been allotted to him.

The infirmary turned out to be a good place to spend time, for he did not have to work and food rations were delivered. The surroundings, however, were dismal. Prisoners were crowded onto the tiered bunks and the noise and smell of the suffering and dying were overwhelming. Because Gabi was not seriously ill, he spent his time observing the Greek doctors treating the other patients. They had no surgical tools and almost no medication—consoling words were the only salve they could dispense. The other prisoners referred to these men as angels. Gabi thought about how difficult it must be for them as physicians, trained in modern hospitals, to have to practice under such appalling conditions. Most of the time all they could do was watch their patients die. And even when they cured someone, they were usually doing no more than buying them a temporary reprieve.

At the end of his second day in the Rivier, Gabi lay in his bunk listening to the work parties returning. He stared at the wooden plank above him, glad to be inside. It wasn't warm and it wasn't comfortable, but it was better than standing exhausted through roll call in the snow. Soon after he heard the dismissal order shouted by one of the guards, a prisoner he didn't know appeared next to his bunk. The man pulled a small loaf of bread from his pocket—a week's worth of rations—followed by a lump of something wrapped in paper, and gave them both to Gabi. The man explained in a whisper that he was a member of a labor party that worked with inmates from another camp. Bertha's cousin Hugo was a capo in the other camp and, upon learning that Gabi was in Wolfsberg, had sent this gift.

The unexpected present gave Gabi a renewed sense of confidence. Gabi hadn't known Hugo well; he was older, in his early forties, and hadn't lived in Beregszász, so Gabi had only met him occasionally while growing up. Yet this distant relative was looking out for him. The loneliness that Gabi had endured since being separated from his father was eased by this knowledge. When he unwrapped the parcel, Gabi discovered that the lump inside was honey. A hard chunk of artificial honey, actually, but Gabi didn't care; he hadn't seen any sort of honey in months.

The prisoner wished Gabi luck and quickly left. He may well have taken some share of the goods, which would be no more than his due for having smuggled these gifts into the camp. In fact, Gabi was impressed with his fellow inmate's honesty; some would have kept it all for themselves. Gabi savored a few bites of the bread and honey immediately, then stashed the rest in his pocket to eat later.

The next day brought further surprises. A capo entered the infirmary to make an announcement. All work would stop immediately, he informed the prisoners. The camp would soon be evacuated. Those who could not walk would be taken by truck to the new camp. It didn't take Gabi long to decode the announcement. Anyone who couldn't walk also couldn't work, which made them useless to those in power. The trucks, he guessed, would go to the nearest extermination camp, where the occupants would be gassed. The decision was simple: he had to get out of the infirmary. The fact that the work had stopped meant that he might at least have a few more days of rest before the evacuation.

His leg still hurt and he could barely walk, but Gabi got himself discharged the following morning. He spent the remainder of the day resting in his tent, where the prisoners shared their theories about where they were going and what would happen to them. Whatever was coming would surely happen soon; the artillery sounds that used to come from far in the distance were now much closer. At night, an orange glow could be seen on the horizon.

At roll call the next morning, an officer announced that they would be walking to another camp. Gabi watched the prisoners from the infirmary struggle to the trucks and felt fortunate that, at least for the moment, he was in good enough shape to walk. He didn't know how long he would be able to keep up, though, and he worried about how well his leg would withstand the coming journey.

The prisoners marched in their columns, a phalanx of hundreds heading west on a road that wound through forested mountains. Gabi's leather shoes were strong, but he had no socks—only a few shreds of cloth he had managed to find and put in his shoes—and the snow was so deep that his feet were wet and painfully numb. Some prisoners collapsed, only to be assaulted by the shouts and blows of capos and guards. Any prisoner unable to rise was thrown onto one of the trucks carrying the weak and sick. Gabi started to doubt whether any of the marchers would make it to their destination, wherever it was. The terrain was uneven, with strenuous inclines and slippery descents. When the sun started to set, they were still marching, leaving Gabi to wonder if they would be forced to walk all night.

As Gabi had suspected, those in the trucks were not bound for the same place as the others. In the evening, shortly before the marchers reached their destination, the trucks turned off onto a different road. Gabi and his comrades, still in their rows of five, staggered, limped and stumbled through the gates of the Schotterwerk camp. Once inside they were counted and assigned to a barracks. As at Auschwitz, these were wooden buildings with tiered bunks along each side and a pot-bellied stove at each end. A pipe covered by brick ran between the stoves, creating a long bench the length of the room. The barracks was already crowded when they arrived. Some prisoners were in their bunks, while others sat on the bench that was warmed by the pipe. Those in the bunks slept alternately with their head or feet to the aisle, which allowed them a little more room. Gabi and the other new arrivals climbed in where they could. There was a thin layer of straw covering the wooden sleeping surfaces, but not enough to provide much comfort. It didn't matter; the exhausted prisoners soon fell asleep.

They were not called to work the following morning. Gabi learned from another prisoner that there was no work performed at this camp. Schotterwerk was both huge and very crowded, filled with inmates who were arriving daily from other evacuated camps. The daylight revealed thousands of prisoners. Gabi stood in line with the others for a minimal breakfast: some ersatz coffee and a small piece of bread. He guessed that if they were not working, their food allowance would be even less than the meager rations they had received in Wolfsberg.

While many prisoners were too fatigued or too ill to leave the barracks, the rest milled around outside. Gabi decided to use this freedom to visit other barracks in the hope of finding someone else from Beregszász. By now he had come to accept that his father had probably been killed that first day in Auschwitz. But maybe there was an uncle or a cousin, someone he knew from home. He went into the nearest barracks and asked if there was anyone from Beregszász. No one replied, so he went to the next building. At the fourth barracks he tried, a weak voice answered. Gabi followed the sound through the crowd and found a middle-aged man lying in his bunk. He looked to be in terrible condition, emaciated and frail.

His name was András, and he came from a small village outside of Beregszász. András asked Gabi for his father's name, and when Gabi told him it was Herman, András asked if his father had owned a housewares store in town. As soon as Gabi confirmed this, the older man instantly became more animated, telling Gabi that he had been a customer of Herman's and had visited the store regularly. In the past, András had received letters from relatives in the United States and, as he knew no English, he would bring the letters for Herman to translate. It was evident that he admired Herman, and Gabi felt proud as he listened to András talk about his father.

After a while, Gabi could see that András needed to rest. He left, promising to visit again soon, and indeed he returned the following day and the day after that. The two of them traded stories about home and reminisced about happier times. Once again, a connection to his past strengthened Gabi's will to survive and make it back home. But the talks were not enough to reinvigorate András, who seemed weaker each time Gabi saw him.

For Gabi, these daily visits provided a sense of purpose, as well as a welcome routine that helped relieve the aimlessness of days structured only by mealtimes. Breakfast and dinner were the same: coffee and a small serving of bread. Prisoners were dying from starvation and disease in great numbers. Every morning, inmates in each barracks collected the dead, stripping the uniforms off each body and writing a prisoner number in large, blue letters across each skeletal chest. The bodies were carried in blankets and left outside the door, where they were gathered by other prisoners and loaded onto a cart. The barely living took the newly dead to a building where they stacked the corpses and sprinkled them with a lime powder. A prisoner who worked this particular detail explained the later stages of the process to Gabi: the bodies were taken from the building to mass graves near the camp, which were filled with alternating layers of corpses and lime. The building was refilled almost every day.

The one-day walk from Wolfsberg had not taken the prisoners much further from the front, so they continued to hear distant artillery and planes. Gabi wondered if they would be moved west again, or if they might be lucky enough to be liberated before they were evacuated. There was a lot of time to ponder such things: the days seemed endless, the hours passing interminably, with hunger a constant presence. There were no roll calls and they had little interaction with the guards, most of whom were Wehrmacht and were visible only in the towers and at the gated entrance.

On Gabi's fourth morning in the camp, he went once again to talk with András. But as he approached the barracks he saw two prisoners carrying a corpse down the steps, and he recognized his friend, bouncing lifelessly on the blanket. András's prisoner number was written in cruel blue marks across his chest. Gabi bowed his head. He had seen many people die in the past year, but since those first months in Wolfsberg when the Mermelstein brothers died, most of the dead had been nameless and unknown to him. Gabi thought he had become inured to death, but the loss of András pulled away the cloak of dispassion that he had gathered around himself. He was, once again, lost and alone, and he wept.

Days passed. Though it was cold, Gabi stayed outside whenever he could. The barracks was a house of horrors: depressingly dark and filled with the moans of the dying. Most of the prisoners seemed simply to be waiting for death to arrive. The stench was nearly unbearable, making the freezing outdoors more attractive than the heated brick bench inside. Gabi knew that he needed to find younger prisoners who, like himself, still had plans other than dying. He started conversations with teenagers he met, most of whom were from Poland. Two Polish boys his own age became friends: Mirek and Jacek. Their experience with ghettos and camps predated his own by years; they had already survived unfathomable months in captivity and Gabi marveled at their tenacity.

In spite of everything, Mirek and Jacek were optimistic about the chances of liberation. Gabi derived new strength from spending time with them. Together they spent the days and weeks talking about the possibility of freedom and debating whether they would be moved again before their liberators arrived. They scanned the night horizon for evidence of the advancing front, and listened for the planes and artillery. Yet even as they hoped that they would soon be liberated, they feared in equal measure that the SS would never let them live to bear witness to the atrocities they had suffered and seen.

THE WALK

There is not far to go. I need to figure out where the entrance to the building is located, and get Herman down the stairs to the changing room. I will leave him at the entrance to the gas chamber; I will not go inside with him. I should. I should go in with him and stay with him until the very end, but I can't. I don't want to have to research or describe what it would be like to suffocate in a room crammed full of naked, suffering people. I don't want my father to have to read those details.

I find blueprints and photos of Crematorium II, which show me that the changing room for the fictitious showers would have been to Herman's right as he faced the building. I learn that the gas chambers were built underground and that victims descended a set of stairs—positioned at the far end of the subterranean part of the building—to get inside. In the Yad Vasham online archives I find a photo of workers building the roof for these underground chambers.[1]

---

1. Yad Vasham photo archives, FA157/388.

On the United States Holocaust Memorial Museum website, I find a model of Crematorium II.[2] From this and the other blueprints and maps, I see how the victims would descend the stairs to the changing room. Upon exiting that room, they would be led to their right toward the gas chamber.

There are multiple accounts of what was inside the changing room and what happened there. Survivors of the *Sonderkommando*—the crematoria workers—have provided detailed descriptions.

> At right angles to the gas chamber was the largest room in the extermination complex, the so-called changing room.... They entered from the yard down wide concrete steps. At the entrance to the basement was a signboard, and written on it in several languages the direction: To the baths and disinfecting rooms. The ceiling of the changing room was supported by concrete pillars to which many more notices were fixed, once again with the aim of making the unsuspecting people believe that the imminent

2. Model sculpted by Mieczyslaw Stobierski based on documents and SS testimony. This recreation of the original model appears at the U.S. Holocaust Memorial Museum. <http://resources.ushmm.org/inquery/uia_doc.php/query/4?uf=uia_Biv-LQt>, most recently sourced March 28, 2013.

212

process of disinfection was of vital importance for their health. Slogans like Cleanliness brings freedom or One louse may kill you were intended to hoodwink, as were numbered clothes hooks.... There were other multi-lingual notices inviting them to hang up their clothes as well as their shoes, tied together by their laces, and admonishing them to remember the number of their hook so that they might easily retrieve their clothes after their showers.[3]

---

3. Filip Müller, *Eyewitness Auschwitz: Three Years in the Gas Chambers* (Chicago: Ivan R. Dee, 1979), 61.

Herman turns to the left, and over his shoulder he watches Gabi go off to the right. His son moves further away, and is soon lost from sight, obscured by the men who fill the growing space between them. Together with the other older men, Herman rounds the front of the train, where he sees a barbed wire fence and, through the wire, long wooden buildings. He follows those in front of him as they approach the wire and then turn right. He scratches his face and registers the unaccustomed sensation of stubble under his fingers. In his other hand he turns a comb.

After three days of being unable to move, his muscles and joints ache and disobey. After three days of constant motion, the dusty ground under his feet seems to shift. He is tremendously thirsty. He struggles to keep pace with those around him who are also struggling to keep pace. He wants to stop and rest, but the dogs and machine guns deny him this choice.

A row of trees appears on his left, lining the fence. Shortly afterwards, he and the others turn left through a gate in the fence. Ahead of him, Herman sees a brick building with a large, tall chimney. As they enter the yard in front of the building, an SS guard shouts to them that they will soon have a shower and be disinfected. Herman anticipates the water that will finally quench his thirst.

Herman follows the men ahead of him down some stairs and into an underground room. The entrance is signed: "To the baths and disinfecting rooms." The walls are lined with numbered hooks, and more signs tell them to hang up their clothes and to remember the number so that they can retrieve their clothes after their shower. A poster on the wall proclaims: "Cleanliness Brings Freedom." Once he has removed his clothes, Herman joins the other naked men as they exit from the long changing room and turn to the right.

Chapter 20
SPRING FASHION

On Sunday, February 4, 1945, after nearly two weeks of writing whenever they got the chance, Oli and Lilly "published" the first edition of the "Grey Papers."[1] They went from barracks to barracks reading their newsletter to an appreciative audience.

```
GREY PAPER - 1st Edition
Editor in chief: Lili Klein²
Correspondent: Olga Klein

WELCOME
To the tune of the world-famous "My Hat
Has Gunpowder on It."³

I. Lager exclusive
The publishing of this newspaper
Guess who wrote it?
Lili, Lyca and Olga

II. Will be published once a week
Or more frequently in the night shift
More can be written
Without fear of Meister Bush.

III. We hope that there will not be
More than three editions
By the time the fourth is published
Our train will be taking us home.

IV. We hope that you will give
A warm welcome to our newspaper
And it would give us joy
If our wish were to come true.
```

1. The complete "Grey Papers" can be found at *www.wegotthewater.com*.

2. Lilly's full name is Livia, but she was called Lilly, which is sometimes spelled "Lili" in Hungarian.

3. *"Puskaporos a kalapom,"* a popular Hungarian folk song.

COMRADE
By Anni Pauk
Comrade, don't watch the grey and sooty
ground
Comrade, don't let tears come to your eyes
Comrade, look at the nice, blue sky
It looks down on you like an old friend.

Comrade, our hearts feel the same sorrow
Comrade, your heartache can't be worse
than mine
Still, look at the clear blue sky
And see how the sun is shining down on us.

There will come a new springtime
There will come many happy summers
There will be freedom and happiness
O, how nice it is!

Comrade, don't look at the grey and sooty
ground
Comrade, don't let your tears come to your
eyes
Comrade, laugh again
Our eyes are watching the sky.

DAILY TOILET NEWS
H.N.A.[4] The Führer has died once again,
after the third resurrection.
H.N.A. The late Pál Teleki[5] is reclaiming
the Jews.
H.N.A. The Russians are banging on the
gates of Berlin.
H.N.A. Apartments with all modern
conveniences are waiting for the Jews in
Palestine.
H.N.A. The captain is putting on civilian
clothes and taking off the skull.[6]

---

4. Haftling News Agency (*Haftling* is the German word for prisoner).

5. Prime Minister of Hungary from 1939 to 1941.

6. SS uniforms had a skull insignia.

```
ECONOMICS
The Haftling News Agency informs you that:
- Beans and cabbage arrived at the kitchen.
- We will have beans on Saturdays and
cabbage soup in the mornings.

Daily price of margarine: one sausage
Daily price of soup: one portion of  bread
Daily price of jam: half a portion of
bread

FASHION
Ladies! Attention!
The first snow of the season is here. We
can't wear shabby clothes any more. Before
I answer the questions of our dear readers,
please let me write a few words about our
new arrivals. Coat selection: light yellow,
deep red, green checked and black for young
girls. The back is conspicuously draped and
decorated with a patch of another color.
Blue-grey striped English-style caps,
tied in a discreet ribbon below the chin,
similar to the afternoon dresses worn under
the coat, are extremely fashionable.

GASTRONOMY
Housewives! We are living in difficult
times, so we need to give up a lot; not
only on clothing, but also on food. Still,
we can give our husbands a varied lunch.
Here are some foolproof recipes:
Monday: potato soup
Tuesday: potato with soup
Wednesday: potato with noodles
Thursday:  noodles with potato
Friday:  noodles without potato
Saturday: potato without noodles
Sunday: Attention! Milk soup
```

The women's laughter told Oli and Lilly that they had been a huge success. The bread the women gave them in thanks—and as encouragement to write more—was an added bonus. They decided to start on their second edition right away.

The next day, the women who worked the night shift were awakened by an air-raid siren at about eleven in the morning. The horn was on the roof of a nearby house, so the noise was ear-piercing in the barracks. The women leapt from their bunks and Lilly, Oli and Bertha huddled together. After a while, some of the women went back to sleep, which Oli found amazing. But the raids terrified Bertha, and her daughters had to work hard to assuage her fears. Oli was just as scared, but she pretended not to be for her mother's sake. Still, she hated being inside during the raid; as soon as she was sure that her mother was calmer, she left Lilly with Bertha and went outside.

Oli was joined by three others: Agnes, the middle-aged opera singer; Csilla, an old acquaintance from Beregszász; and Duci, another friend. The four of them usually gathered outside the barracks during air raids, both to see what was happening and because they felt safer being together outdoors. Many of the planes flying overhead were German, and the women suspected that they must be coming from nearby. The POWs had told them that Allied planes had been bombing Weimar, which was only 32 kilometers away. They guessed that Berlin, which they knew to be about 250 kilometers from them, was now also a target. The eastern front was getting closer: German refugees were flooding into Sömmerda.

On the following day, February 6, the air-raid sirens sounded while they were at work. The factory went completely dark and the machines stopped. Lilly made her way to her mother's worktable, where she put her arm around Bertha and told her she would bring some coffee, while Oli took her mother's hand and tried to calm her. Lilly struggled to find her way to the coffee urn in the blackness, eventually returning with a hot drink for her mother.

The air raids now started happening every day and every night. On some days the hours of bombing outnumbered those when the sky was silent. Everyone was on edge. Both Lilly and Oli wrote in their diaries about the raids; both expressed the stark contrast between their present circumstances and their past lives back home.

Lilly's Diary, February 10, 1945:

7:00 pm In the factory. We are deathly afraid of the air raids—it lasted over 2 hours. We could see the planes. What a view! Our only hopes are these planes yet they can kill us too. They were bombing about 20-30 kilometers away and you could hear the machine guns too. I am so afraid, but at the same time I pray to God that if he asks for somebody's life from our family—it should be me. I am afraid to die—I would like to live in happiness with all of you—Mother, Dad, Gabi, Oli and George. The weather is lousy, rainy, dark—but somehow this is the way I like it. It goes with the way I feel. Very little work in the factory. Our machine stopped altogether.

10:00 pm A year ago today—we were probably in the movies, after that at home listening to the radio. I was working with the beads making necklaces—Mother was taking a nap near the fireplace. Oli was playing the piano, Gabi was reading and you Dad were making goose liver sandwiches for us. Now the five of us are suffering in 3 different places—we are cold and hungry and working.

Oli's Diary, February 17, 1945:

It's the 17th today, I'm sitting in the factory thinking while working. I'm looking out to the foggy courtyard, it may rain soon and I'm happy about it. You must be surprised, you know I used to love sunny weather and the bright sky. Both of us were the children of the street and we loved nature. But now I'm afraid of the fine weather and I remember that once I saw tiny blue points in this sky, they grew bigger and bigger and brought death. That's why I don't like blue anymore,

*although at home it used to be my favorite color
and I remember my dear Laci that sometimes you
deliberately chose blue presents, brooches, manicure
sets for me. So many things have changed since then.
Only now do we see how wonderful everything was,
although then we used to think that we couldn't bear
the "impossible" situation at home any more. It would
be so nice to be hiding, living in a flutter all the time,
fearing only dad, moving apart when an acquaintance
is approaching and then cuddling again happily.
Sometimes I ask myself if all that was true, if I ever
lived without starving, sleeping in a soft white bed,
wearing clean clothes without being scared?*

The women continued to get news from the men on the day shift, and it was from them that they learned about the bombing of Dresden. Oli mourned both the loss of life and the destruction of the city's architectural heritage. She found it amazing that there were still Germans who insisted on the certainty of a German victory in spite of the damage inflicted by the Allies. The guards and the factory foreman made a great show of their optimism: anyone suggesting a German defeat, the warning went, would be shot. It seemed to Oli that everyone was complicit in a grand charade.

The mounting tension felt by the prisoners was accompanied by a decrease in rations. By the end of February there was little work to do at the factory, so the women were fed very little. In the camp, there were so many raids that it was difficult to get any rest. The constant sirens took their toll on Bertha, who complained of chest pains and often had to stay in bed—an indulgence the authorities allowed due to the scarcity of work in the factory.

One night when the women weren't at work, they heard detonations closer to their barracks than ever before. Most of the prisoners ran to a trench that had been dug outside the barracks, but Bertha did not want to leave her bunk. Lilly and

Oli desperately tried to coax her to come down. Oli found that she grew braver when her mother needed her; she finally persuaded Bertha to move to the relative safety of the ditch and, once there, she helped keep up the spirits of the other women.

A few hours later, Lilly and Oli went to work at the factory on the day shift. Their mother stayed behind, so when another air-raid siren sounded, they worried terribly about her. The factory, of course, was the absolute worst place to be when the bombs were falling. The underground bunker they huddled in would do little to protect them—gunpowder was everywhere and one explosion would shatter the entire facility. They were painfully aware that one bomb could be the end of them, so close to the conclusion of the war.

The two weeks that followed were a roller coaster of fear, hope, anticipation and despair. Lilly wrote less and less in her diary, instead writing for the "Grey Papers" whenever she had the time and felt calm enough to concentrate. By contrast, Oli devoted even more time to her diary, using it—and her connection to Laci—as a lifeline to help get her through the difficult days. Bertha grew weaker and often could not come to work with them. Food rations continued to be reduced. Days of hopeful news were interspersed with days of silence that brought renewed anxiety. Oli suffered from severe headaches at this time, yet continued to go to work. There was more peace in the factory than in the barracks, where the enforced idleness led her to brood about her situation and the whereabouts of her father and brother.

By the end of February, work in the factory had virtually come to a halt since supplies were no longer being delivered to produce the bullets. Most of their nights were spent in the barracks, where they lay in their bunks listening to the planes flying overhead and the detonation of the bombs. It was maddening. The one consolation was the change in the weather as spring made its way to Sömmerda, permitting the women to spend their days outdoors.

On the first of March, Oli sat outside contemplating the green buds on the trees and the tiny new blades of grass that had pushed their way up through the soil. She thought about how much her world had changed since she had watched spring arrive in Beregszász just one year earlier, and also about how much she herself had changed. She wondered what Laci would think of her now. If she did finally return home, she hoped he would still like this person she had become, this new being forged by arduous months in the camps.

Oli's Diary, March 1, 1945:

People have become much more religious, even those who never prayed at home. Now they are making vows to wear a wig and become religious. This is all very nice but only if it is kept. I believe that most of them are fearing God now but they will forget about their vows when it comes to that. I can't make such promises because if I made a vow to become religious I would have to give you up first of all and I can't promise that. I think that God does not consider our love a sin. It's not a sin if people love each other, is it?

This reminds me Lacika, that I promised something. I promised that I would be good to people and it is so difficult to do it as they don't deserve it, but I will try.

Naturally, everybody is much more nervous than at home and there are a lot of disputes and quarrels. I've realized that it's better to stay out of them because they just make you anxious and nervous. It's no use arguing with people, I retire into my own shell and arrange everything within myself and I realize it every day how dishonest people are and how awkward their way of thinking is. I hope that there comes the time when I will be happily living in a small family and I won't need any company, only my family, my good friends and You.

Lilly found solace in the company of others. During air raids and other times when they couldn't sleep, Lilly and her friends talked about their school days, their boyfriends and their plans for the future. Éva, her good friend from home, was often with her, along with several other young women from Beregszász. When there was no work, they huddled together on their bunks in the barracks. When the air-raid sirens sounded at the factory, they gathered together in the bunker. They chattered like the girls they had been a year ago—girls who had gossiped over ice cream at a café after a day of school.

On Sunday, March 4, 1945, the second installment of the "Grey Papers" was ready for public consumption.

```
GREY PAPER - 2nd Edition
4 March 1945

Two Klein kids are writing a newspaper
I wonder what news it will contain.
It is thanks to the Tommies[7]
That it is not published weekly.

Because there are a lot of alerts now
We don't feel like writing rhymes.
We hope that next time
The Tommies will come on foot.

That would be good news,
My dear haftling comrades
But it won't be a big tragedy
If the Russians come along with them.

_____


The girls are sitting side by side at the
long table in the factory, and they are
working. The two on the end are paying
attention to everything but work. They are
chatting about love and memories, among
other things. The first one says: "Look
```

7. British soldiers.

Éva, yesterday I was in this hall cleaning
and we did a thorough job." Éva looks at
the wall opposite them and purses her
lips. "Well, look at all those stripes of
dust on the wall." The third girl next
to them hears this despite the rattle of
the machines and asks, "Striped?" "Yes,"
the other one answers and turns back to
her friend, continuing the chatter. The
fourth girl at the table asks, "What are
Éva and the others talking about? Something
striped?" "You don't know yet? It is said
that men in striped clothing will come
here." "Oh, good!" Karola gets excited and
turns to her right to share the news with
Etuka. "Guess what, Jewish men have arrived
at the factory." "Really? Is it true?"
She puts the bullet down on the table and
tells the news to Zsuzsika, who just came
back from the toilet. Zsuzsa says: "This is
still news for you? A German worker just
told me that in the courtyard—and who would
know it better?"
Etuka sits back and tells Magda that the
men will live in our camp.
Magda gets very excited, but just to be
sure, she asks where the news came from.
"It came from a reliable person. Éva is the
one who told me."
The news spreads from one place to another.
In the meantime, the tidy Éva is still
producing the bullets and asking herself
how someone could leave the wall so dirty.

PLANS GONE UP IN SMOKE[8]
While homeward bound I've thought about
How good or big today's portion will be
Will it be sausage or only butter
With a little piece of bread
Oh my Lord, how sad is
This haftling life

---

8. The title and first line are from a popular poem by the renowned Hungarian poet
Sándor Petőfi.

And I've thought about so many tasty
homemade morsels
That we ate with pleasure for so many years
Fried chicken and delicious foie gras
Oh I can still taste it in my mouth
But now I am awake
And in we go through the camp gate.

I'M SITTING BY A SCALE (Lili)
I'm sitting by a scale in the factory
Thinking hard and chewing on my pencil
What shall I write to the girls
Grey paper or verses
Chewing my pencil I'm thinking hard.

I write down two verses and weigh a bullet
When somebody hits me on the head.
It is Muki and he asks, "Darling, are you a
poet or a haftling?
There is no demand here for poets.

Schiller and Goethe are gone forever.
We only need the Führer and no one else
You should weigh the bullet, that's
your task"
And away he runs
And I keep on doing the same
Weighing a bullet and writing 100 verses.

GASTRONOMY
Unlike before, now it's extraordinary if we
can cook something in the block.
Our scared haftling fellow who had two
potatoes during the control put them on her
two thin breasts and she avoided trouble.
What can women with bigger breasts do?

FASHION
Ladies, spring is here. We throw away our
winter clothes and go out for our evening
walks in our beautiful spring garments.
Our smart ladies often wear beige and dark
blue balloon coats while the lower workers'
class unbutton their winter coats then
throw it over their shoulders. With the

arrival of the hot weather they will
put their coats in storage, most likely
without lining, buttons, shoulder pad,
belt or loop.
Mongolian materials are fashionable. I can
recommend making blouses from the lining,
they'll make wonderful "imprimes" with some
pattern. You can wear them with a skirt
from the lining of the blouse and put on
colored spring socks, since we don't need
our scarves anymore.
Let's wear grey-brown socks with our grey
clothes.
If you can't get hold of them, then order
them from the store of Katalin Balder.
Concerning shoes there are not too many
changes, ugly blunt-toed ones are still
fashionable. Some men's shoes with pointed
toes have also appeared but I don't
recommend them now, wait 1-2 weeks then
you can wear your heels that you took off
a year ago.

Ladies, if you grieve for your husband or
fiancé, I can comfort you with the fact that
their presence would be dangerous because
our beautiful blond, brunette and redhead
German women guards would turn the head of
your beloved ones.
Hopefully, it'll be over in a few weeks'
time.

Once again, Lilly and Oli received thanks for their efforts in the form of bread, pats of butter and marmalade, and even the use of a much-coveted needle. Their humor helped the other women get through the next week, which was punctuated by some of the worst air raids yet. One midnight raid sounded like a thousand airplanes overhead. The prisoners were spending more and more time in the bunker at work. Most of the women gave up crowding into the trench in the camp, deciding to trust to their luck in the barracks.

Oli's Diary, March 6 -7, 1945:

Yesterday we spent three hours in the factory bunker and plenty of planes flew over us. Thank God they passed without any trouble. Most of the girls fell asleep after having eaten their food, they were not at all interested in what was happening outside. We, however, were sitting side by side listening to the planes although I told Mum that it was just the wind blowing. I was out twice and I could see and hear the planes. Thank God they flew away but I went with them in thought wondering where they were going and whether our beloved ones were there or not. Please God, be with them and with everyone...

It's the night break and everybody is sleeping around me. I have chatted with the girls then I started to sing at their request. Sometimes I sing like a machine, sometimes I put all my heart into the song and the melodies revive so many memories. Is there a single Hungarian song which does not remind me of you? No.

The Love of Lauretta and the Schubert serenade are our love songs. They sound so sad in this grey arms factory. How nice it was when they were played by the gypsy violinist at night in May or when you were humming them in my ear.

By the middle of March, shifts in the factory were rare. Occasionally small contingents of women were sent to work in nearby fields, but for the most part the prisoners spent their time in the camp. Their industry continued, however. The women sewed, tailoring their dresses for the spring weather. Oli and Lilly worked on another edition of the "Grey Papers." Lilly was impressed by Oli's ability to maintain a sense of humor and to write lines that brought roars of laughter from the women. Her own capacity for humor had diminished over the past weeks, worn down by hunger, fear of the bombs, and the tediousness of daily life. For Oli, writing continued to be her consolation, and less work meant more time to write:

Oli's Diary, March 16, 1945:

10 am. I'm in the grey factory again. I've been working in the warehouse since yesterday. I'm completely alone, I'll be here until the stock-keeper comes back from holiday. There's no one else, so I can let my thoughts wander and think about You all the time. ...The hall is huge, full of ammunition cases and its floor is concrete. I've just swept it like a good maid. I've opened the door letting spring in. The air is fresh and I forget that I'm sitting in the warehouse of an arms factory. The spring breeze and the sunlight are lifting me. I imagine that I'm swaying in a golden carriage. Now You are in front of me, good and beautiful. I'm trying to recall your face in all its details. Your eyes were light green and your long eyelashes that I liked so much shaded them . . .

If You saw me now, You would either start to cry or laugh. Even I can't decide whether the way I look is sad or ridiculous. I'm not wearing any stockings because they are being mended by a nice colleague of mine and I have only one pair. So I'm barefoot today and although I was cold early in the morning, it's quite pleasant now. I have two big wooden shoes, I could put both my feet in one of them.

I'm wearing grey prison clothes, it's quite boring but they are always nice and clean. I've tightened my belt to see if I could still be pretty in a nice dress. (There's an air-raid warning again but hoping that everything will be all right I continue writing.)

I used to have shoulder-length, nice, long and wavy hair and many people looked at it when it was shining in the sun. Today it's short, dim and is squeezed under a shawl.

My eyes haven't changed except for the fact that they forgot how to smile and they are all too often in tears.

That's how I look Lacika, that's how I've been tried. But I can feel that I would revive and be the same as I used to be if God gave us back our freedom and the people that I've been separated from for almost a year.

Later the same day, Oli's friend Anni Pauk, the musician who had sung so beautifully at Christmas, wrote her own letter to Laci in Oli's diary.

Dear Laci, coming towards me from distant obscurity your figure becomes more and more vivid. Retreat into yourself when taking this booklet in your hand. Remove the armor from your heart, pray and listen to the voice of love. You are chosen and you are lucky because this book provides you with music not everyone can hear. Be happy about it and appreciate it. I'm not reading this book, I don't want to disturb the harmony of the two of you. But I can still hear more than You, my dear distant Laci because I stand next to Oli in those moments when you feel that if you take one small step in the dark you'll get to the end of the line. I'm standing next to her but I'm not holding her hand, she's holding mine. She's little, weak and young but she gives the grown-up strong person, me, strength. She's holding my hand and transfers her strong faith to my poor soul. These times only God and You are with us. Thank you ever so much for existing, for being good, for being worthy of this book. Thank you that Oli can love you and that I can have some of her faith in you.

You, who live on the other side where the sun is shining, remove the armor from your heart and hear the voice of love.

If ever we shall get to the sunny side again, take the fragile yet strong hand of your Oli, hold it and never

let it go again. There's no prejudice, there are no
family objections, only the Two of You. Take God's gift
and don't care about people. We are fighting against
death and it's perhaps your personality and your
wishes that give us strength. I can feel this strength
and I'm grateful for it my dear, distant Laci. Would to
God it be so.

As you are coming closer and closer from the
unknown, you are becoming more and more vivid. I'd
like to look into your happy eyes shining with joy when
we meet. Everything that is harmonic is so beautiful.

Anni Pauk

A few days later, all work at the factory ended, and the
women sensed that their situation was about to change. They
could tell from the sound of the artillery that the front was
moving closer, and they had real hope that liberation was near.
There was much less food now—the loaves that had once been
split to make five rations served to feed six, then seven—and
they all struggled with this new deprivation.

Oli's Diary, March 26, 1945:

I'm hungry. You are the only one I'm telling it to,
nobody else knows it, I don't want to confess it not
even to myself. We've received much less food since
we're without work. We can eat only 2-3 slices of
bread each day. I try to eat even less, so that Mum
and Lili can have more. I try to overcome my hunger
and don't eat. I'm talking to You, Lacika, instead. Life
is so strange. You must have everything and I'm sure
you would like to share it with me, wouldn't you? Still
it's not possible. How happy would I be if I could eat
the leftovers from your plate. Now I could eat any
food, even the food we used to give to the beggars at
home saying that only they can eat it. I'm sorry, Laci,
but now I'm extremely hungry, so much that I tell it to

You as well, although I never wanted to grieve you. It's distressing for you, isn't it? But I'm not sad, no not at all, and I take it because it's not eating that's important. I don't want to complain, honey, my stomach just rumbled while writing and it made me remember that I hadn't eaten anything today. It doesn't matter, I hope that I'll live to see the day when I have enough food and I won't have to sleep or talk to an acquaintance about old times to forget about our hunger.

I'm sitting on a green bench, four people are busy with something near me. One of them is making an elegant blouse of her shabby shirt. She's our old friend, Jáger "Cunci." The other one is writing camp poems on the paper taken from the factory, the third one is knitting a striped pullover of her undone scarf and the fourth one is crouching in front of me beating a nail back into her worn out shoe on top of the covered trench. I'm sitting among them writing to You.

Lilly was busy preparing for Oli's twenty-third birthday. She saved every bit of marmalade she could from their rations—a difficult task given its scarcity—so that she could make a tiny birthday cake for Oli from bread, using the marmalade for frosting. She had made a new diary for her sister, and she also managed to obtain a slip to give Oli as a present from Bertha, and a dress that was ostensibly a present from Herman. Oli's gift from Gabi was a small hand-painted plate. Many of the other young women prepared presents as well.

At the same time, a number of the prisoners began planning for the observance of Passover, which started on March 29—but Lilly wanted nothing to do with the holiday. Passover was about her father saying the prayers, her mother lighting the candles and Gabi asking the four questions, as mandated by tradition. None of this could be done in the camp, so Lilly vowed to ignore it altogether. Instead she simply dreamed that by next year the family would be reunited and they would all observe the holiday together around their own dining room table.

On the morning of Sunday, April 1, the women celebrated Oli's birthday in such style that she wondered if it was possible to have a nicer birthday party in a camp. The presents and cake represented so much thought, effort and sacrifice that Oli was overwhelmed by what had been done for her. Adding to the excitement was the very real hope that they would be liberated in a few days. The party felt like a commemoration of their survival, a going-away celebration.

Afterwards, Oli wrote to Laci, reliving in memory past birthdays that they had celebrated together. She then went around to the barracks with Lilly to read the third edition of the "Grey Papers."

```
GREY PAPER - 3rd  edition

Here's our third issue
Only one more will follow
We'll keep our promise
If God helps us.

If you still remember
We promised you
That by the time we publish the fourth
Our train will be taking us home.

BLUE CORNFLOWER
Blue is the cornflower
Nice is the world
And I have no problems
If my bread is not stolen
But if my stomach rumbles
Then the sky darkens
Camp food is never enough
Cornflowers aren't blue
And the world is not nice
Ugly is this life.
```

My new dress is made of three scarves
But there's no one whose heart I could win
I square my shoulders every night
And the girls are green with envy.
My top is striped
The sleeves are checked and striped
But they still match.
It's like a nice "Paton" cut.

We have no work to do
Let Otto grieve
That work is not
For Jewish women.
One or two months will pass
And we shall work for ourselves at last.
We won't have to
Get up early
And will be happy
To awake
Everything will be fine
And we shall live happily
With our loved ones.

FASHION
The style of our coats is still the same,
the only change is that we don't put
lining in our spring coats any more. This
way they will hang much better. The binding
gathered in front with different patterns,
polka dots or embroidered monograms, are
very fashionable and they match with the
coat color.

As sunny spring arrives, our woolen blouses
and dresses have brighter and brighter
colors, with striped or checked patterns.
We can even see some handmade pullovers
on aristocrats. Our blouses are widely
different, with beautiful buttons.
Our buttons made of leather camp numbers
are really cute. I recommend the camp
numbers, these are just enough for five
buttons. Try them even if you're not very
good at mathematics.

> If you cut the handle of a basket into
> small pieces, you can make buttons
> from them.
> Women like blunt-toed shoes so much that
> they still wear them.
> Some lucky ladies managed to get summer
> sandals with stripes.

In the evening, Oli wrote to Laci again. Looking up from her diary, she watched her mother light two candles for the fourth day of Passover. Bertha prayed before the candles, and with tears flowing down her face, she asked God to keep Herman and Gabi safe and to bring them all back home again. In their bunks that night, the women heard the sound of gunfire in the distance for the first time. They knew that the Allies must be getting very close.

On the morning of April 4, they were ordered to ready themselves to leave the camp. They were told they would be walking because there was no transportation for them. The guards did not tell them where they were going, but the point of the evacuation clearly was to keep them on the German side of the front. Though frightened by the nearness of the fighting, Oli knew that the occupation of Sömmerda by the Allies, for which she had been praying, was imminent.

The women gathered their paltry belongings, using cloth torn from their mattresses to create makeshift satchels. Oli also had a wire basket, which she used to carry food that she had squirreled away in the previous days: bread, half an onion, some margarine and a huge, extremely moldy carrot. The last was so disgusting that she didn't know whether she could really eat it; but she also knew that the time might come when she, Lilly and Bertha would be hungry enough to devour even a rotting vegetable.

They waited nervously, listening to the sound of distant machine-gun fire. Finally, at 3:00 p.m., the two thousand women prisoners of Sömmerda marched out of the camp. Over their shoulders and on their backs they carried their home-made rucksacks. They wondered whether the front would over-take them before they had traveled very far. After their many months of suffering, they hoped that their journey would soon be at an end, and that deliverance by liberation—rather than death—would finally be theirs.

RECOLLECTION

March 19, 2012

Lilly is dying. She has a few weeks left, maybe only a few days. I talked to her a couple of days ago and promised that I would get her liberated in this book before she died. But it's going to be a close call. I want to be able to read her my account of her liberation. Of how she took off her uniform and put on a German woman's clean dress. Of how she put on lipstick and posed with Oli, as a handsome American soldier took a photograph that now hangs on my wall.

My dad and I were with her only a month ago. We had no idea she was dying. True, she wasn't as well as on our previous visit; then, she had been able to go out to lunch with us and seemed in good shape. She loved being with my kids, and Sam, now twenty, was fantastic with Lilly. Thai children are raised to respect the elderly and Sam's Thai parents had taught him well. He had been constantly by Lilly's side, while Lilly had worn a coy smile—familiar from those old black-and-white photos from Beregszász, back when it was still called Berehovo—that said, "I have a handsome young man on my arm."

Lilly's health had declined precipitously between the two visits, and my dad and I found her looking worse than we had ever seen her. Fluid had gathered around her lungs, and a procedure to aspirate the fluid with a needle was not working. The doctors were saying that surgery might be required, which, at ninety-one, would have been a big risk. We were in "wait and see" mode. A burly young man from the hospital brought in an oxygen tank, and arrangements were being made for twenty-four-hour care. Still, Lilly, my dad and I were able to talk, eat and watch TV together. She had more than enough strength to ask me several times a day when I was going to finally finish the book, and she was able to answer my questions about the camps—her memory sharp as ever. When we said good-bye, she appeared to be stable, and we made plans to visit again in the summer.

The day after we left, she took a turn for the worse, and there was no longer a choice about surgery. When the doctors operated, they found cancerous tumors in her lungs that had almost certainly metastasized throughout her body. The particular cancer that she had is usually caused by exposure to asbestos, so it is more than possible that its seeds had been planted almost seven decades earlier, when she was clearing rubble in Gelsenkirchen. The doctors decided that further diagnostic work was unnecessary, as she was unlikely to survive treatment.

That decision was made three weeks ago. Lilly can still talk on the phone some days when I call, though usually only long enough to tell me that she loves me. I tell her, every time, that I will be finishing the book very soon, and that I will get her liberated while she can still hear me read to her. I go back to my desk, and I write of the crisp dress that smelled wonderfully of soap, of the taste and feel of lipstick on Lilly's lips, and of the doctor with his extraordinary Polaroid camera. She always loved a man with a camera.

March 21, 2012

I have a question for Lilly, but it is too late to ask her. She is still alive, but is rarely coherent, and for the last two days she hasn't spoken. The question is about Oli's birthday on April 1, 1945. On April 2, Lilly wrote in her diary:

> *Saturday I put out all the so-called gifts for Oli's birthday. A dress from you Dad, a slip from Mother, a small [?] from Gabi, flowers (from wire and wool) from [?] on the table. It was a beautiful table with a lot of cake—make believe put together from bread and some saved-up marmalade. The whole barracks was there to wish her a happy birthday.*

As I have explained, Lilly took pains on Oli's and Bertha's birthdays in Sömmerda to make sure that every member of the family was represented by a gift. The question marks from the translator of Lilly's diary mean that the word could not be deciphered, but Oli wrote in her diary that the gift from Gabi was a hand-painted plate and the flowers were from Laci. Oli also mentioned receiving the dress, and in her Shoah interview she told about getting her second diary. The question that I want Lilly to answer is: "How did you manage to acquire the dress and the slip?" I think she might have bartered with civilian laborers at the factory, but this is just a guess. It's possible that Oli would be able to answer the question, but Lilly might never have told her—and even if she had, Oli could well have forgotten this detail. Her birthday arrived at a chaotic time, full of air raids and upheaval, just before they left Sömmerda. Until three weeks ago, I could have called Lilly and asked her, and she almost certainly would have been able to tell me, probably with lots of details about the clever way she went about procuring the clothing. Now I doubt that I will ever know their provenance.

I talked to Lilly's son Tom a couple of days ago. He told me that even though Lilly is asleep most of the time, when she is awake she still tells stories about Berehovo before the war. So I called Tom and his sister Debby today on the off chance that Lilly was awake, or to see if they could ask her about Oli's birthday next time she is talking. But Lilly hasn't spoken more than a couple of words at a time for two days, and it is unlikely that she ever will again. Debby wrote down my question, just in case tomorrow is a better day and Lilly is able to talk. Debby also promised to tell her that, in my book, they are now only three weeks away from liberation.

March 23, 2012

I called Lilly's house. Debby answered and held the phone to Lilly's ear so I could read her the paragraph I had written just before calling. It describes the moment she learned that she was liberated. I have not yet reached the point where she changes into the clean dress.

I had been writing for hours, in prose of poor quality and questionable grammar, to get them out of Sömmerda and into their long march away from the front, through the bloody battle they found themselves in the midst of, and then to their liberation. Cleaning up the writing can wait; I just wanted to reach that moment where she was freed.

As I typed maniacally, I knew that the phone could ring at any moment. It was tempting to skip ahead and just write that one paragraph, but I felt I owed it to Lilly to get all the details down, to tell her whole story up to the moment of her freedom. As soon as I typed the final word, I called Debby and asked her to hold the phone to Lilly's ear. I could hear Lilly's raspy breathing. I told her she was liberated—that I hadn't gotten her home yet, but that she was free—and then I read those last paragraphs. I was crying, and I thought I heard her breathing quicken. Then I told her that I loved her, that she was a hero, and that future generations will read her story and admire her courage. She died a few hours later.

WE GOT THE WATER

Chapter 21
FREEDOM

In March of 1945, a few cracks appeared in the hard, inflexible surface of winter. Spring chipped at the edges of the departing season, temporarily melting the snow under a weak afternoon sun, only to lose the battle at night when winter reasserted itself. By the time April arrived, Gabi was thinner and weaker than he had ever been. He, Mirek and Jacek spent most of their days outdoors; the lingering winter weather was less awful than the grim sights, sounds and smells of the barracks. Others had been dying around them for weeks: every morning a new pile of bodies lay outside each doorway.

The burning horizon told them that the fighting was near. For some weeks the front had seemed to be stalled, but as April progressed it was clearly advancing again. Instead of artillery rumbling in the distance, the prisoners could now hear distinct explosions. Bombers flew overhead, arousing a mix of hope and fear. So far, the planes had not targeted the camp.

One day, as Gabi sat outside with Mirek and Jacek, an open truck with wooden slats on the sides and back pulled up at the gates of the camp. The gates were opened and, as the truck drew to a halt inside, they saw that it was filled with loaves of bread. It seemed like a mirage; they could not believe what they were seeing. Prisoners converged on the truck from all directions, pushing and shoving each other to get to the food. Gabi decided that the bread wasn't worth the risk of getting caught up in the mass of rushing men. He was unlikely to be hungry for long: the front was approaching and he reckoned that, very soon, he would either be liberated or be dead. Jacek and Mirek had come to the same conclusion: the three boys stepped back as the crowd surged past.

A German soldier got out of the truck and climbed up onto

the siding. He shouted at the prisoners to stay away, but the men paid no attention to him. As several prisoners started to mount the truck, he fired his gun into the air. Almost everyone immediately backed away, but two men still clung to the side. The soldier aimed his gun at the closer of the two, who had just taken hold of a loaf, and fired. The prisoner fell from the truck with a bullet in his head.

Gabi was stunned. He had seen many people die and had witnessed repeated brutalities, yet—perhaps surprisingly—this was the first time he had seen anyone killed outright. The murder had its desired effect: the prisoners backed away, though they still pushed and fought one another as the bread was distributed. Gabi and his friends remained on the periphery. There was clearly not enough bread for everyone. Each loaf looked to be three or four days' worth of rations, and the boys craved the unexpected allowance as much as anyone. Yet it just wasn't worth fighting for. They left empty-handed and returned to where they had been sitting.

Each morning, Gabi, Jacek and Mirek woke early and walked around the perimeter of the camp. At one point the boundary fence passed close to the SS kitchen and, as they made their rounds one morning, they noticed that the kitchen garbage pile on the other side of the fence was growing. If it were not collected soon, the refuse—which included a rising mound of potato peels—would stretch almost to the fence. That day and the next, the boys anxiously watched the area. On the third morning, the peels were within reach. In accordance with the plan they had formulated over the previous days, they split up and searched the barracks for the discarded wire belts of dead prisoners. Before long, they had enough wire to fashion the tool they needed.

Knowing that they could be shot or beaten for stealing the peels, Gabi and his friends hid behind the barracks nearest the kitchen, where the soldiers in the guard tower couldn't see them. They twisted the pieces together, building in plenty of overlap for strength. The tool had to be long enough to reach from their hiding place, across five meters of open space, through the fence, and then over to the potato peels. They bent one end to form a sharp hook and inched it slowly toward the fence—any sudden movement might catch the attention of the guards. They edged the hook under the bottom layer of barbed wire, pushed it deep into the pile and then gently, carefully, pulled it back, dragging a few peels toward them.

They continued like this for about an hour, until they had a handful of peels each. They brought the contraband back to the barracks and laid the peels on one of the stoves to cook. The potato sizzled on the hot metal and the aroma was, in their starved state, extraordinary. The other prisoners noticed what was happening, but no one challenged the three boys or attempted to take their food. The boys turned the slices to brown them on both sides, trying not to burn their fingers. When they finally put the potatoes into their mouths, they were overwhelmed by the flavor and extremely proud of their resourcefulness. As they ate, they placed new peels on the stove, cooking and eating until they had exhausted their supplies.

The next morning they were able to repeat the process. The morning after that, they emerged from the barracks and went again to see if the pile was still there. What they saw made them forget about potatoes completely. The guard towers were empty and the guards were nowhere to be seen. Cautiously, the boys approached the front gates of the camp. For months they had worried that the SS might exterminate the inmates of the camp before the front arrived, and they were extremely apprehensive about these new and unexpected circumstances. The gates, as usual, were chained shut. There were no guards anywhere.

In the far distance they could see a man on horseback leading a second horse; Gabi squinted to try to make out the soldier's uniform. He asked Mirek and Jacek if they thought he was a German. They replied that his uniform appeared to be the wrong color for a German soldier. All three stared as the horseman drew closer. Mirek was the first to notice the red star on the soldier's cap. Bursting into tears, he told the others that the man was a Russian soldier.

Gabi stared in disbelief. It felt as unreal as the moment when the cattle car doors opened at Auschwitz. By the time the horseman reached the gate, all three boys were crying. Mirek and Jacek, who spoke a little Russian, learned that the Germans had fled and the Russians had taken control of the territory. The soldier pulled out his pistol and took aim at the padlock on the gate. With one blast, the lock shattered and fell to the ground. The soldier yanked the chain away and threw the gates open.

Gabi and his two friends ran from barracks to barracks as fast as they could on their skinny legs. In every language they could muster they shouted, "We're free! We're free! The Russians are here!" Within moments, the newly liberated men were gathering outside—some walking, others crawling, their ability to celebrate limited by illness and starvation.

More soldiers arrived, along with trucks bringing food. The trucks were mobbed as bread and soup—real soup—was distributed. Once again, Gabi, Mirek and Jacek decided to bide their time and avoid the crowd. Those who had received food were eating so much, so fast, that Gabi worried about them. It seemed dangerous to consume such large quantities after so many months of deprivation.

The boys went back to the entrance and watched the Red Cross set up tables outside the gate. They were told that everyone would have to be seen by a doctor before leaving. When it was Gabi's turn to be examined, the doctor told him that he had a high fever, and diagnosed typhus. Gabi had not even realized that he was sick. The doctor judged Gabi's condition serious enough to require hospitalization, so he wrote a prescription, then pointed at a nearby table with medicines. Beyond the table was a waiting truck that would take him to the hospital. But Gabi had no intention of boarding the truck. According to the doctor, medication was being dispensed at every train station, so Gabi decided to head straight for home, collecting his drugs along the way. He picked up an initial packet of medicine from the table and went back to join his friends.

Gabi, Mirek and Jacek headed toward the town. Because they were among the first to leave the camp, they walked through empty streets. The homes closest to the camp, which had housed SS officers and guards, were now largely deserted. So it was a surprise when a window opened and a German woman leaned out and handed them a large chunk of bread—real bread, dusted with real flour, and smothered with sweet marmalade. They divided it and ate it hungrily.

The next few houses appeared to be empty. Mirek stopped in front of one and announced that he was going in. Jacek joined him while Gabi waited outside. A few moments later, an upstairs window opened and Mirek leaned out. Clothing and shoes rained down on Gabi as Mirek emptied a bedroom closet. Gabi picked up a pair of brown pants and some leather shoes that he thought might fit him. He slipped off his worn clogs and peeled away the cardboard that wrapped his feet. Now the house was raining food, so Gabi picked up a bag of sugar. He looked at it in wonder, thinking it was the most precious thing he had held in his hands for many months.

Joining the others inside, Gabi found the bathroom, where he turned on the shower and felt the water. It was warm. He stripped off his clothes and stepped under the showerhead. None of the last hours had seemed truly real to him. But as hot water ran down his body and he washed himself with scented soap, his new existence began to sink in. He was no longer a prisoner.

He dried off with a towel—his first in a year—and put on the pants and shoes. He looked at his discarded uniform and wondered whether he should wear his worn, striped shirt all the way home, so that everyone could see what had been done to him. But then he stamped his foot down on his old clothes, over and over, until he was performing a triumphant little dance. No. He had survived. They—the Nazis, the SS— had lost, and he had won.

Gabi found Mirek and Jacek raiding the kitchen. He told them that he was going to find the train station and try to get home. His friends did not have as far to travel, so they were going to stay near the camp in the hope of finding a ride. They said their farewells. Jacek and Mirek had been like brothers to Gabi, and he knew that he was unlikely ever to see them again. But home was waiting, and he had to find out what had happened to the rest of his family.

Carrying his precious bag of sugar, Gabi pulled a shirt from the pile of clothes outside the house and headed in the direction from which he had heard train whistles in the past. It was not hard to find the station. Soon a train pulled in, but it was heading in the wrong direction. An hour later a train of cattle cars arrived. Through the open doors Gabi could see other liberated prisoners, still in their striped uniforms, as well as men who appeared to be POWs. He asked which way the train was heading, and was told it was going east. Gabi jumped aboard.

The women had been marching from their camp in Sömmerda for days. They walked eastward, led by guards on motorcycles. Resting was not an option; anyone who could not keep up was shot and left by the roadside. There were no rations. They had only the little food they were able to carry with them when they left the camp. The moldy carrot was eaten—Oli shared it with Lilly, Bertha and some of the other girls. Oli's wire basket grew too heavy after the first couple of days, so she left it in a ditch, taking the remaining scraps of food with her. Each night the women were allowed to rest in farmers' barns along the way. If they were lucky, the farmer threw in some fresh hay for them to sleep on. They were awakened while it was still dark. Each morning, many felt that it was impossible to continue, yet somehow they got up and joined the others. Estimates of how far they were walking varied, but the women guessed they were averaging about twelve to fourteen kilometers a day.

They walked in their sleep, trying to keep up a sufficient pace to avoid notice. If they slowed down too much, a guard screamed at them to speed up. Those who failed to respond quickly enough felt the sting of a leather strap on their backs. Oli and Lilly were terribly worried about Bertha's condition; she often seemed on the verge of collapse. Anxiously, they watched their mother's muddied face, barely visible beneath the sweaty locks that hung down in front of her eyes, to make sure she was well enough to go on. They had already relieved her of the little she had been carrying, and they took turns holding her hand and dragging her behind them. In their desperation, they discarded almost all of their belongings.

Some days it poured with rain. Other days were so hot that their woolen dresses hung heavy with sweat. Miserable as they were, they couldn't help but notice the beauty that spring was bringing to the Thuringia hills. The trees burst with color, and picturesque villas with beautiful gardens were visible from the road. Increasingly, they also encountered evidence of the war, a stark contrast to the natural serenity of the surroundings. In the first days of their march, they had seen many pristine villages, but now they were walking through devastation and ruins. They passed other prisoners, as well as refugees fleeing from the encroaching front. Bombers often flew low overhead, causing the women to hurl themselves into roadside ditches until the planes had passed.

Oli described the scene a week later in her diary:

Oli's Diary, April 20, 1945:

Almost every day several bombers and planes with machine guns flew over us and whenever it happened we lay down on our stomach in the trench scared to death and praying for our lives. Only God could save us and he did. If we had been seen from the

*airplanes, we would have been taken for soldiers and
none of us would have survived. We were in danger
all the way, several times we could hear bombs
exploding in the neighborhood. Everywhere we go
there are bombed houses, the fields are full of craters,
on the roads you can see destroyed German military
trucks, the bridges fell into the rivers, the factories are
demolished, there's not even one single intact house,
or peaceful place, you can only see the horrible
traces of war and death.*

After a week of walking, the prisoners arrived in Altenburg, at a camp with both male and female inmates. Lilly, Oli and Bertha were assigned with some other women from Sömmerda to a block where the roof was partially caved-in from bombing. They huddled inside, while bombs fell nearby and planes strafed the area with machine-gun fire. With each new barrage, they were convinced that they would not survive.

Two days later, they were ordered to march once more, now being allowed only four hours a night for sleep. A few days after that, they were ordered to continue walking through the night with no rest at all. The darkness that night was so complete that the women in front were nothing more than vague, bent shadows. Occasionally, there was light from a burning military truck, or from electrical poles and wires that had caught fire. Much of the time they could not hear one another over the artillery and the detonation of bombs. The acrid smells of destruction filled their nostrils.

As a thin band of grey began to appear on the horizon, the women saw that they were entering the town of Glauchau. Oli felt strangely agitated, sure that something was about to happen. Lilly pointed to distant houses where they could see white sheets of surrender hanging from the windows. Without warning, the motorcycle that had been leading their procession turned around and raced back past them, the sound of its motor diminishing in the distance. A German munitions truck stopped nearby and Oli saw a soldier jump off and disappear among the houses.

Suddenly, planes were flying low overhead and machine-gun fire was blasting around them. The women dove into the trench by the side of the road. Lilly flattened herself against the ground, with her friend Éva on one side of her, and Oli and Bertha on the other. As the machine-gun fire abated, Éva started to get up—and was struck in the head by a stray bullet. She died instantly. Lilly was convinced she would be next.

When the gunfire finally stopped, Oli grabbed Bertha and ran to a nearby fence, pulling her mother behind her. Lilly followed. Oli jumped the fence and pulled Bertha over while Lilly pushed her up from the other side. Lilly had just started to climb the fence when the planes returned and the machine-gun fire started again. She ran back, threw herself into the ditch, and covered her head with her arms. With unexpected calm, she thought to herself: *This is where I'm going to die.* Oli and her mother had made it to safety, she was sure. They had survived and they would go home. At that moment, the thought that Oli and Bertha would live was all that mattered to her.

Oli and Bertha ran to the nearest cellar, but the door was locked. Over another fence they had better luck: a cellar door was open. Oli guided Bertha down the stairs, then ran back to help Lilly. During a momentary lull in the firing, she climbed the fence again and ran to the ditch. Lilly felt a hand on her back and heard her sister shouting her name. Oli tugged her by the arm, yelling for her to get up. Lilly followed Oli over the fences, and down into the cellar to join Bertha, where the three of them hid for the next two hours. The sound of cannon fire told them that this was more than an air raid. A battle was raging outside, in which the fate of the town was clearly in the balance.

During another pause in the fighting, they heard the sound of steps on the cellar stairs. A man appeared and ordered the three women to leave. They crossed the street to another house, but were again denied entry. Crying, Lilly and Oli begged the inhabitants to at least let their mother in, to no avail. They sat on the front steps of the house, weeping, not knowing what to do. More women joined them, seeking shelter from the fighting, but too frightened by the sporadic gunfire to venture far from the immediate area.

As day turned to early evening, a man approached them. He told them that he was the owner of the house they had been turned out of earlier, and that he was overruling the wishes of his tenant. They were welcome to shelter in his cellar. He also relayed the news that the Americans had taken a bridge in the city. Twenty-four women crowded down the cellar stairs and through the laundry room. The smell of soap and clean clothes was both strange and familiar to Lilly and Oli, conjuring memories of home and doing laundry with their mother.

The fighting went on and on. They knew that, at any moment, a bomb could bring the two-story house down on top of them. Nearby explosions shattered the cellar windows as the women lay huddled on top of each other. From time to time a middle-aged German woman came in with food, which they ate gratefully. During the second night of the battle, they heard tanks passing on the main road. Then, the following morning there was unaccustomed quiet. The cellar door opened and the German woman came down the steps. "It's over," she said. "You are free."

The women ran to the broken windows, where Oli and Lilly saw a young man in the street. They recognized his uniform at once: he was an American soldier. Two dozen former prisoners climbed the cellar steps and followed the German woman through her home and outside. American soldiers were carrying the injured and dead from the ditch by the road. Only when all of the women had emerged from the nearby houses was it possible to take stock of who had survived. Oli and Lilly's good friend from home, Ilona, had died in the gutter. Like Éva, she had endured all the hardships of the camps, only to die in the final hours before liberation.

Several American soldiers approached the women to ask if there was anything they needed. Oli knew some English and asked one of the soldiers for food. Though she was hungry, the first thing Lilly wanted was a toothbrush, so she told Oli to ask for one. The soldier smiled at her request and came back shortly afterwards with canned army rations; he hadn't been able to obtain a toothbrush. The sisters brought the food back to the house and ate the rations together with milk and more food provided by the German woman, who introduced herself as Gerta. The Germans in nearby houses were ordered to shelter and feed the former prisoners. Gerta invited Lilly, Oli, Bertha and a few others to stay with her.

Later that day, Lilly, Oli and another young woman named Sára walked into the town. At a small bridge they met two soldiers, who also gave them some food. Oli asked them where their military kitchen was, in the hope that they could eat there the next day. After the soldiers gave them directions, the women returned to the house, laughing and joking about the good-looking Americans. Local shops were ordered to provide the newly freed women with toiletries and other goods that they needed. Lilly finally got her toothbrush. In the afternoon, Lilly, Oli and Bertha took their first bath since leaving their home in Beregszász, luxuriating in the warm soapy water, washing their hair and drying themselves with proper towels. That night they slept in white linen.

The next day, Oli and Lilly, dressed in their clean grey uniforms, followed the directions they had been given to a large villa, where many of the soldiers were now billeted. The house was both enormous and charming; it was clear why the Americans had chosen it for their headquarters. The sisters approached three soldiers who were standing out in front. They explained to one of them, who looked as if he might be Jewish, that their mother was with them in the village and that they did not have enough food. He went off in search of rations for them. While he was gone, Oli and Lilly struck up a conversation with the other two soldiers. One was named Jack, while the other, who had a red cross on his sleeve, introduced himself as "Doc." They told Lilly and Oli to come back at three o'clock when there would be more food available. Lilly was quite taken with Doc. He was handsome and kind; Lilly wished that she weren't dressed in such horrible camp clothes.

The first soldier returned with a generous package of provisions, including canned food, Hershey's chocolate, white bread, soap and cigarettes. When Lilly and Oli returned to the house, proud and happy about their acquisitions, they found Bertha and Gerta talking at the table like old friends. The heads of the two older women were nearly touching and both had tears in their eyes as they consoled each other over the hardships they had endured. But they brightened when Lilly and Oli unpacked their riches on the dining-room table. The chocolate was pure heaven, a forgotten taste from a world they had left long ago, while the white bread was what bread should be: soft and moist, not the dry bricks they had been eating for almost a year.

At three o'clock they returned to the villa, where they found Jack and Doc waiting for them. Doc asked Lilly and Oli to follow him. Lilly hesitated, but Doc had such a kind face, and besides—after all that they had been through—she was confident that they could handle difficult situations. Doc led them into a large yard where about twenty-five soldiers were standing. A serious-looking officer entered, called the men to order, and led them in a series of exercises, in which they sang to the rhythm of their movement. Oli and Lilly found this all very entertaining, just as Doc had anticipated they would.

The men were dismissed and, in the silence that followed, Oli and Lilly could hear a piano being played somewhere nearby. Both sighed. Doc asked them what was the matter and, when they told him they were piano players, he invited them to go inside and play. The three of them walked through the beautiful gardens and into the villa. The furniture was magnificent and the rooms were enormous. Doc led them up a carpeted staircase to a huge room that contained a black baby grand piano. As had been the case during much of the past twenty-four hours, Oli was having trouble believing that any of this was actually happening. She took her seat at the piano, but hesitated, unsure what to play. Then an old French tune came into her head, so she started with that. Next, she selected a piece that she knew from one of the music books lying nearby—Liszt's "Harmonies du soir." She performed as if the events of the last year had never occurred, as if she were still at home playing in her own living room.

Lilly sat down next to Doc to listen. As Oli played, Lilly looked more closely at the medic. He was a handsome and serious young man, with brown hair, lovely eyes and a mustache. Though he was clearly engrossed in the music, Lilly could tell when he turned to look at her that he was interested in her as well.

Soldiers came in from the exercise yard and began to gather around the piano, until the room was filled with men listening to Oli play. Some had tears in their eyes. When she played the final chords of "Harmonies," the soldiers broke into applause. Oli felt a joy and pride that she had not known for more than a year. Doc and Jack told the sisters that they could take anything they wanted from the house. "They've taken so much from you," said Doc, "so you should have whatever you want." The house, which had belonged to a wealthy industrialist, was filled with beautiful crystals and porcelain figures, but these did not interest Oli and Lilly. Mostly they still wanted food.

They were also desperate to get out of their uniforms. The men found clothes that had presumably belonged to the industrialist's wife, and Lilly and Oli each picked out a dress, along with sandals and silk undergarments. Before Oli changed her clothes, Doc took a photograph in which Lilly is smiling in her new civilian outfit, while Oli is still in her prison clothes, looking sad. After he snapped the picture, Oli also went to change.

It was not merely a joy to dress in real clothes again: throwing away their horrible uniforms and their terrible wooden shoes was a deliverance.

Doc and Jack went to dinner and promised to return with food. True to their word, they were soon back with many delicacies. Oli and Lilly feasted on beef, potatoes, peas and corn, and even some pineapple, accompanied by soft white bread with orange jam. Most wonderful of all was the coffee: real coffee made from real beans! The two men then walked them home.

On the way, Jack and Doc told them a little about their lives. They were younger than Lilly and Oli—only twenty and twenty-one. Jack made them laugh with his terrific sense of humor. He was fun and cute as a puppy, Lilly thought, and clearly smitten with Oli. Doc, like Jack, was married, but had lived with his new wife for only three weeks before shipping out to Europe. He had since learned that she had been cheating on him and planned to divorce her when he got back home. Remarkably, home was Scranton, Pennsylvania, where Lilly and Oli's Uncle Manny lived; they still remembered the address that their father had made them commit to memory on the train. When they got back to Gerta's house, they introduced the young men to their mother. Jack and Doc presented the older women with oranges and chocolates, and Doc promised Bertha he would get word to her brother as soon as he could that she and her daughters were still alive.

Oli's Diary, April 20, 1945:

I sleep in a white bed as long as I want and the owners of the house give me everything. We get excellent food and we aren't hungry any more as the American soldiers provide us with everything that's necessary. But we are still sad, we long to see Dad and Gabika more than ever. That's what we wish for, another miracle to see Dad and Gabika again and then we can forget about all the evil. God, please, let this miracle happen. Prisoners arrive from everywhere, now we have the priority, we are considered even more important than the German population. They are hiding now just like we did when the Germans came. There are piles of German arms and helmets in the streets. They are all burned by the Americans, only the ashes remain of these glorious arms. The houses are full of holes made by machine-guns, the windows are smashed and you can see thousands of English cartridges and cannonballs in the streets. That's how the town of Glachau and all Germany looks today. The German eagles, the flags with the swastika and the pictures of the Führer have been taken down, nobody promotes German victory any more and no more lifted hands celebrate German victory and the evil theories of Hitlerism. The German arms backfired and after all the murders, pillage and tyranny the young American troops have arrived and taken the white flag. Hopefully this white flag will soon be fluttering above Berlin, Prague and the other cities. Then we can take the train to see our home again and I hope that we shall meet Dad, Gabika and You, Lacika because You will also be there waiting for me as you used to do.

Chapter 22
HOME

Gabi continued east, sometimes in cattle cars and sometimes in freight trains, accompanied by other former prisoners making their way home. Some had been prisoners of war, others had been in concentration camps; all, like Gabi, had survived a horrendous ordeal. Their gaunt faces and emaciated physiques testified to the brutality and deprivation they had suffered, although the former POWs generally appeared to be in better shape.

At various stops along the way, Gabi disembarked to obtain food and more medication. At the stations, he saw trains filled with happy Russian soldiers. They carried treasures looted from the homes of Germans: artwork, lamps and furniture stuck out from the windows of the trains. There had not yet been an official surrender, but it was clear that the war was effectively over. At one station, Gabi was able to obtain a formal document attesting to the fact that he was a camp survivor. Below his name, which was displayed prominently at the top, it listed the camps he had been in and his prisoner number. The information was in four different languages, so that he could travel freely.

As the train crossed from Germany into Czechoslovakia, Gabi became increasingly apprehensive about his return. As he passed through the Czech countryside, he continued to feel a mixture of astonishment and joy at his recent liberation, but also a gnawing fear that he would be the only one in his family to make it home. It had been so difficult for him to survive—and there had been so many instances where luck had been on his side—that it was hard to be optimistic about his mother or sisters having lived through the last year. He had no idea what he would do if he was alone in the world.

And then, while waiting in line for some food at a station,

Gabi felt a tap on his shoulder. He turned around to see a young, thin woman in a striped dress. "Are you Gabi Klein?" she asked.

"How can you recognize me?" he asked, indicating his wasted body.

"I went to school with your sisters," she said, "and I have good news for you. I was in the camp with your mother and sisters, and we were liberated together by the Americans. They survived!"

Gabi was elated as he rode the next train. The loneliness of the past year, which had persisted even after his liberation, suddenly evaporated. This was beyond any realistic hope: his mother, Lilly, Oli, all still alive. He imagined that very few survivors could be so lucky. Although he was almost certain that his father must have been killed on their first day at Auschwitz, Gabi continued to ask other liberated prisoners whether they had seen Herman Klein during their captivity. No one had. Gabi knew that he was unlikely ever to see his father again. But now, for the first time since he arrived at Auschwitz, he knew he was not alone: he had his mother, and he had his sisters.

Buoyed by this knowledge, and fortified by the nourishment and medicine he received at the stations, Gabi felt himself growing stronger with each hour of travel. On the final train to Beregszász, he drank in every image as they passed through the outskirts of town, then scanned the waiting faces as the train pulled into the station. George! George was standing on the platform looking intently at the arriving passengers. George's friend Csányi Donat was standing next to him. Gabi yelled to George and saw the surprise register on his face.

As soon as Gabi was off the train, he told George and Csányi the news about Lilly, Oli and Bertha. George was taken aback by Gabi's appearance. He had always been a skinny child but now, George thought, he looked like a toothpick. George told him that he was the first of the family to return. He also told him that the Kleins' home had been stripped bare. Even the doorknobs had been stolen. George's house had been emptied too, so he was staying in his family's hotel; he invited Gabi to stay there with him. Csányi, who had recently returned from the camps himself, also offered Gabi a room—in *his* family's hotel—but Gabi wanted to be with George.

On the way to the hotel, George explained to Gabi that when he had arrived home several months ago, in the dead of winter, all of the Jews of Beregszász were gone. In the past weeks, people had begun to return from the camps, telling terrible stories of what had happened. George had feared that he would never see anyone from his family or from Lilly's family again. So far, he had no news of his mother or his brother, Frank. He wasn't optimistic about his mother's chances, but still harbored hopes that Frank was alive.

In the days that followed, Gabi was nursed back to health by George and Csányi. With the news that Lilly was definitely coming home, their respective plans to marry her had been rekindled. Gabi was the beneficiary; both young men wanted Lilly to be impressed by the care they had bestowed on her brother. Together they kept him well fed.

Meanwhile, George prepared a room in his house for Lilly, Oli and Bertha. He managed to scavenge some old furniture and fixed up one of the empty rooms to provide at least a minimal level of comfort. He wanted to be sure that they came to stay in his house rather than in Csányi's hotel, where a room was also waiting for them. Gabi, George, and Csányi went to meet every train. Laci—who had been thrilled to learn of Oli's survival—joined them whenever he wasn't at work outside of Beregszász. George watched every passing window for his mother and brother, or even a cousin, aunt or uncle. No one from his family returned home.

While Gabi was making his way to Beregszász, Oli and Lilly were still in Germany, paying regular visits to the villa to play the piano and visit Jack and Doc, who continued to provide them with food. Every evening the two young men would walk them home. The women were not yet permitted to travel, so they simply enjoyed their new freedom and the affections of the soldiers. Though Lilly and Oli were quite taken with Doc and Jack, they remained faithful to their boyfriends back home. As a safety net, they told the men that they were married. Lilly did admit to her father in her diary that Doc had asked her for "a few kisses," but she does not say whether she complied with the request.

Above all, Oli and Lilly wanted to go home, but they had to wait until the Americans could arrange safe transportation for them. Incredibly, the Germans still had not surrendered, and fighting continued to the east. Oli and Lilly didn't know how long they would be delayed, but they knew their ordeal would not truly be over until the whole family was reunited.

Jack and Doc were transferred to a town about twenty kilometers away, but continued to visit Lilly, Oli and Bertha. Their visits had to be short: the walk took two hours and they could not be away from their base for long. In the rest of their time, the sisters busied themselves with sewing. They enjoyed having colorful, soft material to work with, and getting their thread from a spool instead of from the fringe of their uniforms.

Oli's Diary, April 30, 1945:

I'm sitting in the nice and clean kitchen of our landlady wondering what You can be doing on this Sunday afternoon. It's about 5 o'clock. At this time You usually put on something nice and go out somewhere, to a cinema or to a confectionery. I often ask myself if You still grieve for me or think about me and the only thing I can imagine is that there has been nobody else in your life ever since I was taken away and you are still waiting for the day when I come back to You. Maybe it's not true, maybe I will be bitterly disappointed, still this is the only way I can imagine You. Whenever

*I remember your love, the way you behaved in the
ghetto and everything you gave me before we parted
I can't believe that anything or anybody could change
your deep emotions for me. That's what gave me hope
in captivity, and that's what gives me hope during
the happy hours of liberation. I don't want to talk
about what I feel when I think about Dad and Gabika
because I would be unable to express it. My heart
is bleeding even more after the liberation than in the
camp. I heard a lot of bad news about the SS having
destroyed several camps before the Americans
arrived. I'm optimistic by nature and I believe in God,
so I don't want to believe all this horrible news and I
hope and firmly believe that God will help Dad and
Gabika, too.*

Oli decided to write a final short edition of the "Grey Papers." She wanted to finish her task and deliver on her promise that the fourth edition would be circulated in freedom.

```
GREY PAPER - ISSUE No. IV

Ladies, it is not a trick,
Neither a sham, believe me.
This is the fourth issue of our paper
And my dear Johnny is sitting by my side.

The camp leader is kicked in the ass,
Otto is discarded
Ristis has vanished
No one is left from the gang.

No more aufstehen and no more appell
We can sleep until we want to
I don't care about carrots or potatoes
I want English canned food.

I won't write reports anymore
Because I'm going home
Farewell dear comrades
Don't forget about us.
```

For several days, Doc and Jack failed to show. Lilly and Oli worried about them. They knew there were only two reasons they would have stopped visiting: either they were prohibited from leaving the base, or they had moved again, perhaps to the front lines. There were rumors that the Germans had pushed back the front, and the women were all terrified of being recaptured. However, they soon learned that this was untrue. On May 1 there was another rumor—that Hitler had been killed while fighting the Russians in Berlin. Over the next couple of days, more details reached them about Hitler's demise and the end of the Nazis.

Lilly's Diary, May 3, 1945:

We are still here—but just for a few more days. The Americans are going to take us by trucks—about 100 km. from here—where they are going to put us on a train. Last week we were given clothing rations for shoes. We are sewing dresses, etc. Yesterday the radio said that Hitler died—a heroic death fighting against the Russians in Berlin. He sure didn't deserve this easy kind of death. They say that Berlin fell today. I have such a terrible tension in me. Everything is fine but I have such a longing for you, Dad, and Gabi. I would like to fly home like a bird and see you both at once. Please God let both of them be well.

Oli's Diary, May 3, 1945:

We have been preparing to go all week. It's probable that we shall leave one day but it's always delayed. They say that we'll be collected somewhere and then taken home as soon as the road towards Beregszász is open.

I'm longing to go home. I'm fed up with doing nothing, I would like to be at home so much and live like I used to do.

*The Russians are already in Berlin and the greatest
news is that the Führer died on 1 May. One year ago
we may have been shouting with joy but Hitler's death
is too late now, after millions and millions of innocent
people have died due to his cruelty and inhumanity.
It's a pity that he died in such a simple way. Of course
we know that he didn't die a glorious death but he
should have gone through all the suffering of the world
first and only then should he have been killed like a
dog because there was so much innocent blood on
his hands. The Germans have changed sides and
now they talk about the Führer with hatred because
he has brought Germany to ruins, their houses have
been bombed and their children have been killed. A
few months ago however they trusted Hitler and his
theories implicitly and they greeted each other with
"Heil Hitler" in the streets.*

*By now they have woken up from their poisonous
dream, now they can see clearly all the theories of
their Führer that led to destruction and slough. The
great words of "Mein Kampf" have proved to be
untrue and Hitlerism has lost all its roots with the
death of Hitler . . . It makes my blood boil whenever I
think about what happened in the past. I can't believe
what I've gone through, I can't believe that mothers
were separated from their children, that 2-3-week
old babies were left alone, that millions of people
perished in the crematoria within a few hours, that
the most beautiful ornament of women, their long and
wavy hair, fell in the dust in an instant, that we lived
as prisoners for a year, our heads were bald, we were
wearing prisoners' clothes, we were starving and
we were cold. We can never pay it back, there's no
adequate punishment for it and this kind of treatment
is unprecedented in history. I think that this era will be
described in history books with even more horror than
the Spanish inquisition.*

When several more days had passed without any sign of Doc or Jack, Lilly and a few other women decided to walk up to the soldiers' camp. Oli was not feeling well and did not think she was up to the twenty-kilometer journey, so she stayed in the house with her mother. Though it was a long walk, it was a beautiful spring day and Lilly did not feel tired at all. She was wearing real shoes, and the sensation of strolling in comfort and without fear was still novel. Lilly did not expect to see Doc—she didn't have his address and the town was full of soldiers—but in fact the first group of men she met knew where he was. She and one of the other women got a ride to where he was staying. When he came outside and Lilly saw his face, she knew he was in love with her. He couldn't speak, and his eyes were full of tears. He explained that Jack was being punished and couldn't leave, and that he had been transferred to a medical facility that required him to be there most of the time. Doc took the two women to see Jack, who could not hide his disappointment that Oli was not with them. Right then and there, he wrote Oli a letter for Lilly to deliver.

The next day, Doc was able to leave the base and visit. Jack, unfortunately, was still confined to his post. Lilly, Oli and Doc found a beautiful meadow where they had a picnic. Doc had brought his camera and Oli took pictures of him with Lilly. Inevitably, the conversation turned to the fact that the two women would be leaving soon. Saying that it would be terrible if he and Jack came to say goodbye and they were already gone, Doc promised that both of them would come back the next day.

At six o'clock the next morning, May 18, the women were awakened and told that they had to be at the train station in ninety minutes. Lilly and Oli could do no more than scribble hurried notes of goodbye to their American boyfriends. Bertha said a tearful farewell to Gerta and the three of them hurried to the station. They boarded their train but had been traveling for only a few hours when they were forced to stop because the tracks ahead had been bombed. Sitting outside in the hot sun,

Lilly imagined that at that very moment Doc and Jack might be arriving at the house, after having walked for hours in the heat. She saw the smiles on their faces disappearing as they reached the house, only to find two envelopes waiting on the doorstep. Her heart ached for them and for the days that they had spent together. Now she had to face what lay ahead—returning to a life perhaps without her father, her brother, and George. She prayed that they would be there.

Two days later, Oli wrote about their trip:

Oli's Diary, May 20, 1945:

The train arrived at Glauchau station. Red Cross trains crowded with wounded people are slowly advancing to the interior of the country. The surviving sons of Germany are going home with these trains, without arms and legs, some of them have only their trunk left. Their eyes are scared and abnormal, their look reflects all the horrors they've gone through which ruined their nerves and they are gazing vacantly. They must have regretted that they had blind faith in the Führer and it would have been better to stop the war earlier and not to be heading for disaster. There are corpses in blankets on the bumpers and there's a contagious, unhealthy smell everywhere at the station, we can hardly wait to go on.

Now the train is taking us on a romantic route again, through the town of Heinsberg, to arrive in the badly damaged covered station of Dresden.

The train is going slowly among smoky ruins and only the chimneys tell you that there used to be houses. The factories that once produced the world famous iron, coal, stockings, cocoa and chocolate are now only deep craters with grey smoke, the rails are broken up, the trains and the engines are lying shot to pieces at the huge station. My God, is this the beautiful, huge Dresden? Was there ever life in these

*burning ruins, was there a library that used to be
visited by foreigners and mentioned even in history
books? Was there a famous theatre and a beautiful
castle?*

*Today everything is in ruins, and it's the irony of fate
that the only intact wall of a destroyed house says,
"Sieg Wird Unser Sein" (The Final Victory is Ours).*

Their homeward journey proved frustrating and difficult.
There were frequent lengthy delays because so many tracks had
been destroyed. Often they had to leave their train, walk around
a bombed-out bridge, and then wait for hours on the other
side until another train arrived. Sometimes they walked long
distances, and once they had to wade across a river. At some
point, they passed from territory occupied by the Americans
and British to land that was controlled by the Soviet Union.
Lilly, Oli and Bertha were afraid of the Russian soldiers. They
met women on the trains who spoke of rapes they had heard
about, witnessed, or of which they had been the victim. Whenever the train stopped, the three women stayed close together.

The trains were filled with former prisoners returning home.
Lilly and Oli asked everyone they met whether they had seen a
Herman or Gabi Klein from Beregszász. With each person who
responded in the negative, they became more and more dis-
heartened. Still, they knew that the camps had been spread far
and wide, so they held on to the hope that Herman and Gabi
were somewhere out there, also making their way home. And
then, on May 22, they received terrible news: a man at one of
the stations told them that he had known Gabi, and that Gabi
had died. Beside themselves with grief, the sisters nonetheless
managed to hide this news from their mother, and clung to the
hope that the man might have been wrong. After all, they told
each other, there were several Gabi Kleins from Beregszász.

The next day, which was the eve of Lilly's twenty-fifth
birthday, they received better news. They met a man who told

them that he had been liberated with Gabi. This news, either because it was relayed in greater detail or simply because it was what they wanted to believe, seemed more credible to them, and they shared it with Bertha. But of Herman there continued to be no word. As they got closer to their destination, their fellow passengers were increasingly people from Beregszász; but still they met no one who had seen Herman since the day of his arrival at Auschwitz.

Oli's Diary, May 24, 1945:

The railway bridge next to Valevska Mezirici was mined and exploded by the Germans when they retreated so we couldn't continue our journey by train. We relaxed for a day then crossed the bridge and after elbowing our way we managed to get on a crammed train with people everywhere, on its top and on the engine as well. Hardly did we travel 30 km when we had to get off again because we had no train from Velky Karlovic. We spent the night in a school with Russian female and male soldiers.

Now we are sitting in an inn with our packs and are trying to get a cart to be able to go on. Maybe we shall have to walk to Zilina. I heard that unfortunately the Germans have destroyed the railway and the bridges, otherwise we would have arrived home a long time ago. We are together with a lot of Slovak passengers. Unfortunately they are quite unpleasant fellows because they still harbor a prejudice against Jews.

I think that the Jewish question will never be completely solved and I often wonder how we could continue our lives without facing the same old Jewish problems. This past year has been enough for a lifetime, I'd like to spend the rest of my life in peace.

From Velky Karlovice we took a cart and then a car to Mokov where we learnt that there was no railway at all in Slovakia and we had to continue our journey on foot. A lieutenant talked us out of walking home saying that it wouldn't make sense etc., etc. so we went back to Kromerizya with military carts. It took three days. We met a lot of friendly soldiers in the Czech legion who were very kind to us. We spent one night in a monastery where the nuns weren't too tidy. It was awfully dirty, there were fleas etc. so we got away the next day. A young, 18-year-old, kind Czech soldier supported us and he rented a nice and cozy room at a timber-merchant. We stayed there for two days and I can't tell how kind the owners, a Czech family, were to us. From Kromerizya we went to Nitra where we stayed for three days, although we didn't want to. There was a crowd everywhere. I can't stand staying with too many people. Fortunately, Árpád Donáth took us to a lovely hotel and we were far from crowded places.

The Nitra station was crammed with people, it seemed impossible that we could ever leave. I was worried about Mum getting on a crowded train so we talked to a friendly railwayman who took us to the train standing near the station and told us to get in. We sat down comfortably and all of us fell asleep thinking that the train would leave in half an hour anyway. Every now and then we woke up and saw that our train was still at a standstill although it should have left a long time before. Then we realized that our train had already left and we got into the wrong train. We went back to the town sadly and it was only the next evening that some Yugoslav soldiers helped us get on a train and we could go to Pest.

Somewhere in all of these stops and starts and getting on and off trains, Oli set down the "Grey Papers," forgot she had done so and left them behind. The pages were one of the few possessions she had kept when she discarded nearly everything else on their long march from Sömmerda. Now they were gone. She and Lilly held on tightly to their diaries.

They arrived in the center of Budapest, passing rubble-filled ruins and collapsed bridges. From the station, they went to the Földis' house. Once the couple got over their surprise, they were overjoyed to welcome them into their home. The Földis wanted them to stay for several days to recuperate from their journey, but Lilly, Oli and Bertha were anxious to get home. They stayed the night, then went to the station the next morning and found a train to Beregszász. There wasn't enough room for all of them on the crowded train, so they located a seat for Bertha inside, and Lilly and Oli joined some others on the roof of the car. For several hours, they rode with the wind in their hair, passing familiar sights and feeling triumphant in their return.

Near the end of the trip, they found seats inside, near their mother. As they approached the Beregszász station, they pressed their faces against the window, straining to catch a glimpse of the men they hoped would be waiting for them. The train was still moving when Lilly spotted George, with Gabi standing next to him. She yelled and pointed for her mother and Oli to see. On the platform, they all took turns hugging Gabi and kissing his face. Then Lilly collapsed into George's embrace. Csányi Donát was standing next to him, but Lilly knew that she was where she wanted to be. She pressed her face into George's chest and cried.

Bertha asked Gabi where his father was. He told them that he hadn't seen Herman for over a year, not since they were separated in those first moments at Auschwitz. They all knew what this probably meant, but, just like Gabi, they would need time to accept the idea that Herman was truly gone. Then Oli asked George about Laci, and learned that he was working in a neighboring town and would be able to see her when he returned the next day.

George was relieved that Lilly was holding him and not Csányi. When he offered the room in his house, the women readily accepted. Before they parted, George and Csányi had a brief private conversation. They agreed that neither of them would propose to Lilly until she had had some time to recover from her journey. George and Gabi got the women settled into their room, then they all had dinner together. The women were tired, so George and Gabi left them and returned to the hotel.

But George could not stay there. Late that evening, he returned to his house and stood outside the bedroom where the women were sleeping. The windows were high above the street and George had to jump to knock on the glass. Lilly came to the window and George motioned for her to come to the front door. He got right to the point: "Let's get married!" Lilly found herself back in George's arms.

Oli awoke early the next morning. She dressed and waited in front of the house for Laci, her diary in her hand. She would present it to him as a gift: all of her pain and hopes, all of the terror and suffering of the past year. He would read it and understand what she had been through. She saw him in the distance, looking just as he had before she left, but this time his face was filled with anticipation instead of sorrow. He was so handsome, dressed in an elegant summer suit. Oli ran straight into his embrace. He said her name over and over again, as she repeated his. All her worries that she would be so changed, that he would not recognize her, that he would not want her, dissolved. They were together, the way they should be. They vowed never to be apart again.

Betrothed within a day of arriving home, both Lilly and Oli were thinking about the future and all it promised. But they wanted their father. Every day, the entire family went to the station and waited. Two days into their vigil, they heard some promising news: a disembarking passenger had been with a Herman Klein in one of the camps. Gabi was skeptical. This man had not known Herman before the war, and he had not known his fellow prisoner well. He had no information to link the man he knew in the camp to the Herman Klein they were waiting for. There were hundreds of Kleins in the region, and the name Herman was far from rare. Gabi watched his mother and sisters' excitement and refrained from saying anything.

They hoped for the best. Every day that Herman did not appear, they left the station deflated, often in tears. Nonetheless, the women found reasons to remain optimistic. Perhaps, they thought, Herman had been liberated by the Americans and was delayed because he was working as an interpreter. Their hopes diminished each day, but they still watched every arriving train, staring through the windows and searching the figures stepping from the doors. Each of them, even Gabi, could picture Herman emerging from the train, thinner than before, yet still their strong father or husband. Each could imagine the relief and joy on his face when he saw them waiting for him. He would jump from the train. He would run to them. He would encircle them in his arms: his entire, whole, family.

THE WALK

This is the part that we all know, but no one remembers.

But now, I have enough detail in place to make the scene real to me. Herman need no longer make his walk alone. I can be with him. I can hold his hand.

Herman turns to the left, and over his shoulder he watches
Gabi go off to the right. His son moves further away, and
is soon lost from sight, obscured by the men who fill the
growing space between them. Together with the other older
men, Herman rounds the front of the train, where he sees
a barbed wire fence and, through the wire, long wooden
buildings. He follows those in front of him as they approach
the wire and then turn right. He scratches his face and
registers the unaccustomed sensation of stubble under
his fingers. In his other hand he turns a comb.

After three days of being unable to move, his muscles
and joints ache and disobey. After three days of constant
motion, the dusty ground under his feet seems to shift.
He is tremendously thirsty. He struggles to keep pace with
those around him who are also struggling to keep pace.
He wants to stop and rest, but the dogs and machine guns
deny him this choice.

A row of trees appears on his left, lining the fence. Shortly
afterwards, he and the others turn left through a gate in
the fence. Ahead of him, Herman sees a brick building with
a large, tall chimney. As they enter the yard in front of the
building, an SS guard shouts to them that they will soon
have a shower and be disinfected. Herman anticipates the
water that will finally quench his thirst.

Herman follows the men ahead of him down some stairs
and into an underground room. The entrance is signed:
"To the baths and disinfecting rooms." The walls are lined
with numbered hooks, and more signs tell them to hang up
their clothes and to remember the number so that they can
retrieve their clothes after their shower. A poster on the
wall proclaims: "Cleanliness Brings Freedom." Once he has
removed his clothes, Herman joins the other naked men as
they exit from the long changing room and turn to the right.

He steps through a doorway.

AUTHOR'S NOTES

It is with love and great admiration that I thank my father Gene (Gabi) Klein, my aunts Oli Klutsik and Lilly Isaacs, and my uncle George Isaacs. They spent hours telling me about their past and responded to hundreds of questions. Though I was often asking for details about events that were painful to remember, they always answered willingly and thoughtfully.

Lilly and George were married three weeks after Lilly returned home. They had only been married for a few hours when my father heard on the radio that their region of Hungary was about to be ceded to the Soviet Union. He knocked on Lilly and George's window at 3:00 a.m. to tell them the news. The three of them left Beregszász a few days later. Oli stayed behind with Laci and Bertha, hoping to join Gabi, Lilly and George sometime shortly thereafter. But the Soviets closed the border, and the two halves of the family were not reunited until decades later.

My father and his sisters lost nearly all of their extended family: out of 107 living in and around Beregszász, only seven survived. George's mother was killed at Auschwitz (according to a witness, she was selected to die because she was carrying a friend's child). Though George's brother Frank never came home to Beregszász, he did survive and immigrated to Palestine after the war.

George and my father lived in a displaced persons' facility in Austria for two years. Lilly gave birth to my cousin Tom in 1946 and they all immigrated to the United States in 1947. Uncle Manny and his family met them off the boat at Ellis Island (and promptly changed Gabi's name to Gene). Manny sent my father to art school in New York, where he learned calligraphy and sign painting, My dad had to leave New York when he was drafted during the Korean War, but his linguistic skills allowed him to work stateside. While he was in the army, Lilly and George moved to Miami, and my father joined them there when he was discharged.

My mom, Barbara, worked as a buyer for a department store in downtown Miami, and was spotted by my dad as he decorated the display windows for Easter. He presented her with a plastic golden chick, asked her out on a date, and they were married within two years. My sister Monica was born in 1959, and I was born just under two years later. My father spent his career as a display artist and sign painter, and my parents still live in Florida. My dad speaks frequently to schools and other groups about his Holocaust experiences, and the two of us regularly give business seminars on resilience.

Oli and Laci were married in December 1945. They lived with Bertha and had two daughters, Zsuzsa and Ágnes. Laci died of a heart attack in 1979. A few years later, Oli moved to Hungary, where she still lives. Bertha was allowed to join Oli soon after and died in 1987.

Unfortunately, my father does not remember the name of the German civilian engineer. I give him the name Fürst in this book, because it means "prince" in English. He saved my father and he will always be a hero to us. All of the friends that my father met in the camps have fictitious names because, while my father clearly remembers the individuals, he does not remember their names. I use the real names of the women who were with Lilly, Oli and Bertha. Writing this book has left me with great admiration for these women, and indeed for all the women of Sömmerda: their creativity and strength are an inspiration. The names of the people described in Berehovo/Beregszász are also real, thanks to Oli's and Lilly's vivid memories.

There are many people who helped provide me with documents, photos and other information that I needed for the book. Steven Spielberg's Survivors of the Shoah Visual History Foundation provided the detailed interviews that were essential in reconstructing my family's history. Suzy Snyder at the

United States Holocaust Memorial Museum (USHMM) provided the photos of the diaries, as well as copies of Lilly's camp identification documents. Ben Neufeld, Sari's grandson, gave me the translation of her diary, which is on display with Lilly's at the USHMM. Yad Vashem provided photos from *The Auschwitz Album*. My mother, Barbara Klein, has done painstaking genealogical work on both sides of our family. She was able to provide me with important dates and names of extended family members. I am grateful to Lilly and George's son, Tom Isaacs, and his wife, Angela Aofner, for helping me with some of the interviews, and I owe a special debt to Lilly and George's daughter, Debby Isaacs, for holding the phone to Lilly's ear while I read the account of her liberation.

Several historical sources helped me better understand the details of the Holocaust, and so enriched my comprehension of my family's experiences. I have cited a number of these in the book, but I should also acknowledge the many memoirs I have read about life in the concentration camps. Particularly helpful were *Night* by Elie Wiesel, *Survival at Auschwitz* by Primo Levi, *Speak You Also* by Paul Steinberg, *Upon the Head of the Goat* by Aranka Siegal and *Chasing Shadows* by Hugo Gryn.

To survive the Holocaust, as these memoirists and my family members did, you had to be resilient, but above all you had to be lucky. The history of the Holocaust is largely a chronicle of innocent people being torn from their homes, separated from loved ones, and killed, either through mass extermination or through work and starvation. My family's story can be written, but they deserve no more admiration than do those whose stories are lost. I hope this book, in some small way, honors every victim of the Holocaust.

I write papers for scientific journals and have done so for three decades. Writing this book required a completely different set of skills. I would never have found my voice in this book or have been able to tell this story without a lot of help. Foremost, I thank my husband, Andrew John, who has edited every passage in this book many times over, bringing great improvement each time. We live hectic lives; I am grateful for the time he has put into this project, and for his helping to make this book what it is. Further, I am indebted to Jon Hofferman, my editor and graphic designer. He contributed a tremendous amount to the quality of the prose, and did a masterful job on the graphics and layout work.

Several others also improved this work. Anne Swardson and Charles Trueheart read through early versions of the first chapters and provided critical advice that helped me give the narrative more depth and direction. Matt Ross helped me make the prose more vivid. Allison Itterly ensured that readers could picture the people and their surroundings; her encouragement during this project was invaluable. My niece, Claire Hoppens, made some key suggestions for improvement. My two proofreaders—Isabel Harrison and Yolande McLean—were meticulous in finding errors and advising on the writing. My translators Zsuzsanna Palasthy (Oli's diary and the "Grey Papers") and Kinga Katus ("Grey Papers") worked painstakingly to accurately convey in English the thoughts expressed in these Hungarian documents. The USHMM provided a translation of Lilly's diary, and Heni Kaman recorded an oral translation of Oli's Shoah interview.

I am very fortunate to have such encouraging parents, and I am grateful to them. I have already acknowledged my husband's copyediting, but here I thank Andrew for his support and for bringing more love and friendship into my life than anyone has a right to expect. Finally, I am thankful to my children, Paris and Sam, resilient survivors of the Asian tsunami, for bringing me joy, love and fun every day.